SEMINA

Also by John Cornwell

The Pontiff in Winter
Hitler's Pope
Breaking Faith
The Power to Harm
A Thief in the Night
Nature's Imagination (editor)
Consciousness and Human Identity (editor)
Explanations (editor)
Earth to Earth
Hitler's Scientists
Powers of Darkness, Powers of Light
Coleridge: Poet and Revolutionary, 1772–1804
Seven Other Demons
The Spoiled Priest
Strange Gods

SEMINARY BOY

JOHN CORNWELL

FOURTH ESTATE · *London*

First published in Great Britain in 2006 by
Fourth Estate
An imprint of HarperCollins*Publishers*
77–85 Fulham Palace Road
London W6 8JB
www.4thestate.co.uk

Copyright © John Cornwell 2006

1

A catalogue record for this book is
available from the British Library

ISBN-13 978-0-00-723243-7
ISBN-10 0-00-723243-8

Typeset in PostScript Minion with Serlio Display by
Rowland Phototypesetting Ltd, Bury St Edmunds, Suffolk

Printed in Great Britain by Clays Ltd, St Ives plc

For Gabrielle

AUTHOR'S NOTE

In the absence of diaries I have relied mostly on unaided personal recollections for the writing of this memoir. In some instances I have concealed the identities of the living.

The wounded is the wounding heart.
RICHARD CRASHAW, 'The Flaming Heart'

PART ONE

FATHER FIGURES

1

ON MY LAST summer holiday at the minor seminary I ran into my father in the east London suburb of Woodford. His heavy limp, a handicap from childhood, seemed more laboured than I remembered. As he toiled up George Lane his hand motions were like a man steadying a skittish horse on a leading rein. His hair was plastered down with brilliantine and he was wearing a new raincoat, collar turned up in the manner of Humphrey Bogart. He accosted me affably with his familiar limelight smile, as if greeting an invisible audience somewhere above my head. He betrayed no remorse at having left my mother and his five children a year earlier. Standing outside Woolworth's, chatting about the new soccer season, he was fishing for something in his trouser pocket. I glimpsed a ten-shilling note. Then he fetched out a large bright horse chestnut, a conker. Buffing it on his sleeve he handed it over, saying: 'Cheerio there, Jack.'

I stood watching him until he was swallowed up in the lobby of the Majestic cinema where a matinée was about to begin. He did not look back. I was missing him, but he had always been more of a troublesome sibling than an ideal father. In any case, I had other father-figures to contend with.

2

FATHER JAMES COONEY, pastor of my early adolescent years, was an austere soul. He had a drawn grey face and blood-raw eyelids. His cracked celluloid clerical collar was the colour of soiled snow. It was the rigid cheap sort that priests and seminarians could launder in seconds with a damp cloth. He would kneel at the altar rail in our empty church, eyes shut tight, grizzled head listing in concentration. When he looked up towards the tabernacle, he seemed to be adjusting his vision to the scene of his life's mission – the east London district of Barkingside. Father Cooney was in resigned exile from Skibbereen, County Cork.

From the age of eleven until I departed for the minor seminary aged thirteen to begin my education for the priesthood, I served Father Cooney's Mass at seven o'clock every weekday morning in what he called his 'old bit of a church', dedicated to Saint Augustine the missionary to the English. On Sundays the people stood three deep in the aisles, latecomers huddled out in the churchyard. To reduce the pressure he celebrated an extra Mass in a disused army hut next to a pet cemetery where dogs, cats and horses were buried beneath headstones. Father Cooney would gaze bleakly out of the hut window, disparaging 'the pagan English customs over the way'. I served Mass at the Camp, as we called it, before cycling up to Saint Augustine's to assist as censer bearer at the sung High Mass. In the afternoon I returned to serve at Solemn Benediction when Father Cooney led the singing of his favourite hymn:

> Lord, for tomorrow and its needs
> I do not pray.

Yet Father Cooney was struggling to supply the needs of tomorrow in the form of a larger church. Holding up the offertory plates he would reproach us: 'Copper! Copper! Where's the silver?' In the meantime he was watching the pennies. Around the church and the presbytery he wore a frayed, black-trying-to-be-green cassock. In winter he went shod in army boots; in summer, black canvas plimsolls, sometimes without socks. He chopped his own hair. Standing close to him in the sanctuary on summer days, he smelt like a sack of fertiliser.

At High Mass, the segment of charcoal cake, painstakingly excised with a razor blade, was minuscule, the incense grains sparse. When I swung the censer high to make the smoke billow, he would come suddenly out of his meditative mode: 'Not so briskly, child!' he would hiss. When we buried parishioners in the Catholic section of the local cemetery, the charcoal was a morsel of white ash by the time we reached the graveside. It seemed to me strange, Father Cooney swinging a cold smokeless censer at the coffin. At Low Mass he would ease a tear-drop of wine into the chalice. The candles on the altar were dark guttering stubs appropriated from Our Lady's votive rack. He lit them at the last moment, and snuffed them with a singed pinch before he had even finished the words of the last Gospel.

He was a withdrawn man. If we met outside church he would incline his head, silently acknowledging the bond between himself and his daily Mass server. Sometimes he made a peculiar noise, a substitute for saying anything definite: 'Wisswiss ... wisswiss.' When the children gathered around him in the school yard he would make a nuisance-fly gesture: 'Very good! So! ... wisswiss ... Run along now!' Addressing women, young or middle-aged, he would stand sideways on to them, bleakly descrying objects of curious interest in the distance. But I had also seen him comforting in his arms a widow wracked with grief at her husband's graveside.

He was tireless in the service of the sick and the dying. I would see him out in all weathers on his rusty bicycle, visiting the inmates at Claybury mental asylum and the bedridden at

King George V hospital. Careering unsteadily along the street, narrowly missed by buses and lorries, he gripped the handle-bars with one hard-knuckled hand; the other nursed the sacrament within his breast pocket.

He was self-effacing. When he dropped an object from his arthritic hands, he would whisper to himself, bending over painfully: 'Wisswisss . . . Imbecile it isS!' If he caught the servers fooling around before High Mass, he would mutter: 'Boys will be boys as the hills are green far off!' But he could get exasperated with our choir when they droned on beyond the Offertory: '*Orate frates* . . . Enough of that! . . .'

My mother used to say that when you confessed your sins to Father Cooney it was 'like going on trial for your life'. Often he made me repeat my purpose of amendment: 'Say it again . . . As if you meant it, now!' But he always ended with the heartfelt murmur: 'Be sure now and pray for *me* – the un-worthy sinner.'

On Sundays he preached on the Gospel of the day before straying to his weekly hobby horse, the *News of the World*, which 'desecrated the Sabbath by its very existence', lingering hissingly over that final sibilant. Then he would excoriate the barbers' shops which sold 'prophylactics', which I associated in my innocence with mysterious idols of a false religion. 'No dacent, upright Catholic gentleman,' he said, 'should give custom to such a one as does the Divil's business now!'

3

FATHER COONEY recruited me as a candidate for the priest-hood in this way. One Sunday evening I arrived at church early for Solemn Benediction. After vesting I looked into the sacristy. The room was silent, deserted. On the press stood the chalice in readiness for Mass the following morning. I had an urge to touch the receptacle. I went on tiptoe across the parquet flooring and grasped the embossed stem of the sacred cup. At that moment I heard a gasp. Looking back I was seized with terror at the sight of Father Cooney perched on a stool behind the open sacristy door. He followed me with his eyes as I walked slowly past him, trembling, as if I had committed a sacrilege. He said not a word.

The following day, after early morning Mass, Father Cooney asked me what I hoped to be when I grew up. I said confidently that I hoped to be a priest. Within a day it was settled that I should apply to the bishop to try my vocation at a minor seminary, a boarding college where young boys began their long training for the priesthood. When Father Cooney put my name forward to the bishop I was approaching my thirteenth birthday. I was already a Johnny-come-lately: many boys of my generation had begun their priestly formation at the age of eleven.

On the appointed day, my mother took me to an interview with the Right Reverend Bishop Andrew Beck of Brentwood. She was dressed in her purple coat with padded shoulders which she kept for special occasions; it was smart but her dress showed a few inches below the hem. I was dressed in my elder brother's navy blue jacket temporarily stitched up at the sleeves. We sat at the front of the upper deck of the London Transport bus because Mum thought it a treat to have a view of the scenery on a journey. Riding northwards from the bus-stop outside Trebor's mint factory, we passed Hill's car showroom festooned with bunting snapping in the spring breeze. Then we crossed the River Roding with its smell of the sewage plant and passed under the Central Line railway bridge on our way to the towering Majestic cinema. In all that journey, I reflected, there was not a single sacred image to be seen. That was how I had begun to think.

Bishop Beck's diocese took in the county of Essex with its

new towns and the poor districts of London's East End, but he lived in the prosperous suburb of Woodford Green. The bishop's house was set back from the road amidst clipped shrubberies. A gleaming black limousine stood on the gravel drive. Monsignor Shannon, the Vicar General, greeted us at the door. He was a stout man in a black suit, a cigarette perched between his fingers. He had a flushed face as if he had just climbed out of a steaming bath. He spoke to us softly, advising us to address the bishop as 'My Lord'. He ushered us into a room where the bishop sat at a desk with his back to French windows. He got up and held out his ringed hand for us to kiss.

He was a lean, dark-haired, exhausted-looking man with a sallow face. He was watching me intently through half-horn-rimmed spectacles. I sat bolt upright on a straight-backed ornate chair trying to look alert and decent. He spoke for a while about Father Cooney's recommendation. Looking up at the ceiling, he said: 'How lucky you are to have Father Cooney as your parish priest.' Then he asked my mother if she would mind waiting outside.

He handed me a piece of paper and a pencil and dictated a passage from St John's Gospel, which I wrote down accurately. Then he wanted to know how many bedrooms we had in our house, and about the sleeping arrangements. I said that my three brothers and I, and sometimes my father too, slept in one room sharing three single beds. He asked if my father and elder brother went to church, and I said that Dad never went to church even at Christmas. He wanted to know how I liked my school. I said I liked it well enough. I had no inclination to tell him of the fights in the school yard, and the impure larks in the evil-smelling latrines.

'If you are to be a priest one day,' he said eventually, 'you will have to study hard to be an educated man. Ordination alters your entire soul . . . You must become a holy man.'

He asked how I felt about going away to a boarding school,

the minor seminary. 'You might be homesick,' he said. 'What do you think about that?'

I tried not to betray my anxiety. I was afraid that I might say something that would make him withdraw the suggestion. 'I would like that very much,' I virtually whispered.

Then he called my mother back, and it was my turn to go out into the hallway where Monsignor Shannon was at the ready with a biscuit and a glass of milk.

When Mum emerged accompanied by the bishop I could tell from her expression, a pious look she wore in church after taking Communion, that everything had been agreeably settled. The bishop explained that since our diocese was poor it had no minor or senior seminaries of its own. He would have me lodged in a seminary owned by one of the larger, more prosperous dioceses of England. 'It will be a long way from home,' he said, with a warning look.

I tried to appear intrepid.

On the bus, I surveyed the Godless landscape, rejoicing inwardly that I was soon destined to depart for a very different world where there would be constant visible reminders of the Mother of God and the Kingdom of Heaven. Eventually Mum patted me on the arm and said she was proud of me. When we reached home, the house that went with my father's job on the sports ground, she looked down at me with her lustrous grey eyes. 'I just wonder whether it's really you,' she said. 'But we'll see ... I should be so proud! And as your saintly grandmother used to say: gain a priest – never lose a son.'

Later Dad came in from the sports ground wearing his overalls. Dad and Mum had not been speaking to each other for some days. He had not been consulted about my visit to the bishop or its purpose. He appeared less pleased than Mum as she reported the proceedings of the morning. He was blinking frequently, as he often did when he was puzzled or nervous.

He said: 'Are you sure, son?'

I had not the capacity to consider what it meant for Dad to

be informed, without reference to his opinion, that I would leave home that autumn to begin my education for the priesthood. I did not consider his feelings or his opinion of any significance. I was filled with a sense of glowing ripeness and anticipation.

4

MY MOTHER, KATHLEEN, whose maiden name was Egan, told me that she became desperate on discovering in the autumn of 1939, days after Britain declared war on Germany, that she was pregnant again. She was twenty-five years of age. It would be her third child under three. In those days the family lived in East Ham, a working-class district close to the London docks north of the River Thames. Dad was out all day seeking casual labour by the hour on the wharves. He had a withered, unbending left leg and was always among the last to be hired.

If she had another baby, how would she manage? And to bring another child into a world at war! Mum began to pray day and night that she would lose the baby. Then she felt guilty. Wasn't it a mortal sin for a pregnant mother to pray for a miscarriage? She went to see Father Heenan. Father Heenan, who would one day become Cardinal Archbishop of Westminster, was in 1939 a young, East End parish priest. According to Mum, the priest, from where he sat, extended both his legs, stiff at the knees, to reveal the holes in his shoes right through to his socks. He said: 'Don't be afraid, Kathleen, we're all poor. Trust in God: he *will* provide!' She began to pray fervently to Saint Gerard Magella, patron saint of childbirth, for the safe delivery of the baby that was me.

In the early summer of 1940, as a test air-raid warning wailed over London, I came dancing into time in my parents'

John 'Blitz Baby' Cornwell, 1941.

bed in Carlyle Road. Our accommodation, which sheltered my parents and elder brother and sister, was two rooms of a terrace house backing on to a busy rail route that ran from the conurbations of Essex to the City of London. I was to be named in baptism after Father Heenan: John Carmel. In Saint Stephen's church Father Heenan blew in my face in the form of a cross, commanding my unclean spirit to depart. Even as he touched my tongue with salt to preserve me from corruption, the air-raid sirens were singing out again. It was not a test warning. The priest cut the rest of the service, save for the cleansing waters of baptism, dropping my intended second name: Carmel. The baptismal party, myself cradled in my godmother Aunt Nelly Egan's arms, made for the public shelter even as Father Heenan called after me: 'John, go in peace . . .'

5

I HAVE DIM early impressions of East Ham, the shunting steam trains, clashing couplings and buffers beyond the yard fence; fog horns echoing from the docks in the night; a medley of nostril-scorching stenches. Later I learnt that the bad smells came on the wind from the Becton gasworks, the factories in the Silvertown basin, the polluted waters of the Thames at Woolwich.

I feel my father holding me under my armpits in his strong hands, to a rising and falling chorus of sirens. Then I see it: flying high, caught in the searchlight shafts, a growling black flying object shedding fountains of fire. Dad is holding me up, arms outstretched, to watch one of Hitler's 'doodlebugs' crossing the night sky.

The shelter smelt of dank clay. Lying on the top bunk wrapped in a blanket, I watched Mum gazing imploringly at the image pinned to a cross of wood, her lips moving constantly. Eventually the sirens stopped and the night was silent. Through her bowing and whispering before the figure, Mum could control the fiery black thing in the sky and the hideous wailing across the rooftops.

6

DAD WAS THE eldest son of Arthur Cornwell, a former pub manager, and Lillian Freeman, a Jewish barmaid. When Dad was born his father had charge of the Horn of Plenty at Stepney Green in the heart of London's East End. Granddad was the eldest sibling but he quarrelled with the family because of his liaison with Grandma Lillian. She had 'got herself into trouble' and the result was my father. After they married, Granddad sulked. He buried himself in the dockland slums of Custom House, taking a scullery job in the works canteen at Spiller's flour mills.

Dad was lean and compact, his hair raven black. He might have been a sportsman, but his athletic potential along with other prospects were dashed the day aged three he fell down a flight of stairs. His left leg was badly injured; it was neglected to begin with and complications set in. He spent much of his childhood lying in a body-length wicker gurney in various hospitals far from London. He emerged on to the streets of Custom House aged thirteen, his left leg sans kneecap permanently stiff and thin as a willow stick. He dragged that stick-leg behind him, hopping frantically to keep up with three younger brothers until he found his special rhythm. At a walk his gait was awkward and laboured. At speed he looked like a ballet dancer careering across a stage, his bad leg whizzing forward from the hip in a stiff-legged arc, arms balancing his body with an elegant rhythmic breast-stroke. He even managed to play a bizarre game of football and could put an impressive spin on a cricket ball.

My mother had Atlantic grey eyes and prematurely grey hair. She had nervous eczema across the temples, and a tendency to mottle instant crimson across her chest and neck when roused. She had large hips, strong hands, and an erect bearing. She had left school at fourteen and graduated through unskilled jobs in one reeking local factory after another: Tate & Lyle (sugar, syrup), Spiller's (flour, dog food, fertiliser), and Knight's Castille (soap, detergents). My mother's people on her father's side were descended from Egans and Sheehys, second-generation immigrants from County Kerry. Her mother was a Sweeney, a Catholic Scot from Leith, but originally from Donegal. Mum was the only daughter, with six brothers; there had been a second daughter who died aged five.

Granddad Thomas Egan's people had come over from Ireland with nothing but their Faith and the family. Two of my Egan uncles would become involved in a minor way with the IRA: guns up the chimney, running 'messages'. In truth, Granddad Egan's children were by their generation belligerent cockneys with a vulgar sense of humour, albeit ghetto Roman Catholic to the core.

Granddad Egan worked in boiler maintenance; he knew precisely where to hit a cylinder to eradicate a dent. He met Grandma Catherine at a Catholic church social evening in Bow and they married in their teens. When Mum was a girl, her family, all nine of them, was squeezed into a two-bedroomed house on North Woolwich Road, Silvertown. Old Silvertown, before Hitler and the London County Council planners re-shaped it, was isolated from metropolitan London and its suburbs by the geography of the river and the dock complexes. Rural Essex was a day's walk away. Transport was minimal and there were few social amenities other than the pubs and churches. Eventually the Egans were joined by a tenth family member, Grandma's destitute and ageing Sweeney uncle who had walked down from Scotland. Nobody in need was turned away.

Mum was an expert mimic, mocking the follies of pretty well everybody outside the Egan–Sweeney circle. She would hold herself tight as she dissolved into high-pitched, tearful laughter. But she was quick to anger when sensing an affront to her dignity. She thought class a matter of personal aspiration rather than accident of birth. She loathed socialists and the unions because they were 'against bettering oneself'. She believed that a 'real man' is 'clean' and 'truthful', and 'never raises his hand to a woman'. Raising her own hand to a misbehaving child was another matter.

She had an unqualified respect for the priesthood. Priests, she knew only too well, were hardly immune from individual lapses. Yet one never judged a priest; for one day, she would say, these men would come face to face with Almighty God to answer for their deeds. She had stories to tell about priests. As a girl, her route to school passed through a Protestant enclave. One morning there was a street fight. The Catholics inflicted a lot of pain and injury, and a delegation complained to Father Fitzgerald. The suspects, led by Mum (big for her age and sporting a broken front tooth and a terrible cast in her right eye), were summoned to the school hall. A cantankerous Father Fitzgerald picked on Mum first. Had she taken part? Even as she said: 'No, Father,' he punched her in the chest, sending her flying against the wall. 'When that priest *tumped* you,' she used to say, explosively imitating his brogue, 'you *stayed tumped*.'

Despite a restricted education, Mum had a remarkable if occasionally shaky vocabulary ranging from surprising archaisms to odd vulgarisms. She had an outlandish way of undermining well-worn clichés: 'It's so quiet in here you could hear a bomb drop!' And she routinely subverted key words as if striving for the caricature status of a malaprop cockney. Anything surprising was a 'relevation'; while missing the point was always 'irrevelant'. 'An erring priest,' she used to say, 'will be judged more harshly than any other before the *trinubal* of God.'

Mum maintained that she acquired her religious piety from her own mother, whom she described as a 'walking saint'. Grandma Catherine Egan was a lay member of the Franciscans. She venerated Saint Anthony of Padua and the Carmelite Thérèse of Lisieux (the French saint widely known as the Little Flower of Jesus). She attended a Franciscan church at Stratford East. Mum would relate how Grandma Egan would collect her as late as eight o'clock on Saturday evenings from her Saturday job at a grocer's store to take her to confession at Stratford.

Mum was eighteen when her parents died in the same year, both aged fifty. The event cast a shadow of remorse across the whole of her life. It was as if her parents continued to reach out from their graves to clutch her by the ankles. Granddad

Egan, the boiler man, a worrier by all accounts, died first of a perforated ulcer. Mum used to say that days before his sudden death she saw a figure in a black cloak leaning over her father as he lay sleeping on a daybed (my mother's bed at night) in the living room. Her mother died a year later of breast cancer. Towards the end there was a lapse in Grandma Egan's piety. As she lay in agony, Mum brought up from the yard a rose her father had planted a week before he died. She said: 'Remember the Little Flower of Jesus, Mum.' Grandma turned her face to the wall and said: 'Don't be stupid!' Dressed in the Franciscan habit, she was buried in Leyton's Catholic cemetery along with six strangers in a common grave, close to Granddad Egan's common grave.

Mum, being the only girl, looked after three brothers who were still at home, and the aged and cantankerous Scottish uncle. She also became responsible for shopping, cooking, cleaning and laundry, as well as being the breadwinner – a factory worker on early morning shifts. Her brothers abused her verbally, and sometimes physically, although not without explosive retribution. She continued like this for three years until she met Dad at a dance in the Spiller's factory social club. She found him handsome and funny. But she married him, she would say later, as a result of his determination and her pity for his handicap. She was twenty-one; he was twenty-four.

My father became a Catholic to satisfy the virtual ban on mixed marriages. Mum says he was an eager convert. Once married, however, he seldom went to church. We grew up thinking him a lost soul. His mother, Grandma Lillian, being a Jew, was deemed doubly a lost soul. The contempt of some East End Catholics for Jews was matched only by their hatred of Protestants. I once heard an Egan uncle referring to my genial Grandma Cornwell as 'that Yid their father's mother'.

7

MUM'S DISILLUSIONMENT with Dad began with a wartime episode. To escape the air raids in London, Mum and we three children went to stay in the market town of Bicester in Oxfordshire while Dad stayed on in East Ham. During our absence, Dad got involved with a girl he met in a public air-raid shelter. Mum discovered this when she returned to East Ham without warning and found an intimate letter written from an address on Canvey Island in the Thames estuary.

Mum set off on the train to pay the girl a visit. When she arrived at South Benfleet, the station for Canvey Island, she saw Dad on the opposite platform. He waved nonchalantly ('As if to say: "Here we are again!"') before nipping on to a train bound back to London. So she proceeded to the address where she found the girl, aged just nineteen, living with her mother. Mum discovered that Dad had constructed a web of fantasies about himself. He claimed to be a master carpenter and had offered to take on the girl's younger brother as an apprentice. To Mum's fury in the those times of wartime food shortages, he had turned over his ration book to the girl's mother.

Retrieving the precious book, Mum set off for London determined to end the marriage. Back in East Ham she confronted him. He confessed all and begged forgiveness, but she was adamant, absolutely adamant, until she went round to see my devout godmother Aunt Nelly. After many tears and over many cups of tea Aunt Nelly persuaded Mum that Dad's erring behaviour was a consequence of 'this terrible, terrible war' and that God would surely wish her to forgive him and stay with him. So Mum did what she believed her Faith expected of her. We all moved back to East Ham, to Dad, and the bombing.

Some nine months later, brother Terry and my sister

Me, aged four, outside my grandparents' basement flat, East London.

Maureen were evacuated to the north of England in the national scheme to save children from the flying bombs and V2 rockets. At the departure point Mum was carrying little Michael in her arms, the product of her post-Canvey reconciliation with Dad. My elder siblings looked down at us from the bus that would take them to the railway station: two sets of huge sorrowful eyes gazing accusingly through the window. They had labels bearing their names tied into the lapels of their raincoats. I have an impression that I could not wait for them to go.

8

BY LATE 1944, and after four wartime home removals, I was attending a Catholic primary school run by Irish nuns and spinsters. The yellow brick building surrounded by a fenced-in gravel yard was like a stockade surrounded by a hostile world of unbelief. One Sunday a V2 rocket destroyed a nearby Anglican church killing most of the congregation. The next day Miss Doonan, who taught us so piously to make the sign of the Cross, informed us that these people had been punished by God because they were Protestants.

My understanding of the Faith had been marked since infancy by wonder and illusion. The people sighed and bowed and sang together. Why did they do that? When the man at the front turned and raised his arms, he made the bells ring. The man was holding up what looked like a gold clock. When the people bowed their heads deeply, Mum said we were bowing towards God. 'God', then, was a clock, and the clock made people bow and sing and walk in circles.

These operations of cause and effect were puzzling. The day before we celebrated the end of the war in Europe, I was humming to myself, skipping ahead of the girl who took me to school, when two bull terriers hurtled around the corner and sank their teeth into my plump legs. I spent the morning in a doctor's surgery being stitched up and painted with iodine. According to the policeman who visited our house on Victory Day in Europe, the dogs' owner claimed that I made the animals bite me by my singing and dancing.

That autumn my elder siblings came back from evacuation. They had been lodged in Bolton, Lancashire, with two indulgent spinsters. My sister Maureen wore a red frock and her hair was in ringlets tied with silk ribbons. She spoke in a strange accent, laughing excitedly. I thought she had an adorable face and I fell in love with her in an instant; yet she would not deign to look at me, despite my attempts to be noticed. My brother Terry, a few weeks short of his ninth birthday, and raven-haired like my father, did not take his eyes off me: he was like a black cat with very still yellow eyes. He had returned from exile to find a younger brother living on the emotional fat of our mother's affections. At tea I blew a raspberry at him. Then he invited me to step out into the yard where, I informed him with a wave of a small hand, 'All this is mine.' Why, I wondered, was his face swollen like a boiled tomato? The next thing, I was lying on the ground with a mouthful of blood and three milk teeth down my throat. My sister's home-coming rapture did not last long. I have a re-collection of her bitter wailing that evening as Mum took the scissors to those 'silly' ringlets which would only harbour nits.

With the arrival of a fifth child, brother Jimmy, the product apparently of Victory euphoria, our financial situation became ever more precarious. Mum and Dad worked hard to keep us respectable, clean and well fed, but we brushed our teeth with soot from the chimney (an old East End tactic), had our hair washed with carbolic soap, and ate bread and margarine for tea on a kitchen table covered with newspaper. A tongue-tied Irish lodger supplemented the household income. Terry, Michael and I shared a bedroom with him. He put curlers in his hair each night and smoked in bed. Dad grew cabbages out back and Mum kept five chickens.

Mum's mood darkened, a circumstance linked in my mind with two physical misfortunes. Before dawn one morning, looking for eggs in the run, she trod on a rusty nail planted in a piece of wood carelessly left by Dad; it went right through her foot. Not long afterwards, she had her top row of teeth out, a popular practice in those days since dentists earned more for extractions than fillings. They were replaced with ill-fitting false ones. Mum's new menacing melancholy was also associated in my mind with churchgoing, and what the nuns told us at school. One day Sister Paul unrolled a picture which she hung on the wall for a whole day. It showed naked people standing in beds of fire. 'These are the souls of the dead who died in mortal sin,' she said. Talk of sin made me think of dirty cinders in the fire grate. 'They are burning there for ever,' she said. The next day she showed us a picture of the 'holy souls in purgatory', where people stood in pits of grey ash. Mum spoke often of praying for 'the holy souls in purgatory'. But when I first heard those words I heard 'the sorry holes in the lavatory'.

Eventually I came to understand that the clock-God was a glass case that held a white circle of wafer bread. The round white wafer was God, which I came to eat. I put out my tongue and there he was. God was sour and soggy in my saliva. You must not bite him, Sister Paul said. You must not let him touch your teeth or the roof of your mouth. Let him rest on your tongue until you are ready to swallow him whole. I could feel him sliding down inside me, the slimy little God inside me, in under my roof. I was a little house and God could sit inside my tummy. As we walked in twos back to school for our First Communion breakfast of custard and jelly, I passed Mum standing by the school gate, gazing down at me with a peculiar expression of sadness.

9

IN THE YEARS before I became devout and felt called by Jesus to follow Him, I had been as wicked as was possible for a child washed in Christian baptism. Sister Paul informed Mum that I had a 'black streak'. I was physically strong for my age, demonically restless and sudden to anger. My childhood agitation was like a fever. It was as if I was permanently waiting, on edge, for the sound of the old wartime sirens; hankering for a heart-stopping explosion.

I suffered the stigma of one 'lazy' dim-sighted eye, just like Mum's. When I was tired my eye turned inwards as if straining to see inside my brain. It provoked taunts from other children, who would imitate my affliction to my face until they knew me better. My knuckles would be covered in their blood. The nuns called me 'sly-boots', commanding me to look them 'properly in the eye like a dacent fellow!' When I looked at myself in a mirror I could see what they meant. My shifty myopic eyes were at war with each other, swivelling and blinking in a restless head. Mealtimes at home were the worst. Through poor hand–eye coordination I tended to make scraping noises, knock over cups, miss my mouth and spill food down my front and on to the floor. Eyeing me from on high, fork-hand trembling, as if at any moment she would skewer and devour me, Mum would struggle to maintain her patience. Crying out between her new false teeth, she would throw down her cutlery and set about me.

Yet Mum herself was no less clumsy. Dishes leapt from her hands, needles pricked her fingers, the stove burnt the porridge, and our cat, despite Mum's training regime, peed on the kitchen floor. We all of us, including the porridge, felt the avenging Egan hand. As for the cat, I have seen our poor drop-kicked Moggy, paws pedalling frantically, crash-land on the yard fence with a scream.

After a visit to an optician I was made to wear an evil-smelling black bakelite 'colluder' on a pair of wire spectacle frames to blank out my good eye and so to encourage the weak and wayward one, now assisted by a lens as thick as a magnifying glass. I was always taking off the colluder. I hated the comments it evoked: ''Ere comes Punch's sore-eyed dog,' quipped Uncle Mike, ever the creative and well-meaning genius of the Egan vulgarism. So Mum took to covering the good eye with a large square of sticky plaster. Since the sight in my lazy eye provided no more than peripheral vision, I was always walking into trees and lamp-posts. I would rip off the plaster, a prelude to retribution.

Desperate for companionship, reckless of punishment and danger, I became an under-aged thug. I trailed a gang of older lads, haunting bombed-out houses and tenements. Others had been there before us, but there was always something to smash. The blasted staircases and sagging floors, especially on the higher storeys, were terrifying. My talent for atrocious mayhem earned me the respect of my elders. One day, at my prompting, four of us struggled to place an iron girder on a railway track, aiming to derail an express train bound for Liverpool Street Station. Our attempt at mass murder was fortunately spotted. I was chased by police and railway workers for throwing bricks at the windows of passing trains, thrashed by a builder for setting fire to a house he was rebuilding, hit by a car as I ran away from a shop where I had stolen a pack of cigarettes. I did a lot of hitting myself. I nearly killed the boy next door by whacking him over the head with my elder brother's cricket bat. He had contradicted me. I lied to the nuns to get a goody-goody boy into trouble, alleging he had misbehaved on the bus. With vicious associates I assaulted a girl in a disused bomb shelter, putting our grubby hands down her knickers. She was in my class at school and she had earlier shown a liking for me. She looked at me in silent sorrow as I urged the others on.

Was there no one in my childhood who calmed me with tokens of affection? My Aunt Rose, Tommy Cornwell's wife, was a vivacious young cockney woman with thick blonde hair, a smoky voice and a husky laugh. She had two children of her own, Sylvia and young Tommy, but all children were her own children, and she seemed in a state of tearful, permanent wonder at their lovable natures. Her voice, full of heartfelt affection, filled me with joy. She was the light of my life, but she appeared all too seldom.

And what of my uncles? Mum's six brothers were garrulous egotists who loved to put children down. Only Uncle Mike, Mum's youngest brother, displayed an affectionate interest in us. He told us jokes and would sing popular songs in a pleasant crooning voice. Dad's three brothers were in the Royal Navy. They would appear briefly on occasional leave, smart in their spotless uniforms. They were hard men and talked with nose-blocked accents. When angry they would screw up their lips in a silent whistle. Uncle John, a submariner, could be spiteful. He had a wife, our Aunt Edie, who wore a wig, but they had no children.

Uncle John: 'How would you like a tasty bar of chocolate, Jack?'

'Yes please, Uncle John.'

'Well, I can't give you one see Jack 'cos I ain't got none!'

Then he would hoot with laughter, looking down on me with a mad gleam in his eye.

10

I WAS HAPPIEST at the cinema. When *Scott of the Antarctic*, starring John Mills, was shown at the Plaza, I stole money from Mum's purse and skipped school every afternoon to enter the darkened auditorium from which I faced the lands of brilliant white light. The world of the cinema merged with the world of church, everybody facing one way. Sometimes I found myself genuflecting towards the screen as I came out into the cinema aisle.

All the children in our school were taken by the nuns to see Bing Crosby and Ingrid Bergman in *The Bells of Saint Mary's*. I was bored and kept up a facetious running commentary, with screeches of forced laughter as I identified each ill-favoured nun on the screen as one of our own: 'Watch out! 'Ere comes Sister Paul again . . .' At one point I got a stinging smack round the ear from Sister Paul who had crept up on me in the dark.

Despite the dysfunction of these years Sister Paul taught me to read and write. When I found a book I liked I gorged on it greedily again and again. I read the class copy of *The Island of Adventure* by Enid Blyton until it fell to pieces. At home there was little reading matter: Mum's *The Key to Heaven* (subtitled 'A Selection of Prayers and Devotional Exercises'), a two-volume illustrated encyclopedia of housekeeping, and the *Evening News*. My craving for reading matter was eventually to be satisfied in an unexpected fashion as a result of what I did to my new class teacher, Sister Magdalen.

Sister Magdalen, with fading freckles and puckering bloodless lips, was a hard-worked, dedicated teacher, with charge of a class of more than sixty children. One day for some trivial playground misdemeanour she pulled me into the empty classroom by my ear while making indentations in my scalp with her knuckles. Enraged, I seized the wooden blackboard T-square which lay handy on her desk and whacked her around the head, ripping her veil off. The sight of her shorn gingery scalp paralysed me with fascination for a few seconds. She stood there yelling, holding her head, before flying at me. So I went on whacking until our plump headmistress Sister Dolores came hurtling in and pinned me to the ground with her superior weight.

Mum was sent for. She towered over me white-knuckled as the breathless reports of my sacrilegious attack were recounted. Back at home, having bruised her hands with walloping me, Mum completed her punishment with the toe of a heavy shoe. In the days that followed there was talk of having me 'put away'. Mum took me to a clinic in a church hall on a street called Snakes Lane. A man and several women sat behind a table covered with a green cloth. He said: 'Take a biscuit, boy!' He was pointing to a tin box of biscuits on the table. As I nibbled at the biscuit my case was discussed over my head. Mum uttered the word 'wilful' a great many times. At one point I reached out for another biscuit, but the man growled: 'One biscuit only!'

I was sent to a 'convalescent home' run by the London County Council in a remote flintstone farmhouse on the Downs near Worthing in Sussex. Lodged in this place were some fifty boys suffering from a variety of physical and emotional disorders. I saw in some of them the same evasive, drowning eyes that I witnessed in my mirror. Many were being treated for additional slum-district afflictions – impetigo, ringworm and scabies; several had cotton wool stuck in their ears or sported suppurating boils on their necks. Some were pale, stick thin. Our beefy minders were known as 'aunts' and 'uncles'. If we misbehaved we were not beaten; we were tied into our beds with skilfully knotted bandage bonds for hours on end like berserk patients in strait-jackets.

Soon after my arrival I became involved with a villainous older boy, whose face was daubed with red antiseptic paint covering an impetigo scab as big as a lobster. One day he invited me to insert my forefinger, after wetting it thoroughly with my spittle, into an empty light socket. He had said to me: 'D'you wanna see an angel?' It was a hard way to learn about the power of electricity. Had I enjoyed a precocious gift for irony, I would have seen it as an apt recompense for my knicker-fingering exploits in disused bomb shelters. The experiment nearly killed me and I ended up in bed swaddled in blankets. When I got better I could not wait to try it out on new arrivals. I spent a lot of my time in that place tied into my bed.

It was in Sussex that I first experienced wonder at the open countryside. One afternoon an 'aunt' took a group of us for a walk along footpaths to Chanctonbury Ring, a coppice of trees high on the Downs with distant views of the sea. I stood on the side of the hill intoxicated by the vistas and the fragrant air. The sea was a distant line of fiery light. A small aeroplane was droning high in the sky, wheeling and glinting in the sunlight like a dragonfly. I threw out my arms as if they were wings and ran in circles, wild with delight. Then I threw myself down by 'aunt's' side.

'Well, John, what do you think of the countryside?' she said. Unusual for the staff in that place, she was young and pretty, red in the cheek and pleasant. She was looking at me expectantly.

Something got into me. I did not want to give the impression that I had become tame and a softie.

'It's shitty!' I whined, making a sour expression. 'It's only fit for pigs.'

She looked away, saddened; and I felt wretched with myself and the world.

11

I RETURNED HOME to London after three months, full of energy for renewed mischief, fattened out on a diet of un-limited porridge, eggs, bacon and doorsteps of bread and jam. Back at school, my terrible sin against Sister Magdalen still unforgiven, I was banished from the set being prepared for the Eleven Plus examination for entrance into academic grammar schools. I was placed, like a villain in the stocks, in a desk for two out in the corridor with an overgrown lad smelling of stale urine who did not know what a book was for, let alone how to read it.

The desk was sited where Sister Dolores could keep an eye on us from her office. She sat very still, with an expressionless face like a Buddha. I was trapped for a year in that desk. On the wall behind us was the shrine to Saint Maria Goretti, the

Italian virgin, stabbed to death at the age of eleven because she refused to 'besmirch her chastity' with the lodger. Details of Maria Goretti's story, which was intended to promote purity in the Catholic young, prompted a darkly pleasurable excitation in my genitals. It was my special task to keep Saint Maria Goretti's votive lamps trimmed and lit.

My formal education in primary school had come to an end the moment I attacked Sister Magadalen, but close to where I sat in the corridor were shelves containing a chaos of battered books: Butler's *Lives of the Saints*, outdated Catholic directories, hymnals, an ancient and incomplete edition of the *Encyclopaedia Britannica*, and a set of novels and short stories by Charles Dickens. I spent many undisturbed hours reading about saints like Simeon Stylites who lived at the top of a pole, or devouring encyclopaedia entries on such mysteries as the history, economy and geography of Bulgaria. Best of all I lost myself in the plots of *David Copperfield*, *Great Expectations*, and *A Christmas Carol*.

At eleven I was released from the corridor and sent, as befitted an academic reject and troublemaker, to a Catholic Secondary Modern school on the Ilford High Road. The building was lit by gaslight, heated by open fires, and surrounded by a caged yard. Saints Peter and Paul was in those days an educational sink for an area that stretched from Barking, east of where my mother had been brought up, to Dagenham where Ford workers and their families lived. The head teacher, Mr J. O. Murphy, a red-necked Irishman, spent a lot of his day spying on boys. He would hide in cupboards, peep through keyholes, and stand on a ladder in order to peer around a corner from a high vantage point. He caned me almost daily, not for specific misdemeanours but on a generalised assumption that I deserved it. My classroom teacher was an exotic middle-aged woman called Roma de Roper, who had once been a professional actress. She devised bizarre theatricals mostly involving magic potions and wizards. She was a civilised contrast rather than a sufficient antidote to the male teachers. Since we had no games facilities, except for the Ilford public swimming pool, the boys' principal sport was boxing, with a vindictive tendency to mismatch troublemakers with heavier partners.

To the glee of Mr Murphy I was knocked out cold in my first gym-friendly by a boy twice my weight and reach. 'We'll get you in shape,' he told me with a chuckle. I soon learnt to keep my guard up and aim for the throat.

The school latrines, housed in an open-air lean-to in the yard, were the scene of grotesque pubescent pranks. One involved bigger boys attempting to ejaculate over the wall into the girls' playground beyond. The mechanics of these larks were a mystery, as was the fact that they possessed enormous penises compared to my own little willy. I came home uttering foul language I did not understand, my clothes filthy and in tatters from desperate playground fights. The beatings I had from my mother left me with bruised limbs and on one notable occasion the purple closure of my good eye. One day, on hearing me call one of my small brothers 'a little shit', she dragged me to the sink, prised my mouth open, and shoved in a bar of carbolic soap. I hid my fear cockily, coming back for more. Sobbing with pain after she had badly bruised her hand whacking my head (which, she said, had the consistency of reinforced concrete), she moaned: 'Oh God! . . . My poor hand! . . . One day you'll weep bitter tears over my grave.' At the time, I seriously doubted it.

She was always there, however, demonstratively supportive for life's big occasions. One of her greatest gifts after the interlude in the Sussex home was to send me at significant expense to piano lessons. The teacher was an indolent fellow called Mr Hall who had a brass plate on the door of his modest terrace house proclaiming 'The Hall Academy of Music'. The piano in our otherwise unused sitting room was tuned and I began to attend the 'academy' once a week. After six months the struggle to pay for lessons prompted her to withdraw me, saying that Mr Hall was useless; which was probably true. But at least I had learnt to read music.

It was in the crucial matters of life and death that Mum proved strongest. One afternoon I watched as a girl I knew was carried shoulder-high out of her house into a waiting ambulance. Her back was arched and she was screaming. She had contracted tetanus, 'lock-jaw', after cutting her hand on a dirty broken milk bottle. When news came of the girl's death, her mother stood in the middle of the street shrieking, her head covered with her apron. On the morning of the funeral I stood petrified on the pavement as the cortège passed.

Later that day Mum found me sitting alone on my bed, head in my hands. I had been struck for the first time with the reality of death. I felt as if I was drowning in a tide of despair and terror. Death had to be a grotesque life-in-death: dead and yet conscious, trapped in a coffin beneath the ground. She gripped me around the shoulders, a veritable wrestler's hold: 'You are never going to die,' she said with a certitude that brooked no contradiction. 'You will grow up and live for years and years ... so many years that it will seem like for ever.'

Ever since I could remember, Mum had kissed us in bed every night with the dire instruction: 'Cross your arms and pray for a happy death.' After the incident in the bedroom, she discontinued this gloomy utterance.

12

AFTER THE WAR Dad became a grounds keeper on various sports fields. Eventually he became the chief grounds keeper at the Peel playing fields in Barkingside, a working-class suburb

Sidney Cornwell, my father, on his tractor at the Peel, 1954.

at the outer reaches of London's East End. The sports facilities
– a twenty-acre field and clubhouse – were used by the
employees of several companies including the Plessey electrical
engineering factory in Ilford. After a succession of temporary
lodgings we had come finally to settle in a whitewashed box
of a dwelling by the gates of the place we were to call 'the Peel'.
The house faced a highway lined with houses and blocks of
flats. In one direction the road headed out towards the industrial wastes of the Essex estuary; in the other it merged into
London's North Circular Road. Frowning down on the district
from a far hill was Claybury Hospital, the principal mental
asylum for the East End. Claybury was a byword for lock-up
wards, a threat not infrequently employed by Mum against
Dad and each of us when we failed to live up to the standards
of behaviour she set for us.

There was one habitable living room which contained a gas
stove and sink, a built-in larder, and space for a small dining
table and chairs. We had two uncomfortable armchairs lined
with canvas, purchased from the Cooperative Society after the
war. A corresponding room on the ground floor, where the

old piano was situated, was too damp for habitation through much of the year. Upstairs there were two bedrooms and a 'box room' where my sister would sleep.

Living on the sports ground gave us an unusual sense of outdoor freedom. To the delight of my sister the former grounds keeper had bequeathed us Gyp, a shaggy sheepdog the size of a small pony. Maureen took over this lolloping animal, taking it for walks around the field. I once saw her clutching an umbrella in the pouring rain as Gyp dragged her towards the filthy, fast-running drainage ditch. For my brother Terry, the Peel was paradise. When the summer came around I watched with growing admiration as he bowled for hour after hour in the cricket practice nets. To my tearful disappointment, he would not allow me to even fetch the balls. He was on the way to becoming a demon bowler and sometimes managed to break a stump in two.

Dad tried hard to make something of the Peel, but when it rained there were gull-infested lakes where the pitches should have been. Despite his handicapped left leg, he managed to drive the pre-war tractor, working the brake and clutch like a gymnast. He became an expert on grass and spent hours gazing at seed catalogues. In 1951 he laid out lawns and flowerbeds at the entrance to the grounds to celebrate the Festival of Britain Year: the theme was strident red, white and blue. He earned five pounds a week, with free rent, and I remember his wry announcement that his pay had been increased by one penny an hour after he had agreed to squeeze another sports club on to the fields. He tried to make a few shillings on the side, bounding with his balletic stride out to the wealthy suburbs to do private gardening jobs.

At weekends Mum managed the cafeteria in the clubhouse, preparing drifts of Spam sandwiches and pyramids of cakes. Mum's cakes hardened on cooking to the consistency and taste of baked mud. We called them 'rock cakes'. When bad weather turned the cricket pitches to miniature lakes, and the matches were cancelled, we would be eating stale Spam sandwiches and rock cakes all week.

There was never enough money, and every household bill was attended by Mum's expressions of shock: 'I don't believe it! Not another one!' The house was oppressed in those days by my parents' exhaustion and tension; my mother's desperate longing for something better. The atmosphere comes flooding back whenever I hear the strains of the radio hit song of those days from *South Pacific*: 'Some enchanted evening, you may see a stranger . . .' Mum would sing it feelingly to herself, gazing longingly out of the window by the sink towards the gates of the sports ground.

For a period, under the influence of a prayer campaign in our parish by Father Cooney, now our parish priest, Mum instituted the daily recitation of the Rosary. The slogan was: 'The family that prays together stays together.' With my father sitting in his armchair by the fire, present in body but hardly in spirit, and the rest of us on our knees, we prayed five 'mysteries' of the Rosary every evening after supper. For a time Dad came to church with us. He half-sat-half-knelt in the pew, breathing deeply and bathed in sweat with the discomfort the posture caused his leg. The experiment did not last.

There were nights when we children huddled together upstairs as our parents brawled in the living room with crockery and kitchen pans, accompanied by the sound of smacks, grunts and curses. There were mealtimes when a bowl of stew or a custard tart would go flying through the air to explode on the opposite wall. No small matter for seven hungry people, and with nothing going spare. After a big fight they would refuse to speak for days and weeks on end, save for tight-lipped requests for basics: 'Pass the salt . . . please.' It usually ended with my father buying flowers, and promising a trip to the Odeon at Gant's Hill, cajoling Mum back to normal communication before the next set-to commenced.

Over the years, Mum's contempt for Dad had infected our

regard for him. Yet I found it hard to dislike him. He often made us laugh with the peculiar literalness of his humour. In the height of the summer season, when he was working outside from dawn till dusk, he would limp in wearily for his supper saying: 'Cor blimey, I'm as busy as a one-armed paper-hanger.' When we were seated, eager for breakfast, five sets of hungry eyes, he would produce like a conjuror a tiny beef-stock cube, placing it in the middle of the table: 'Here we are, kids. How about a square meal?' One day I knocked down a tin of pennies and halfpennies we kept on the mantelpiece. He picked me up and rolled me about in the coppers: 'Here we go, Jack: now you're rolling in money!'

He had a comic sense of mischief which often stoked Mum's anger. One afternoon I was bouncing a ball against the back of the house when the bathroom window opened and Mum hollered out: 'Sid! *Sid!*' Dad was in the garage, but he heard her clearly enough and came bounding along. I followed him into the house.

Mum had been trying to clean up Gyp in the bathroom and the dog refused to get out of the tub.

'Sid!' she called out to Dad, now stationed at the bottom of the stairs: 'Lift this bloody thing out of the bath, will you!' Instead, Dad gave me a wink and made a shrill whistle with his fingers. Gyp came out of the tub like a rocket, flew down the stairs and into the living room where he shook gallons of filthy water over the walls and furniture. Mum's execrations followed Dad as he retreated giggling up the yard path towards the field. By nightfall Gyp had been consigned to a stray dogs' home.

13

THE END OF my delinquency and the growth of my devout life followed a trauma that I was unable to confide in anyone, least of all Dad. From about the age of ten I was in the habit of stealing money from Mum's purse to take the tube up to central London. I would take the tram, clattering along the Victoria Embankment. I would find my way from the Monument, commemorating the Great Fire of London, to the dark magnificence of Saint Paul's Cathedral with its ancient rancid smells. I liked to walk from the Protestant Westminster Abbey to Victoria Station, marvelling at the huge apartment buildings, and the grand façade of the Army and Navy department store. By the age of eleven I had found the museums at Kensington, and I would wander there on Saturdays.

One afternoon on my way back to South Kensington a man walked in step with me along the tunnel that leads from the museum district to the underground station. He was in early middle age, well-groomed and dressed in a tweed suit. He had fair hair and a pleasant fresh complexion. He smiled at me and I smiled back. I had seen boys with fathers like him in the museums. He asked me if I would like to earn some money, showing me five shillings in the form of two newly minted half-crowns resting in the palm of his hand. It crossed my mind that the money would buy me many more trips into central London, but even as I gazed at the coins I was frightened. The tunnel was now empty of pedestrians; we were alone. I started to walk quickly ahead, but he kept pace with me. 'Don't be scared,' he was murmuring. 'I'm not going to hurt you.'

Saying that he was not going to hurt me made me all the more frightened. When he held me painfully by the shoulder, I was terrified of what he might do if I refused to cooperate with him.

In a cubicle of the deserted public toilets at South Kensington the man forced me into a deed for which I had neither words nor understanding. I was conscious only of the dirty cracked tiles, the evil smell, and the noise of flushing urinals. In my child's terror of the man and what he was doing to me, I seemed to understand so clearly what I had somehow always known: that this I, this soul of mine, was a stranger in my body, a stranger in the world.

When he had finished doing things to me, he made me do things to him. Then he stood over me, telling me never to tell anybody. 'Don't let me see your ugly little face around here again!' he kept saying. 'Look at me!' he said. But I could not look at him; I stood frozen, blind. He smacked me hard around the head, and I cried again. 'That's nothing to what you'll get if you tell,' he said. Then he made off. I had forgotten about the five shillings, and so had he.

Some time after this I had an experience in the night which seemed like a waking dream or a deeply buried memory. I was standing, dressed in nothing but a short vest, in an attic room high up in a bombed-out building where the stairs had collapsed. It was a summer's evening and I was gazing through a dormer window over rooftops and chimneys. In the far distance I could see a church tower touched by the evening sun. The sight of the church tower filled me with sadness. I could hear a sound of sighing and wailing across the rooftops like the old air-raid sirens of the war. There was a presence in the waves of sound, like an ageless dark being, and it gathered strength and purpose in a series of sickening, irresistible pulses. I was about to be engulfed by a monotonous rhythm that intended taking me to itself for ever. This I knew was the only reality, the ultimate and inescapable truth without end. As it ebbed away, like a mighty ocean of darkness, I understood that its departure was only temporary. Finally, inevitably, it would return. This and only this was real. It was a presence greater than my sense of the entire world, and it lay in wait for everyone.

After this I began to listen with greater concentration to the words of Father Cooney as he gravely recited the prayer to Michael the Archangel at the end of Mass. He spoke of the Evil One as he who 'wanders through the world for the ruin of souls'. I began to understand the Evil One as a dark power that threatens to devour every soul in the world. What extraordinary words they seemed. How they filled me with dread especially in the night: 'He who wanders through the world for the *ruin* of souls.' *Ruin*.

14

AT MY MOTHER's suggestion I responded to a call from Father Cooney for altar servers. Following an evening's instruction in the rituals, and several mornings serving Father Cooney's Mass, I found that I had an inclination for being on the sanctuary. I discovered an unexpected satisfaction in the dance of the rituals and rhythm of the recitations. The murmured words of the Latin echoing to the church rafters, the bell chimes, the devout movements by candlelight in the cool of dawn filled me with wonder. Lighting candles before the statue of the Virgin, reverently making the sign of the Cross with Holy Water on entering and leaving church, carrying rosary beads on my person at all times, genuflecting with reverence, crossing my forehead, lips and heart in the correct manner at the Gospel, calmed and soothed me.

In retrospect, there was a measure of narcissism. Through all those bad years I had often lost myself in ritualistic play. On the bedroom wall was a picture of the Sacred Heart of Jesus with hungry eyes and blood on his hands. I knew the picture had a life of its own because its eyes followed you about the room. I would offer in my play a piece of bread to the Sacred Heart, holding it up to his bearded mouth as if bestowing on Christ himself the gift of the Eucharist. I put an old satin dress of my mother's around my shoulders. Shaking with excitement, I carried the piece of bread around the room slowly; bobbing up and down, I muttered in pretend Latin over a vase. I jabbered away in a make-believe homily to the four walls. It was as if I was both heroic actor and awestruck audience in a cinema, watching myself on the screen. One day in the midst of these performances I heard a sound: looking towards the crack in the half-open door, I jumped with fright. I saw a sea-grey eye gazing at me, like the eye of God himself. Mum was watching in silence, from the landing. After that my rites became ever more secretive.

When I first began to serve Mass, my religiosity on the altar, for all its apparent self-discipline, was childishly puffed up. Each morning Father Cooney would open the doors of Saint Augustine's church at twenty minutes to seven precisely, to greet me waiting on the steps whatever the weather. There I stood sometimes drenched to the skin, sometimes caked in ice and snow, after the two-mile cycle ride from home without breakfast. These were the days when communicants, including children, fasted from midnight the previous day. Father Cooney, I was convinced, was observing me on my knees before and after Mass. I saw myself as he might have seen me: an angelic child surrounded with sacred light; a glowing little saint in a stained-glass window. I bowed profoundly till my forehead touched the carpeted steps of the altar; I beat my breast heavily at the Confiteor; I turned my head low and devoutly towards Father Cooney, as the ritual demanded; I lifted his chasuble at the consecration, while ringing the sanctuary handbell with a vigorous flourish. I did all this with a show of profound reverence, while I basked in what I imagined to be Father Cooney's approval.

Father Cooney's unspoken admiration was as nothing, however, to the sense of power I believed I had begun to exert over my mother, who still lay abed as I let myself out of the house before dawn and who began to speak to me with grudging respect as if for the clerical estate. She had even taken to rewarding me with the cream that collected at the top of the milk bottle, which she normally reserved for herself. 'You'll need this,' she would murmur, as she poured the cream over my porridge when I returned from Mass, to the sullen envy of my siblings and the wordless amusement of my father. This was holy power indeed.

15

I HAD ABANDONED the bad company of former years, and I now found a friend in an ageing woman of the parish. Miss Hyacinth Racine, who was probably in her late seventies at that time, used to haunt the pamphlet rack in the church porch. Deeply stooped, she had a prominent hook nose with hang-glider nostrils. She spent her days walking between her house and the church, pulling a shopping trolley filled with reading matter. She spoke in an accent I identified as upper class. When I held the plate beneath her bristly chin at Communion, her tongue leapt out like a trembling yellow lizard. Most people tended to shun her. Mum said she was 'a religious maniac'.

One day after Mass at the Camp, she invited me to her home. She lived and slept at the back of her semi-detached villa amid piles of old books, holy pictures, statues and devotional knick-knacks. There were French windows looking out on to a garden wilderness of brambles. On my first visit I asked if she was a widow. She told me that she was once engaged to a man who went 'missing in action' in the Great War. Every year, she said, she went to Leyton station on the date he had departed and stood at the point where he had waved her goodbye. 'For years I used to wear on that day the dress in which I said my farewell, until the moths got it.'

Some day, she assured me, he would come back.

My friendship with Miss Racine started shortly after my eleventh birthday. After that, unknown to anyone, I was often in her house, listening to her spellbound while I ate her stale biscuits and drank the weak tea she brewed in the kitchen where marauding cats had their muzzles into every item of food. She had a stock of gossip about religious books and their authors, religious communities, priests and nuns. I loved her voice. Alone in the street I would practise imitating her speech, making up conversations with myself.

She gave me a relic of Saint Thérèse of Lisieux, the French nun who died aged twenty-four and was venerated the world over as a patron saint of priests and the missions. It was a tiny leather wallet containing a piece of cloth that had touched the saint's bones. On another occasion she gave me a 'scapular', two pieces of brown cloth not much larger than postage stamps attached to each other by silken threads, to be worn beneath one's clothing across the back and across the breast. Those who died wearing this object, she said, were guaranteed an 'indulgence': release from purgatory and entry into heaven on the first Saturday following their death.

Miss Racine was mainly a gossip. She never tried to preach. But she prompted an important event in my late childhood which led to my call to the priesthood. She often spoke of her visits to a Marian shrine at a place called Aylesford in Kent. That year the Saint Vincent de Paul Society organised a free camping holiday at Aylesford priory for boys of poor families in the parish. Mum put my name forward and I was accepted.

16

SIXTY BOYS WERE taken in buses from London's East End to camp in a field next to the gardens of the priory which bordered the banks of the River Medway in Kent. Aylesford had once been the site of a medieval Carmelite foundation from which the friars were expelled at the Reformation. After the Second World War a group of Irish Carmelites had purchased the ruins and rebuilt them as a shrine to Our Lady who, according to tradition, had appeared there in the hollow of an oak tree. In those early days of its revival Aylesford was a romantic place surrounded by the unspoilt Kent countryside.

I watched the brown-and-white-robed friars singing in their renovated church, and walking prayerfully along the cloisters. I was enraptured by the view of weeping willows through clear Gothic windows, the dawn chorus, the tolling of bells marking out the monastic day, river waters lapping below ragstone walls, the smell of baking bread in the kitchens. Aylesford was a haven from the degrading everyday realities of parental discord, the school at Ilford, and dangerous men who lurk near toilets in South Kensington. The singing of the monks, from one side of the choir to the other, created a reassuring rhythm that seemed to echo deep into my heart. At Aylesford I experienced something even more transforming than morning Mass: I felt an *inclining* of my heart and soul, like the opening of a flower in warm sunlight. I was especially happy in the evening when the house martins swooped above the church roof and the scent of the river drifted in through open windows to mingle with the lingering incense.

The Prior, Father Malachy Lynch, was a large man with a great swatch of silver hair combed across the dome of his head. He spoke to me sitting on a stone ledge in the cloisters. He told me that angels had kept guard over the ruins of the monastery through the years when Catholic practice had been banned in England. He said that he had often seen angels, and that he had a sense of the presence of my own guardian angel who 'loved me very much'. One day, walking in the monastery gardens he said something that had a deep and lasting effect on me. It was natural, he said, for human beings to look for God as a son seeks a lost father: 'We are put on this earth to search for God.' He said that some people look for God with greater determination than others: 'That is what we do here at Aylesford. We friars make ourselves free to do nothing but search for God.' Before I left Aylesford to return to London, Father Malachy Lynch gave me a book, *The Imitation of Christ*. It was bound in black leather, the pages were edged in red. It slipped easily into my jacket pocket.

17

AFTER I RETURNED to the Peel and Saints Peter and Paul School, I daydreamed about Aylesford through the autumn and into the New Year. I longed for that Carmelite cloister and the presence of the monks. I began to spend more and more time in Father Cooney's 'old bit of a church' which became for me a haven in the urban dreariness of Barkingside. The smell of candle grease, the flickering sanctuary lamp, the scent of incense, thin as it was, transported me back to Aylesford in my imagination. During school holidays I sat before the blessed sacrament for what seemed hours at a time; sometimes praying, sometimes in silence as if waiting to hear the voice of God. And it now no longer mattered to me whether Father Cooney was there to observe me. Nor did it matter whether Mum knew where I was and what I was doing.

In *The Imitation of Christ* I read: 'If you would understand

Christ's words fully and taste them truly you must strive to form your whole life after His pattern.' My earlier Mass serving and displays of piety had placed me at the centre of my fantasies: the young hero saint. Now I was no longer the single and exclusive focus of my religious life. I was beginning to be interested in the person of Jesus for his own sake, as the admirable father. I saw him as he was depicted on the front of Mum's prayer book, *The Key of Heaven*, which she had possessed since her wedding day. It showed Jesus as a beautiful, mild-eyed, bearded man, pointing to his fiercely burning heart. Protective, understanding, generous, he was a father who loved us more than his own life. In *The Imitation of Christ* I sensed his concern for the poor, for the sick and the dying; his love of the meek and the peacemakers. I felt his love for children: for me. This image of Jesus merged with my memories of Father Malachy Lynch with his flowing gestures and soft reassuring voice. As I knelt in prayer in Saint Augustine's church I had the feeling that Jesus was calling me to himself, just as Father Malachy had described the call of Jesus: the invitation to spend my life seeking to know him; the call to imitate him.

One morning, as I knelt before the Blessed Sacrament, the world of my imagination and the world of daylight reality came together. I heard a low, kindly voice. I thrilled to the sound of the voice, which was even more real than the motor of a passing car on the high road outside. 'Come, John,' said the voice. 'Follow me. I want you to be one of my priests.' It was the voice of Jesus.

I cycled home in a glow of happiness; it was as if the whole world was bathed in warm light. I was filled with the love of Jesus: me for him, and him for me; it was as if I was shedding a warm glowing light on the entire world. As I cycled back to the Peel, past streets of terraced houses, past suburban avenues of little semi-detached houses with their privet hedges, storm porches, bird baths and garden fixtures, this entire Godless world seemed bathed in sacred radiance.

It was the next day that I crept into the sacristy before Solemn Benediction and grasped that sacred chalice, as if I were taking possession of my future calling, only to be scared out of my wits by Father Cooney, perched on a stool behind the door. Then came that morning, when as if by providence, Father Cooney turned to me at the end of Mass: 'Wisswiss . . . now then, John . . . What is it that you want to be when you grow up?'

I told him, confidently, that I wanted to be a priest at Aylesford. I expected his joyous approval. I was not prepared for his retort: 'Wisswiss . . . There are far too many monks and friars . . . Our Lord needs priests for our city parishes, not more Carmelites.'

I was thrown into confusion by Father Cooney's response. His world was a milieu of church building debts, primary school catechism classes, vagrants at the door, hospital visits, Barkingside High Street, the Ford and Plessey factory plants, troubled parishioners like Mr and Mrs Cornwell at the Peel. When I thought of the priesthood, I was thinking of Father Malachy Lynch and a life within Aylesford's cloisters and monastery gardens.

Then he asked me whether I had thought about applying to enter a minor seminary. I had no idea what he meant. But he was telling me, earnestly, that to delay would be a mistake. I must not miss my chance, he said.

'Sure the boy's not got a word of Latin . . . wisswiss . . . wisswiss,' he mumbled, as he took off his vestments. Now he attempted to explain in a halting fashion that a minor seminary was a college for boys who wanted to be priests when they grew up; where they got themselves a decent education.

That day I went to see Miss Racine and told her what Father Cooney had said. Her hand shook with excitement as she handed me my rattling cup of grey tea with its sour milk globules. She seemed to know a lot about minor seminaries, and their histories and locations, and she painted an enticing picture of life in those places. The minor seminaries, she told me, were the best schools in England and they were situated in beautiful locations in the distant countryside. The boys there lived the lives of monks. 'Oh yes,' she said. 'You surely have a vocation for the priesthood.'

She told me that the word 'seminary' originally meant a garden plot where seeds were grown, protected from harsh weather. Then it came to mean a college where 'seminarians' grew sturdily in their religious lives while being protected from the world. God would be my guide in his own good time, she assured me, whether it was to be a monk or a diocesan priest with a ministry in the world. 'But now that Father Cooney has suggested it, it is a sign. You must respond to his call.' She clapped her hands like a child: 'Oh, this is too lovely for words. How happy you will be, John.'

Convinced by Miss Racine that the minor seminary would be a kind of Aylesford for boys of my age, I informed Father Cooney the very next day and without reference to my parents that, yes, I would very much like to go there. He had just turned and bowed to me as we entered the sacristy after Mass. He held his head to one side. 'Ah, do you say so!' he said emphatically. 'Do you say so! Wisswiss . . .'

On that basis, and without further discussion, Father Cooney took action. The day soon came when he arived on his bicycle at the Peel with a letter for my mother, wishing to talk with her alone. I was sent upstairs to the boys' bedroom, where I sat looking out at the passing traffic. They must have talked for an hour. After he had gone, she called me downstairs and handed me a letter. It contained an instruction for me to meet the bishop. Mum looked at me with a mournful smile. Then she said with tears in her eyes: 'If only my mother were alive to see this day. Fancy, me having a son a priest. It's surely an answer to her prayers.'

Mum did not see fit to mention the matter to Dad, nor did I think to raise it with him. So it was that I came to be riding on the bus to the pleasant suburb of Woodford Green, destined for recruitment as a minor seminarian of the diocese of Brentwood.

18

THE SEMINARY CLOTHES LIST with a letter from the Very Reverend Wilfred Doran of Cotton College, North Stafford-shire, caused uproar in the house. Shaking the list above her head, Mum reckoned it equivalent to a month's wages. She accosted Father Cooney after Mass on Sunday. He arrived the next day on his bike, looking gravely askance. Ensconced in Dad's armchair, still wearing his cycle clips, he slurped his tea to the bottom of the cup. The two little ones gawped as if a giant scorpion sat ready to strike.

Father Cooney snatched the clothes list and began crossing out items and altering numbers with a pencil stub. 'Wisswiss . . . five pair of stockings [that's how he referred to what we called *socks*]. *Tree's* more than enough! *Tree* pair of trousers? Wisswiss . . . *One* pair. He'll be growing out of them anyways.'

It was still a whopping prospective bill.

Mum challenged him: 'Well, where did your parents get the money when you went to the seminary, Father?'

'Oh, I was brought up in poor old Ireland, Missus. Not a penny in the house. My dear old Mam went out the back and killed the pig.'

After he had gone, Mum stood by the kitchen sink watching him cycling away up Woodford Avenue. '"Me dear owld Mam went out da back and keeld da peeg!"' she mimicked. 'Wish *I* had a peeg out da back.'

Assistance came from the Saint Vincent de Paul Society. Four crisp five-pound notes, the white ones of those days

46

large as jumbo-sized handkerchiefs. So began the process of purchasing my seminary wardrobe, mainly at the Cooperative Society store in Ilford. The new underwear and shirts were placed in a drawer in Mum's bedroom; the black suit hung in her wardrobe. Alone in the house I would creep in and sniff the unworn items.

Time was at an agonising standstill. I attempted to bring forward the moment of departure by imagining myself sitting in the train as it pulled away from Saint Pancras station. I had chosen the passage I would read from *The Imitation of Christ* as I settled back in the seat of the carriage. What I read drew me into an interior world where I seemed ever more aware of my innermost secret thoughts, known only to me and my God:

> Avoid the concourse of men as much as you can; for discussion of worldly affairs is very bad for the soul, even though they be discussed with a good intention. For we are quickly defiled and enslaved by vanity.

I could not wait to enter the religious life so that I could make a reality of the ordinances of Thomas à Kempis in pursuit of the example of Jesus. But time obstinately refused to pass.

19

THAT SUMMER I took a full-time job as errand boy at a grocer's store on Claybury Broadway, our local shopping centre. The hours were 8 a.m. to 6 p.m. (7.30 p.m. on Saturdays), with a half day off on Thursday. In all weathers – it rained a lot that summer – I delivered boxes of groceries carried in the iron basket attached to the handlebars of an ancient bike. The popular song on the radio that summer was

Frankie Laine's 'I Believe'. Recalling that doleful tune, I see the streets of Barkingside stretching before me as I struggle to keep upright on the heavily laden machine, my toes barely reaching the pedals. When I wasn't weaving perilously on the recalcitrant bike and coping with its faulty brakes, I was blackening and chafing my hands realigning the loose chain, or mending multiple punctures in the decaying inner tubes.

I also gained first-hand experience of the amorous antics of the grocer and his assistant manageress. She was a buxom pretty woman, her peroxided hair piled high on her head. In the storeroom at the back there was a high desk at which the grocer stood doing his paperwork while eating chocolate. He would rip off the foil and bite into the chocolate bar as if it was a slice of toast. She would come up silently behind him and poke two fingers between his buttocks. Then they would go into a clinch, with a lot of tongue kissing, breast and testicle squeezing, moaning and giggling: all as, in sight of them, I attempted to fill my cardboard boxes with orders of tinned baked beans, trays of eggs, bacon, cheese, margarine, jams and marmalade. Their behaviour intrigued and yet repelled me. I prayed for them both every morning at Mass.

Two weeks before I was due to depart for Cotton College, I was fired from the job after crashing the bike while evading a dog that hurled itself at my front wheel. The dog's owner stood smirking down at me. 'That happened to me once,' he said. Then he added: 'You must have frightened him.'

The bike was a write-off, and I was concussed. The money I had earned, less compensation for broken eggs (four dozen of them were spread over the incline of Clayhall Avenue), paid for football boots and a new black blazer. 'You're lucky I didn't make you pay for a new bike, you clumsy little bleeder,' said the manager as I made my farewell.

Suffering a fever, which Mum insisted was due to homesickness in anticipation, I was unable to travel on the appointed day of the new academic year in the third week of September.

For several nights I lay weeping, convinced that I was unworthy and therefore fated never to depart for Cotton. But the Very Reverend Father Doran wrote a revised travel schedule, informing Mum that a car would be waiting at Oakamoor station and that I should arrive at the college in time for Compline, Benediction and supper.

20

ON A LATE September Sunday morning of cool breezes and brilliant sunshine I served Father Cooney's Mass for the last time. In the sacristy he handed me a parcel and told me to open it. It was a new leather-bound Roman missal in dual Latin–English translation. The pages were gilt-edged and there were sumptuous silk markers, purple, red, green, white and gold. I could smell the warm scent of the leather and the sweet aroma of the delicate rice-paper. I was moved to tears, realising the expense of the beautiful object. I attempted to thank him, but he interrupted me: 'Wisswiss . . . Very good! Run along now!' As I left the sacristy he called out: 'And keep the Faith!'

As I made my farewells at home, Terry, my elder brother, was terse: 'Now I'll be able to breathe at night.' My sister, immaculately groomed, and approaching her fifteenth birthday, gave me a quick dry kiss on the cheek. She had a knowing gleam in her eye. Not for one moment, she appeared to be telling me, was she taken in by my devout pretensions. The youngest two, aged ten and seven, stood gaping, incredulous that any of us should be escaping from the Peel. Dad came in from the field. He was blinking with nervous excitement. He lifted my bags. 'Gawd awlmighty!' he said. He sang a bar of 'Pack up your troubles in your old kit-bag', then he lowered his face towards mine for a kiss. Accompanied by Mum, wearing her purple coat, I set off through the gates of the Peel, my arms almost out of their sockets with the suitcases I insisted on carrying by myself. In my unyielding new black shoes I just made it to the bus-stop.

We had lunch in the cafeteria of Saint Pancras mainline station. Mum ordered steak. It stuck in my stomach. She nevertheless ordered treacle suet pudding, urging me to finish every morsel. Her boy was not going to depart unfortified.

The station was a like stage set for the commencement of my spiritual journey: incense steam clouds, amplified pulpit-voice announcements, grand cathedral arches, shafts of lantern-light. I leant out of the window as Mum walked, then trotted alongside the carriage, her eyes suddenly reproachful and gazing into mine. She stopped at the end of the platform, a purple figure frantically waving a handkerchief. Then she was gone.

I sat hunched forward, still suffering from lunch, looking out at the passing immensity of the aged and filthy city war-torn from Hitler's bombs. Taking *The Imitation of Christ* from my pocket I read the passage I had marked weeks earlier with a picture of Our Lady of Perpetual Succour:

> It is no small matter to dwell in a religious community,
> or congregation, to converse therein without complaint,
> and to persevere therein faithfully unto death. Blessed is
> he that there lived well, and ended happily.

Opposite me sat a smartly dressed woman. She smiled, her broad lips thick with orange lipstick. But I avoided her eyes and watched the factory buildings and terraced houses slipping by. In glimpses between tunnels and high embankments, the countryside finally opened out to the horizon. I felt a delicious sense of sadness as the train sped on, carrying me farther and ever faster away from Mum and the family, from Father Cooney, from the huge, bruised city of London. From the World.

21

THE SUN WAS setting as the steam train laboured alongside a fast-flowing river, brassy blue-green in the late afternoon sun. I could see drystone walls bordering steep fields; clusters of pine trees on the summits of dark red cliffs. Eventually there was a line of cottages and a factory foundry with clashing engines. A man lit by the reflection from a furnace stood in a doorway mopping his brow. We had arrived at Oakamoor.

The waiting car was a cavernous pre-war Austin. The driver greeted me with: 'Now then! Cotton!' As we lurched away, he explained that the factory was a copper mill. 'They keep those furnaces going day and night; even on a Sunday,' he said. The taxi paused at a crossing for the train to pass. There was a church in a steep graveyard, dense with decayed head-stones. We crossed a bridge where I could see a broad weir blurred with rising steam. Oakamoor was a settlement of workers' cottages. The dwellings cowered below the wooded flanks of the hills that rose on all sides. There was a shuttered pub.

We began a climb through hairpin bends. The road was narrow, bordered by lush pastures and coppices. At turns I could see back down to Oakamoor, virtually hidden now in mist. Higher and higher we went. Then the driver called out: 'There she is!' We were running along a straight stretch with overarching trees. In the distance, through a break in the woods, I could see a cluster of buildings which seemed to cling perilously to the side of the valley.

We paused at a crossroads by an ancient stone inn and turned left, passing a hamlet of single-file cottages. 'That was the village of Cotton, that was,' said the driver facetiously. As we passed along a level lane, sideways to the hillside, the college came into full view. At its centre was an imposing mansion to which was attached a barrack-like stone building with lighted curtainless windows. To the right of the mansion, silhouetted in the evening light, was a stone church with a spire. The college faced out across a thickly wooded shoulder of the valley; above and beyond were playing fields rising in terraces towards the crest of the valley.

There were iron gates and a driveway ahead, but the driver followed the lane around the back of the buildings and came to a halt on a cinder yard as spacious as a football field. Depositing my bags, he said: 'You go down there to the lower yard ... up the steps, and someone will look after you.' He seemed to imply, by his sympathetic tone of voice, that he felt sorry for me. Wishing me goodnight, he got into the car and shuddered away.

It was now dark, the air shockingly cold and pure. I lugged my bags down the path to the lower yard and entered a door at the top of a flight of stone steps to find myself in a high-ceilinged lobby. A priest in a cassock was standing at a noticeboard lit by a single naked bulb. He turned as I entered, as if he had been expecting me. He had huge shoulders and black horn-rimmed spectacles. His hair was cut close and stood up from his scalp stiff as a brush. He had dark eyes and a strong square jaw.

'Cornwell? I'm Father McCartie, Prefect of Discipline.'

When I said: 'Hello, Father,' he replied unsmiling: 'No, you address the priests here as "sir". It's our custom.'

Father McCartie took my bags and hurried ahead of me up four flights of a worn stone staircase, the thick crêpe-rubber soles of his shoes squelching noisily. We entered a dimly lit dormitory like a tunnel under the eaves of the house. Black iron bedsteads with white coverlets stood close together. Behind each bed was a space for storing clothes. There was a range of narrow dormer windows on each side, wide open to the raw air. A statue of Saint Joseph stood on a pedestal at one end, and a crucifix hung on the wall at the other.

'That's your berth,' said Father McCartie, pointing to a bed beneath one of the windows.

This place was called 'Little Dorm', he told me, so as to distinguish it from 'Middle Dorm' and 'Top Dorm'. There was no talking in the dormitory for any reason, he added. I was wondering why he had not asked me about my journey, or where I had come from. I had an impression of vast chilly space beyond the windows, which looked out across the valley to a pine ridge barely visible in the dusk, and I was aware of the distance I had come from home. It was all so different from what I had imagined. Aylesford and its birdsong, its summer fragrance, bell-ringing, tranquil routines and friendly friars, could not be more different from this cold, unadorned place. I thought of Mum and her protective presence, despite her unpredictable moods.

After I had finished unpacking Father McCartie picked up the two books I had brought from home: *The Imitation of Christ*, and the new Roman missal. Returning them, he said: 'Take them into church . . . Now bring your washbag and towel down to the wash places.'

Leading the way, he paused by the statue of Saint Joseph. 'That was given by the parents of a boy who died of peritonitis within two days of his arrival at Cotton,' he said almost in a whisper. 'He died fifty years ago.'

We proceeded down to the cloisters and descended again to a whitewashed cavern smelling of ancient damp. There were lines of wash bowls and pegs, all numbered. 'Your number is ninety-two,' said the priest, pointing out my bowl and peg.

I said: 'Thank you, Father.'

'No, you call us "sir",' he corrected me once more.

As we returned to the cloister, he explained that the college was founded two hundred years earlier during the penal times, when it was a crime to be a Catholic priest in England. 'The priests of this college,' he said, 'dressed in lay clothes and were addressed as "sir" to hide their true identity. We've carried on the tradition of being called "sir".'

I felt quelled, and it seemed strange that he asked me nothing about myself. Perhaps, I thought, he already knew everything that was to be known about me.

The building was echoing with the raucous clangour of a bell. Somewhere on a higher floor there was a sound of scraping of feet, and a man's voice praying, followed by a roared response. The stone stairs reverberated as a host of boys came into view walking in silence towards the cloisters where they took their places in parallel lines, hands behind their backs. They were dressed in black suits, black ties and white shirts. The toecaps of their shoes were highly polished.

The seminarians of my imagination had been pale and pious, slow of movement, gentle-eyed. These boys were fresh and open-faced, their ears red as if with the cold and the fresh air, their shoulders squared like boy soldiers. Some of the older ones had the tough appearance of farm boys or young building labourers; I had the impression that their eyes were bright, as if with a kind of inner excitement.

Father McCartie led me down the ranks and positioned me between boys who appeared to be the same age as myself. At a signal from the priest we moved forward slowly in step along the terrazzo-floored cloister like a regiment of young undertakers. Many of the boys had metal studs on their shoes giving their precise marching the sound of a metallic drum roll. We passed into a gallery I would come to know as the 'clock cloister', because of the presence of a tall grandfather clock. The walls were lined with pictures, including one prominently large print of a youth whose naked body had been punctured bloodily with arrows (this, I learnt later, was a copy of Botticelli's *Saint Sebastian*, the early Christian boy-martyr). There was a pervasive smell in the gallery, of wood polish, burnt toast and lingering coffee fumes.

Finally we passed through double doors into the church

where our footsteps echoed on the patterned tiles and the cool air was heavy with the smell of incense and candle grease. The ceiling disappeared into the darkness high above. There were simple stone columns, unadorned side altars, and a Lady chapel at the end of a side aisle beyond a wooden screen. The boys took their places in plain pine pews on either side of the main aisle; beyond the altar rails was a spacious sanctuary with choir-stalls, an organ, and a stone high altar in the distance overlooked by a massive east window gleaming in the darkness. The boys were kneeling, ramrod straight; the kneelers were made of hard wood. The boy next to me, a youth with pale limp hair, high colouring in his cheeks, and National Health spectacles, took my missal and found me the page for Sunday Compline.

A procession of boys entered the sanctuary, filing into the choir-stalls, followed by a priest wearing a white-and-gold cope. He was tall and ruddy, and walked casually without a hint of devotion. He bowed at the foot of the altar and intoned in Latin the beginning of Compline, the office of prayers at the end of the day.

The ritual appeals to God for his protection as night falls: 'May the dreams and phantasms of the night recede; keep the enemy at bay, lest our bodies become polluted.' At the *Salve Regina* the boys' voices soared up to the high rafters: 'To you we sigh, groaning, and weeping in this vale of tears . . .' I was conscious of the wild valley in its remote and rugged setting in the darkness outside, deepening the sense of strangeness. Then it struck me that unless I begged to be allowed home the very next day, I had no other choice but to throw myself completely on the person of Jesus. I stole a look around me. My companions knelt with their faces buried in their hands in prayerful recollection.

After the celebrant and the choir processed off the sanctuary we began to leave the pews in strict order, starting with the front row. Towards the rear of the church there were six or seven priests. One older than the rest, bespectacled and with fair receding hair swept back, was scrutinising each of us in turn. I guessed that this was the Very Reverend Wilfred Doran, the superior of the house and headmaster. His face betrayed no emotion, neither severity nor kindliness. Father McCartie knelt on the opposite side of the aisle. He too was watching each boy in turn with those dark eyes through heavy black horn-rims. The others were reading their breviaries.

At the end of the cloisters we passed through a set of double doors into an oak-floored refectory and the warm atmosphere of cooked food. Someone touched me on the shoulder: it was the boy who had knelt next to me in church. He was about the same height as me, his wrists protruding a long way out from his black sleeves. He held his head submissively to one side. 'My name is James Rolle. I've been deputed to look after you,' he said with a reassuring smile. 'Welcome to Cotton.' He placed me next to him in the middle of one of the rows of tables.

The boys were standing in silence, hands joined. Near the double doors there was a table where three nuns stood with ladles poised over enamel serving pans. After Father McCartie said grace we sat down while boys assigned to be servers queued in front of the nuns. Each boy received a portion of beans and a hunk of bread. They fell hungrily on the food, eating at speed. After several minutes there was a sharp rap as Father McCartie struck the serving table, and the boys began to talk all at once.

James said: 'Did you have a pleasant journey?' No sooner had I answered and begun to tell James about my home parish than Father McCartie rapped on the table again and the boys fell silent and stood up, heads bowed for the grace.

Outside the refectory, James took me down to a room in the basement. It was cold and dimly lit, with stone flags and pine benches. Boys sat around talking quietly in groups, occasionally laughing. James was intent on being kind to me.

'On weekdays,' he explained, 'we have Rosary after supper, which you can say either in church or in the cloister. I rarely come in here. I usually go to the library which is above the refectory.' James seemed unusually self-controlled and serious. I decided that I liked him.

'Do you like reading?' he asked. 'What are you reading?' When I said that I was reading *The Imitation of Christ*, he reacted with surprise. Slipping his hand into his jacket pocket, he pulled out a slim black copy of the *Imitation* with red edging, identical to my own. 'I read it at odd moments of the day, and carry it everywhere,' he said. 'But it's spiritual reading, isn't it? One could hardly count it as one's normal reading.'

At the clangour of bells, James said that we would not be allowed to speak until breakfast the next day. I should just follow him. 'Watch out,' he said grimly. 'You'll be beaten by Leo if you're caught talking, and so will anybody you're caught talking to.' Leo, he explained, was Father McCartie's nickname.

Boys were hurrying down the cloisters to the staircase leading to basement level where they took off their jackets and ties to wash in cold water and brush their teeth. I was still brushing my teeth when an older boy told me brusquely to get a move on. James was waiting to accompany me to the dormitory.

About sixty boys were lodged in Little Dorm; they changed into their pyjamas with a uniform set of modest stratagems. They went down on their knees to pray silently for a few moments before getting into bed. I was still undressing when the lights flashed off and on. I nevertheless went on to my knees to pray.

I thanked God for a safe journey and asked for his protection through the night. After a prayer to my guardian angel ('O my good angel, whom God has appointed to be my Guardian . . .'), I was the last to get into bed, where I lay shivering for several minutes. The sheets felt damp and the mattress was as lumpy as a sack of potatoes, but it was the first time I had slept in a bed to myself since my brother Terry had returned from evacuation.

Father McCartie appeared by a doorway situated at the top of a wooden stairway which looked to be a laundry shoot. After a while he began to walk along the lines of beds looking at each of the boys in turn; he had taken off his noisy crêpe-soled shoes and was in bedroom slippers. Then the dormitory was plunged in darkness and silence. How comforting it would have been, I thought, had the priest wished us goodnight and blessed us.

The air, carried on a stiff breeze through the dormer windows, was cold on my face. Soon I made out the night sky through the window above my bed. A scattering of stars sailed between the clouds. I could hear the wind in the trees, then, gradually, in the far distance, the sound of a motorbike taking the steep climb up from Oakamoor, constantly changing gear before surging forward; eventually the sound grew fainter and merged with the rustling of the treetops. I wondered what the family were doing back in London. Dad and my brother Terry were probably listening to the radio, perhaps a cheerful dance number played by the Palm Court orchestra. Sister Maureen the convent-school girl would be doing her homework, while Mum was washing dishes at the sink. My younger brothers would be fast asleep in their single bed, lying end to end.

I lay awake until the breathing of the boys about me became regular. I was dozing off, when I was surprised by the sight of a black figure in the darkness moving silently along the dormitory. I guessed that it was Father McCartie. For an age, it seemed, I could see him standing in silence at the doorway halfway down the dormitory. Eventually he left. As I dozed, I was again conscious of the great spaces beyond the windows and the garret roofs. I felt the wild presence of the woods and hills which were to be my new home.

22

THE NAKED DORMITORY lights were switched on and a senior boy passed at a run, whacking the ends of the iron bedsteads with a heavy book and shouting: 'Up!' It was still dark outside and there was a stiff wind and spots of rain whipping through the dormitory windows. Boys were leaping from their beds, throwing back the bedding for airing; going down on their knees to pray. As it was a weekday, they were donning grey flannel trousers and casting over their shoulders black or navy blazers or sombre tweed jackets in readiness to depart for the wash places. I was the last out, struggling with fingers too stiff with cold to keep up. James, who was several beds down from me, was waiting and gestured for me to follow.

He saw me through my ablutions before leading the way to church where we were the last to take our places in the pews. The boys were kneeling with their shoulders hunched, heads bowed in private prayer. A bell rang and the Mass celebrant and two servers appeared on the sanctuary. I looked at my watch and saw that it was only seven o'clock. The sun was rising, revealing the magnificent detail of the stained-glass window above the high altar – an image of the enthroned Christ the King surrounded by angels and saints. I had grown used to being the only boy at dawn worship in the church at home; it was strange to be kneeling with so many youths at a time of the day that had been special for me and Father Cooney alone.

While the boys concentrated on the main community Mass there was a constant ringing of small bells, muttered Latin, and a flurry of rituals at the side altars of the church as priests came and went with servers to say their private Masses. But the activity died down after the community Mass ended. The last of the priests had returned with his server to the sacristy, and the church was silent.

The period of thanksgiving after Mass seemed interminable. My stomach was churning with hunger, my knees were giving way, and I had a headache and a full bladder. The discomfort was all the worse as I had no idea how long it would last. I felt humbled by the youths around me who seemed controlled and patient in their apparent contemplation.

Father McCartie's rap at last signalled us to leave the church in ranks for the refectory. Breakfast, eaten in a few gulps by most boys, was porridge (grey, salty, lumpy and made without milk), hunks of dry bread and plastic mugs of tea. James accompanied me to the dormitory where we made our beds in silence, Father McCartie lurking in the background. Descending the stairs, James said we were free until the beginning of lessons so he would give me a tour.

The central focus of the array of college buildings was the façade of the mansion he called the 'old hall' where the priests had their rooms and refectory. Before it was a sweep of lawn and a grand cedar of Lebanon. At the back of the old hall was an ugly extension where the nuns lived. James explained that they did our laundry, cooking and cleaning. 'We call them the witches,' he said with a contrite smile. 'They have taken a vow of silence. But the sister matron speaks to us.'

Attached to the old hall were two stone Victorian elevations at right angles to each other, which housed the boys' refectory, libraries, dormitories, classrooms and wash places. A cloister with Gothic vaulting ran through one of the wings. The most recently built section of the college was a square rose brick structure known as Saint Thomas's where the most junior boys, aged eleven to thirteen, had their dormitories under the supervision of a wraith-like balding priest called Father Manion.

James showed me the library, which smelt of beeswax floor polish. There were deep windows with views of the valley and an expanse of tall shelves. A few boys were sitting at the tables reading. Through a far door was another library with oak panelling and stained-glass windows which, James whispered to me, was the sixth form library. He pointed out a periodicals table with several magazines from other schools and seminaries on display. A single copy of the *Illustrated London News* lay on the table. 'There are no newspapers,' he said, 'and we're not allowed to listen to the radio.'

He explained that from among the boys in the final two years at Cotton were recruited the college monitors, house captains and their deputies: they were known as the Big Sixth and had the power to have boys punished by sending them to the Prefect of Discipline or the Prefect of Studies. The teaching staff priests, he said, were known as 'the profs'.

We finally emerged into the chill morning air, descending by stone steps known as the Bounds Steps into an area James called Little Bounds, a yard large enough for two tennis courts. Little Bounds formed a kind of level platform or stage looking out over the panorama of the surrounding countryside, bathed that morning in early autumn sunshine. Several boys were staring like prisoners in a cage through the wire fence that bordered the yard. James and I joined them. The high fence marked the boundary, James told me, between the boys' domain and the lawns and gravel pathways strictly for the use of 'the profs'.

Immediately below these gardens a drystone wall bordered the lush meadows, ending abruptly at a wood that descended into the valley. Beyond the closest canopy of the woods, a mile or so away, rose a corresponding series of meadows on the opposing flank of the valley. An ancient stone cottage stood in one of the meadows, a wisp of smoke rising from its chimney. This was the only human habitation visible in the landscape. To the left of the pine wood was a sheer drop and the distant countryside opened out in a succession of gentle shoulders and folds, each softer and more hazy than the last, until the final ridge melted into the skyline. As I stood there my heart leapt with the immensity of the scene and the bracing air.

James now led the way to a second level by way of a wide sloping path up to the cinder yard he called Top Bounds, where I had been deposited the previous evening. Boys were walking up and down in threes and fours, hands in pockets. James said: 'Shall we take a few turns?'

As we walked we were joined by another boy with severe acne and untidy hair who introduced himself as Derek Hanson from Southend, Essex. He too was a seminarian from the diocese of Brentwood. He skipped about a little as he walked, turning towards me, then suddenly turning away. He was describing the eccentricities of his parish priest at home, while occasionally giving vent to nervous ripples of laughter. After one more fit of the giggles he said: 'Watch out for Father Armishaw.' Then he blushed and excused himself, hurrying down towards Little Bounds.

'Derek is very nice,' said James, 'but he has taken a sort of vow never to talk after mid-morning break.' James seemed to consider the matter for a few moments. 'I do think that his behaviour is rather singular,' he added. It was the first time I had heard the term 'singular', and I was not sure what it meant. (I was soon to discover that it was an important watchword in our spiritual lives, meaning any behaviour that was deemed showy.) Then he informed me that 'Armishaw' was Father Vincent Armishaw who taught English. 'He's a character, a bit ferocious, but he's not too bad. Derek has a crush on him; and he's not the only one.'

23

As we walked in Top Bounds a boy came up and asked me to accompany him to Father Doran, the headmaster. His office was situated on a corridor with a highly polished linoleum floor in the old hall. The boy rapped hard on the door. When a muffled voice called out: 'Come!' he left me to enter by myself.

Father Doran, a thin, slightly stooped man in a caped cassock, was leaning on the mantelpiece in a room filled with light from a set of bay windows that went from floor to ceiling. There was a desk covered with papers, and glass-fronted bookcases. The atmosphere of the room was heavy with tobacco.

He was busy with a penknife and a pipe, attempting to extract burnt-out tobacco into an ashtray at his elbow. At the same time he occasionally looked down on me with penetrating grey eyes through flashing gold-rimmed spectacles. His ash-fair receding hair was brushed back flat on his head and his thin lips were firmly set in a long pale face. He looked about the same age as my father. He stopped fiddling with his pipe, snatched a cigarette from a Senior Service pack and lit it with an almost petulant movement.

'I prefer to smoke a pipe,' he said, the cigarette wobbling up and down on his thin lips. 'But whenever the reverend mother comes in from the sisters' community, I have to put it down. You see, it's never done to smoke before the sisters. Then it's such a business to light it up again.' He took a deep drag and held the cigarette between his fingers as he blew out a long column of smoke. 'She's just been in this morning, wanting to discuss kitchen business and here we go again – down goes the pipe,' he said. 'So I think to myself: "Oh bother, I'll just have a cigarette, it's much less trouble."'

Very Reverend Father Wilfred Doran,
Headmaster of Cotton College.

He stopped to inspect me. 'You don't smoke, do you, John Cornwell?'

I shook my head.

'Well, just make sure you don't. In any case, you'll need to save all your puff for cross-country running, especially when you're sprinting up and down the valley here.'

I smiled, but he was observing me without a hint of humour. He began to talk about the history of the school. He told me that Cotton was the oldest Catholic college in England. Most boys were sent here, he said, by the Archbishop of Birmingham, who was the official owner of the school, but there were also a number of students from my own diocese, Brentwood, which had no minor seminary. A minority of the boys, he added, were 'lay students' who had not dedicated themselves to the priesthood, and whose parents were therefore paying for their education. 'You must understand,' he said with gravity, 'that your bishop has been put to considerable expense to place you here, and that your fees are paid for out of the charity of the people of your diocese. So you will do your very best to make the most of this opportunity.' He said that fourteen former pupils of Cotton had been ordained that year. 'That is your aim,' he went on. 'To become a priest ... Just keep your sights on that and you can't go wrong.'

Father Doran now walked over to the bay windows which had an unhindered view across the valley. He beckoned me to join him. 'Splendid, isn't it,' he said. 'Aren't we lucky to be enjoying all this?'

'It's beautiful,' I said, avoiding the use of the word 'Father'. I found myself thinking of the 'aunt' at the home in Sussex, and how I had described the beautiful countryside as 'shitty'. I was eager to let him know that I was impressed by the view.

'Well, enjoy it now to the full,' he said, 'because one day you'll probably be trapped in a city where there's not a single tree, let alone grass and cows.' For the first time he gave a husky laugh, and I smiled back at him with relief as he took another deep drag on his cigarette.

Now that I was here, standing at Father Doran's windows with the great panorama of the valley below, I had the confidence to say: 'I'm glad that I'm here, Father.'

'Sir,' he said. 'Sir! not Father!' Then he announced with an air of grandeur: 'For the purposes of competitive spirit all the students in the college belong to one of three groups or houses, named after the great founders of the Catholic archdiocese of Birmingham. You have been placed in Challoner House, which commemorates Bishop Richard Challoner who founded the college in secrecy in 1763 when Catholics were still being persecuted by the Protestants for their Faith.' Bishop Challoner, he went on, was a wonderful man. During one of the anti-Catholic riots in London a Protestant mob threatened to burn down his house. 'So there you are,' he went on. 'We have great traditions! And you are now a Challoner man as well as a Cottonian.'

With this he led me out of his office and down the corridor to a room where a priest was standing, reading some papers, his thick-rimmed spectacles up on his forehead. He was robust with a lineless cherubic face and marked dimples. He was almost bald, despite his youthful appearance; but he had a ring of hair that looked like little collections of chick feathers. He was dressed in a cassock over which he wore an academic gown with long drooping false sleeves. 'Aha! Master Cornwell,' he said. 'Let me introduce myself: Father Tom Gavin, Prefect of Studies!'

Before leaving me, Father Doran turned to say: 'I'll be watching you closely, Cornwell. And I shall be informing your good bishop of your progress.'

'Now let me see! Cornwell!' said Father Gavin with a radiant grin. 'Frumentum Bene! That's "corn" and "well" in Latin! I suppose we'd better shorten it to Fru. Yes, I like Fru. You look like a Fru. I take it you have no Latin. No Latin at all, eh, Fru!'

With this he gingerly extracted from his shelves a slim book, grinning back at me conspiratorially as he did so. 'This, Fru,' he said, as if he were a magician producing a tender live animal from a hat, 'is called a Latin primer. And you are going to become well acquainted with its contents, otherwise your bottom is going to become acquainted with that stick there on the bookshelf.' His face was bright red now, his shoulders heaving with laughter. 'Not to worry, Fru,' he said. 'Only joking, eh! But my stick is there to make sure you behave in class, eh!'

I decided that I liked his joviality even if I did not care for his joke.

Placing the book in my hands he said in a low murmur, his small mouth fighting against the compulsion to smile: 'Take it away with you, Fru. In spare moments acquaint yourself with the first ten pages in preparation for the treat of our first lesson.' Before dismissing me, he produced a timetable, specially devised, he said, so that I could catch up with my class year, which was known as the lower fourth.

24

THE MORNING PASSED in abrupt initiations and lessons, punctuated by an unrelenting routine of church visits and religious rituals. I was shown my desk, a capacious box with an oak lid, situated in the lower fourth's area of the study place, a room which ran the length of one of the stone wings and contained more than a hundred such desks. I was summoned to 'the bursary', a room stacked with bars of soap, stationery and clothing, where Father William Browne, a sad-looking overweight priest, issued me with sports gear. I was told to attend 'the dispensary' where the matron prodded and poked me all over. When she had finished inspecting my tongue and poking my ribs she murmured: 'Ah well! Let's be thankful for small mercies.'

Lunch, which followed the visit of the whole college to the Blessed Sacrament, was a dish of tasteless greasy mincemeat, which the boys called 'slosh', accompanied by boiled blemished potatoes, which they called 'chots'. Within minutes of lunch ending, a bell rang and the boys were hurrying to the dungeon wash places to change into sports gear for a cross-country run. Being under fourteen I was assigned to the 'easy' three-mile course.

We streamed up a footpath between drystone walls, green-edged with age, heading for the summit of the valley. I stumbled along, buffeted by a stiff wind. Ahead was a wood of stunted trees; to our right miles of uplands dappled in sunlight to the horizon. To the left was a view of barren hills, their soft green sides broken with outcrops of rock. I was breathless, my legs failing. James hung back, looking sympathetic. We were now the very last of the runners, and the rear was taken up by an older boy who prodded me forward gently with soft little punches in the small of my back. At length we were running on level terrain. Silent woods alternated with swampy open land and we were up to our ankles in the black brackish water that lay below the turf. We clambered over yet another drystone wall and plunged into a pig farm where we were up to our shins in stinking swill and mud.

The college was below, nestling around the church steeple. By the time James and I reached the wash places, most of the boys had doused themselves in cold water and changed back into their day clothes.

The lesson schedule on that first afternoon introduced me to Father Gavin's special class for Latin beginners. My attention kept wandering to the foliage of the trees at the head of the valley while the lesson unfolded quickly and confusingly with explosions of laughter, jokes and Latin nicknames as Father Gavin drove us on, attempting to explain the mysteries of conjugations and declensions.

Afterwards we were guided to Dr Warner's remedial class for Greek beginners. Dr Warner was dressed in an ancient grey suit patched with poorly sewn strips of black leather. His face was sallow and faded, his bald pate deeply wrinkled. After setting the others an exercise on the board, he came to sit next to me. Sighing a little as if weary to the heart, he showed me how to form the Greek letters of the alphabet. He smelt of boot polish and his breath was rancid. As I attempted to copy the letters by myself, he hummed a monotonous little tune: '*Alpha . . . beta . . . gamma . . . delta . . .*'

James met me on Little Bounds to take me in to afternoon tea. He said that Dr Warner was known as Lazarus, or Laz, but his real first name was Leslie. Laz Warner, James said, was a deacon who had studied for the priesthood at the Venerable English College, the seminary for England and Wales in Rome.

Dr 'Laz' Warner.

On the day before his ordination he decided that he was not worthy to be a priest after all. But his diaconate status had left him committed to celibacy. He came to Cotton where he had remained ever since. Laz was a man of immense learning, said James, but he and his strangely patched suit were unfortunately the butt of many jokes. 'He is,' said James, 'like an old bridegroom who changed his mind on his wedding day.'

25

As MY FIRST week passed, the rhythm of the day, punctuated by a huge jangling bell rung by the school captain, settled into a routine of classes, study periods, manual labour, runs, drill and hurried meals. But religious devotions dominated: meditation before the early morning Mass; Low Mass celebrated every day of the week, followed by private thanksgiving; with High Mass in addition on Sundays and feast days. There was a homily, known as 'conference', after High Mass; prayers before and after each lesson, and Angelus recited twice daily. There was grace before and after every meal, community prayers before lunch, spiritual reading after tea, Rosary after supper, and night prayers before bed on weekdays; Compline on Sunday evenings. Confessions could be heard each evening after supper. There was private spiritual direction on Thursday afternoons when confessions were also available. Many boys spent time in church during their scarce leisure periods.

On my second day, coming out of the refectory after tea, I was accosted by Father Anthony Owen. He was a stiff-necked man in middle age with thinning sandy hair and remarkably bowed legs, hence his nickname, 'Bowie Owen'. He understood, he said, that I could read music and wanted to test my voice for the choir. We walked to the choir practice room where there was an upright piano.

After taking me through several scales, he said: 'You'll make an excellent alto, but open it out! Let yourself go!' Choir practice, he said, was every day after tea. 'But there are advantages, Cornwell. Outings, special treats.'

Suddenly the door was flung open and boys of all ages began to enter. Father Owen distributed music sheets for Mozart's 'Missa Brevis'. The youngest boys jostled in friendly horseplay while the older ones – the tenors and basses – affected a sense of disdain.

Father Owen, standing at the piano, took each of the four voices separately. Then he turned to face us as he conducted us in harmony with minimal gestures, closing his forefingers and thumbs at the dying fall of a bar in a gentle pinching gesture. At one point, looking at me directly, he put his hand to his ear as if to indicate: 'Let it out!' When we had finished the Gloria, he bowed and implored us not to be late for practice the next day.

As I was leaving, he took me by the arm and drew me back into the room. 'That wasn't too bad, was it, Cornwell,' he said. 'I think you'll be a useful member of the choir. But let's hope that your voice doesn't break too soon.'

Until then I had never given any thought to the fact of my voice breaking.

26

THE PROFS WERE always and everywhere in evidence: at the side altars saying their Masses in the morning, in the classrooms, and on the playing fields. There was a priest, sometimes two or more, present at every juncture of the day to scrutinise us. We were watched from morning until night, and even through the night, it seemed, by Father McCartie.

Father Tony Piercy made an immediate impression. Built like a boxer, and known as 'Tank', he was to be seen hurrying about the buildings and across the Bounds, propelling himself forward in a flurry of cassock and gown with a springy half-walk-half-run, shoulders squared. He had a head of unruly, wiry hair and his nose appeared pinched at the end, which gave him a strangely fastidious appearance, as if aware of an unpleasant smell about him. He taught mathematics and he was a tireless handyman, James told me, a 'general factotum' around the college, who would cure the ailing plumbing, rebuild a broken desk, mend a boiler, or service Father Doran's car. Beneath his cassock he wore scuffed army boots caked with mud, and invariably carried a variety of tools in his capacious cassock pockets.

Two days after my arrival at Cotton, Father Piercy introduced me to 'manual labour'. This involved digging ditches in a scheme to level and drain the playing fields above the college. The drains were constructed by digging down four feet and laying limestone-grit boulders along a channel two feet wide before replacing and levelling the soil. Boulders from disused drystone walls had to be fetched, sometimes from a mile distant. They were heavy and it was easy to tear one's hands on the jagged edges.

James encouraged me to join Father Piercy's 'Workers' Union', as the ditching teams were called. 'Ditching,' he murmured, 'is, of course, an opportunity for self-denial.' We wore rubber Wellington boots, with rugby shorts and shirts over our second-best clothes to protect us from the mud. Father Piercy, dressed in a filthy blue boiler suit and army boots, leapt in and out of the ditches, directing operations. He never spoke to us directly, nor even looked at us, but appeared to focus his attention inches away from the end of his pinched nose as if he was trapped inside a protective bubble.

On the afternoon of the first Thursday after my arrival I attended Father Piercy's handicraft session. Thursdays were a half-day holiday from games, lessons and manual labour, but boys were expected to do something constructive. One could choose between reading in the library, attending confession and spiritual direction, or handicraft. And it was possible to do all three. The projects in Father Piercy's workshop included the making of rosaries, the cutting and binding of leather cases for missals and prayer books, the carving of crucifixes, or construction of pipe-racks. He set me to work making a case for my missal, Father Cooney's gift. He moved from boy to boy at the work benches, demonstrating techniques for cutting leather, sewing, binding, making the hooks for rosary beads, and carpentry. He spoke in a quiet, barely intelligible, rapid nasal voice, and appeared to be working his mouth nervously.

Another striking prof was Father Armishaw whom Derek had mentioned blushingly when we were walking on Top

Bounds. Father Armishaw taught English literature to the fifth and sixth forms. He was over six foot with broad shoulders, and dressed in a caped cassock, and an MA gown when he was teaching. He could be seen making his way across Little Bounds, a book under his arm, walking with a self-confident rolling gait. He had a swashbuckling posture; but such was his powerful physique and piercing look, it seemed natural rather than boastful or proud. He was also famous for owning a large gleaming motorcycle with a dark green petrol tank. Several times in my first week I saw him flying along the lane at the back of the school, the flaps of his leather flying jacket open to the wind.

I encountered Father Armishaw when I went up to the top corridor in the old hall to deliver an exercise I had written out for Dr Warner. He lived on a passageway known as 'Creepers', as boys were expected to go on tiptoe so as not to disturb the priestly inhabitants. The first door on the left stood wide open; as I glanced in I saw Father Armishaw at his desk in the middle of the room. There was a bed in one corner with a white coverlet like the ones in our dormitory. There were two simple armchairs, and bookcases running from floor to ceiling around the walls. The books, many hundreds of them, were carefully arranged, their spines all evenly regimented and displayed. Everything about the room was neat, and the polished surfaces reflected the light of the coal fire in the grate. On a table beneath the open window was a gramophone playing a piece of music. The priest sat slouched at his desk, a smoking cigarette between his fingers. He had strong, well-proportioned features; jet black wavy hair, strong and glossy like the coat of a healthy animal. He looked up from a book he was reading and stared back, his mouth a little open, his lips slightly curled as if he were mocking me.

'What are *you* gawping at?' he said in a low voice. I was rooted to the spot. Then he said evenly: 'Well, if you don't want anything, bugger off!'

Father Vincent Armishaw.

I had never heard a priest swear or utter a vulgarity, and I was shocked. I moved along the corridor and left my exercise book outside Dr Warner's door as I had been instructed. When I returned, Father Armishaw had come to lean up against the door jamb of his room, all his weight on one leg. He was watching me, smiling. 'And who might you be?'

When I told him my name, he made a gesture with his head as if to show that his curiosity was satisfied. 'You're one of those Brentwood types, aren't you?'

Then he nodded into his room towards his gramophone. 'Listen to that . . .'

Filling his room and resounding into the corridor was the sound of a violin backed by an orchestra. The music was entering its finale, and the priest stood watching me in silence, nodding his head in time with the rhythm. When it had finished, he said: 'Do you know what that was?'

'No, sir.'

'Mozart . . . second violin concerto. Not bad, eh!'

I stared at him, speechless.

'One day, perhaps, I'll play it through from beginning to end for you. In the meantime stay out of trouble.'

As I turned to go, he added: 'And mind you don't take life too seriously.'

The incident excited me. I felt that the priest had engaged me rather than kept me at bay like the others. The following day, walking up and down Top Bounds after breakfast, I reported the encounter to James, and James reported it to Derek when he joined us as he usually did. Derek was avid for every detail and chortled and danced around with glee.

27

IN THE SECOND week my name appeared on the Mass roster to serve Father Piercy. There was no hint of emotion or devotion in his voice or gestures. At Saint Augustine's I had emulated Father Cooney's slow and devout voice; kneeling beside Father Piercy, I found myself trying with difficulty to pace my responses with his rapid recitation. Father Cooney would take almost an hour over Mass, whereas Father Piercy said his in twenty minutes.

Day by day the choir prepared for the Sunday High Mass. On that first Sunday we sang the Mozart Mass, and Victoria's 'O Sacrum Convivium' during the Offertory. The rest of the service, involving the whole college, was sung in Gregorian chant. The long, complicated Mass was celebrated by three priests robed in green vestments and beskirted with lace albs. The pillars of exorbitant incense smoke (Father Cooney would have been scandalised) rose high to the rafters. In their distant side aisle I could see the nuns, some twelve of them, following the Mass with rapt attention.

As I found my feet at Cotton in those first days, struggling with the early lessons, keeping up on runs, shivering under cold showers, and attempting to wolf down the tasteless meals, I realised that the single most important focus of our routine was the sanctuary, where we created a daily pageant of music, precise rituals, and rapid rhythmic prayer. The tabernacle on the high altar, where resided the real presence of Jesus Christ, was the centre of our lives. And yet, I was conscious of another presence, in the wild panorama of the woods and hills and sky outside. I sometimes found myself gazing through a window in the cloister, fascinated by the sight and sound of the bluster-ing winds and the racing clouds. The wild disturbance of the countryside seemed to echo an unfamiliar and troubled excitation in my soul.

I went for confession and spiritual direction to Father Browne, the bursar, who also acted as parish priest for the small community of Catholic farmers who lived in the locality of Oakamoor. Father Browne saw boys in his sitting room off the church cloister. He was a heavy man, with sleepy eyes, pale flaccid jowls and wiry grey hair. He appeared slow of move-ment, as if he was weary. He smelled of incense and the bars of soap in his bursar's shop. There was something gentle and soothing about him, almost motherly. His hands were very white and plump.

He asked me to sit opposite him on a corresponding chair and began by asking about the family and my home parish. Occasionally, moving his head languidly, he would look out of the window at the valley scene where low clouds were rising, trailing rain squalls over the canopy of the woods.

An important first step in the pursuit of the devout life, he told me, was the daily, or, better still, twice daily, examination of conscience. 'I want you to get into the habit of reviewing your behaviour,' he said gently. 'Have I thought unkindly of anybody today? Have I thought less of them? Have I envied anybody?'

He asked me about my spiritual reading. When I told him about *The Imitation of Christ*, he replied: 'Yes, a lot of boys here read the *Imitation*.' He said that excellent as it was, the work was written for enclosed monks and nuns. Had I not heard, he asked, of the greatest model of parish priests, Saint John Vianney? 'He was known as the *Curé d'Ars*,' went on Father Browne. 'You'll find several books about him in the college library.'

That afternoon I took down from the library shelves a book entitled *A Saint in the Making: The Story of the Curé d'Ars*. In the frontispiece was an engraved portrait: the saint's cheeks were hollow and his eyes looked upwards towards the heavens. Sitting in the library with its glowing mahogany shelves and dramatic views down the valley I started to read. The historical setting of the famous priest's life, I learnt, was France in the years after the Revolution: the persecution of bishops, priests and nuns; the suppression of seminaries. John Vianney inherited a parish sunk in drunkenness and fornication and made it a model of sanctity. He was convinced that the root of evil in his village was dancing, since it led to girls and boys touching and exposing themselves to sexual temptation. He was intent on eliminating 'occasions of sin'; he even had the apple trees cut down in his orchard to deprive the village boys of the temptation to go scrumping. John Vianney disdained to sleep in a bed; the floor was sufficient for him, without pillows or blankets. He rose in the middle of the night and went to his church to lie full stretch on the stone flags. For food he would cook a pan of potatoes once a week, hang them in a wire basket and eat them till there were none left. The final potatoes were always rotten and wormy. He wore a hair shirt and flogged himself. What seized my imagination far more than his 'thirst for souls' were his heroic prayer life and self-mortification.

I realised that John Vianney's heroism was impracticable, but I was determined to emulate the saint in so far as I could. Like other more pious boys I had begun to spend regular time in private prayer in church during mid-morning break, and between outdoor activities in the afternoon and first lessons. I had also begun to wear a hairy knitted sleeveless pullover under my vest which chafed my skin – a kind of junior hair shirt. Before going to sleep I pinched myself hard on the legs and on my waist. I was refusing sugar on my porridge at breakfast.

During my next session with Father Browne, I told him of my self-mortification. I wanted to be more like John Vianney, I said, but I could not see how that would be possible until I became a priest. Father Browne nodded sleepily. He said that my frustration was a good sign, because it meant that I was ready to consider what Saint Thérèse of Lisieux called her 'Little Way'. It was not necessary to perform unusual mortifications, such as whipping oneself or wearing a hair shirt, or fasting. 'In fact,' he said, 'you should take sugar on your porridge as you need all the energy you can get to grow strong and healthy.'

Extricating a book from the pile on the table next to his elbow, he said: 'I want you borrow this for the rest of the term. You'll find that Saint Thérèse made heroic sanctity out of the small everyday routines of convent life.' He told me how she knelt in front of a nun in chapel who rattled her rosary beads. 'She could have quelled the annoying behaviour with a single look; instead she chose to endure the irritation.' At times, he said, Thérèse was so distressed as she struggled to resist the temptation to rebuke the nun that she would break out in a sweat.

Father Browne, in his calm motherly voice, asked me to read the book slowly and thoughtfully. It was a fat, dark green book with gold lettering: *Soeur Thérèse of Lisieux: An Autobiography*.

28

FROM HIS HIGH desk Father Gavin fixed me with an alarming rubicund grin of pity and glee. 'Find time, *Magister* Fru,' he said, 'to write out one hundred times the declensions and conjugations I set you yesterday.'

It was my fourth week at Cotton and I was struggling with Latin. Most of my year had come to the college aged eleven and had started Latin two years ahead of me, or even earlier, and the majority of my companions in the remedial class, who had come to Cotton at thirteen, had made a start on Latin in their previous schools. My problems began when I failed to grasp the meaning of the cases: nominative, vocative, accusative . . . I struggled to apply principles I did not understand. Lack of practice in learning by heart was compounded by poor concentration. I was so astonished to be at Cotton, so entranced by the strangeness and interest of the surroundings, that my mind would still wander towards the windows to gaze at the autumn foliage and the sky. I was failing to learn the grammar set by Father Gavin day after day, and I was incapable of attempting the simple composition and translation exercises.

With Greek it was different. The elderly Laz Warner went at a slower pace, sitting next to each of us in turn, making sure that we had grasped what he had taught. He was intent merely to have us read and form the unfamiliar letters. There was not going to be much progress in the remedial Greek class, I realised. But Latin, the universal language of the Catholic Church, was the key to our future studies in the senior seminary, the daily recitation of the breviary, and the year-round ritual.

On waking each morning my first thought was dread of the commencement of Latin drill. Passing the great double doors at the entrance to the Study Place each night, I felt a surge of

Father Tom Gavin,
Prefect of Studies at Cotton College.

relief at the amnesty of Greater Silence and the night. I was not the only pupil in difficulty: there was another ex-Secondary Modern boy from east London, the oafish Patrick O'Rourke, who cried with homesickness in the night and proved incapable of keeping himself clean without his mother's help. He was big for his age, with large clumsy hands and greasy hair. We were both teased on account of our cockney accents: ''Allo, me owld cock-sparrer!' He tried to make friends with me, but I was determined not to be identified with him. He had the stricken look of a boy who was not going to make it. O'Rourke floundered so much that Father Gavin had put him down into the first year, despite his age and size, as incapable of 'catching up'. As it was, my classmates looked at me, I thought, with smug glances every time Father Gavin scolded me. I had seen boys looking at O'Rourke like that.

My class year, the lower fourth, was composed of some fifteen boys who had moved up from the junior section, Saint Thomas's, and about twelve of us who had arrived from a variety of schools mainly around the Midlands. As I got to know my class many of them seemed like any other boys: teasing each other, fooling around, quarrelling about favourite soccer teams back home. But I came to recognise some as peculiar to a seminary community. There were the 'Sanctebobs', a word James had used, who made ostentatious display of their piety even outside church, walking around college with measured gait as if still in the sanctuary, and 'talking piosity'. They were quietly derided by their fellows, and often accused of hypocrisy. And there were the loners, who seemed, in the context of Cotton, monk-like rather than just friendless or stand-offish. Such boys were not considered odd, and their desire for solitude was respected, unless they appeared sanctimonious as well, in which case they were regarded as Sanctebobs.

For some, like James Rolle, being a seminarian seem to come naturally. Although not a Sanctebob himself, he seemed a 'cleric' by nature, a boy born to be a priest. Neat and studious in appearance, good-humoured but never coarse, ever helpful and kind, he swam in the college as though it were his natural element. I liked him, and he quickly became my friend, although there was an aspect of his character that on reflection I found embarrassing. I had yet to learn the meaning of the word 'priggish', but it was a quality that I was beginning to recognise occasionally in myself as well; I sometimes found the former tough boy, Cornwell, sneering at his new self.

It was obvious that some of us had brought personal problems to Cotton. I thought I saw these tensions in the haunted expressions of several boys in my class: anxiety beyond their years, as if they were straining to curb their inclinations. Much as they wanted to be in the college, it went against the grain. Many, it was obvious, came like me from modest and poor homes. Although the uniformity of our 'best' wear – the black suit – might have ironed out the differences, the texture, cut and fit were invariably a give-away. My own black suit was several sizes too big for me, 'so that it will last you a couple of years,' Mum had said.

In the remedial Latin class there was a boy called Charles House whose parents lived abroad. His well-made footwear, the beautiful cut of his blazer, the fit of his shirts, and the way he wore them, singled him out. He walked with a loose-ankled swagger, his right hand inside his jacket pocket. He wore an expression of bored amusement beyond his thirteen years. He had peerless skin; high cheek-bones that gave him an almost oriental look; even, very white teeth; and a head of silken, honey-blond hair. His confident voice came from the back of his throat as if he was mocking the world. He would rub his hands together vigorously before Father Gavin's arrival in class. 'Very good for the mind all this Latin, Fru,' he would say, singling me out for such remarks. 'Keeps us mentally on our toes!' It took me some time to realise that he was mocking me.

Charles had a way of giving the profs knowing looks, and an occasional chortle in class; he even engaged in a little quiet banter. Was it just the stylishness of Charles House that prompted the profs to direct their quips and jests in his direction? Charles had this effect, I noticed, on some of the older boys, too, and coolly played up to it. One such was Bursley, a morose senior boy whom I had got to know in the choir. Bursley had a leathery face with pit marks on his cheeks. He looked old enough to be a man, but he tended to hang around with younger boys at break. One morning, after Father McCartie's routine distribution of letters, I saw Bursley giving Charles a soft, playful punch on the arm. Charles not so softly punched him back and said: 'Bursley, has anyone ever told you that you have a head like a dehydrated beehive?' I thought that Bursley would be furious, but he just smiled at the insult as if happy that Charles had spoken to him.

Charles's odd humour provided occasional light relief from the misery of Latin lessons, but it was Peter Gladden, a tall, stooped youth with a startling Roman nose, who helped me overcome my difficulties. Learning of my plight through James, who had become concerned on my behalf, Gladden took me by the arm one evening after Rosary and said: 'Let's try to sort out this Latin, Fru!' The nickname had caught on.

He led me down to a piano practice room underneath the stage in the assembly hall. With a Latin primer propped up on the music stand he began to take me through the basics. For a start, he explained the cases: nominative, vocative, accusative. As the light dawned, he said: 'You're not unintelligent, Fru. Nobody taught you how to learn.'

Gladden, a born teacher at the age of nearly fourteen, advised me how to learn by rote, by repetition and rhythm. 'Sway slightly to the rhythm,' he said, 'as if it's music. You can do it. Memory and music, don't you know.' That was one of Gladden's favourite phrases: 'don't you know'; not a question but an expression of encouragement.

'You need,' Gladden told me during one of our sessions, 'to brush up either the night before or early in the morning.' He suggested I work on my primer underneath the bedclothes for half an hour at night: 'It will put you ahead,' he said. So he lent me his torch. 'Make sure Leo has done his last round,' he warned.

That night, after lights out, and after Father McCartie had made his final stealthy round in the dark, I began to study a set of irregular verbs under the tent of my sheet and blankets. I had been working for fifteen minutes or so, coming up for occasional gasps of air, when the bedclothes were pulled back sharply and the figure of Father McCartie towered over me.

'My room!'

Leading the way with a torch of his own, he descended the staircase through the laundry room below the dormitory where we emerged into his office. Bending down in my pyjamas,

I was thrashed in silence: six strokes of Father McCartie's bamboo cane on my buttocks. Confiscating Peter's torch, he led me back to my bed and left me without a word, my bottom throbbing agonisingly. At least, I thought, the brutal Mr Murphy of Saints Peter and Paul would have bid me goodnight.

Lying in bed looking out at the night sky through the dormer window, I felt a sense of painful loneliness sweep over me. I had the impression that my companions were gloating. The silence was broken only by an occasional rustle of a mattress as a boy turned. Thinking of home, and the immense distance that lay between our valley outside and London in the far-off south of England, I started to sob.

I was still weeping when I was conscious of a hand touching my cheek. 'Don't cry, Fru,' said a boy's voice level with my face in the dark; then I felt the hand stroking my head. 'Come on! Cut it out! Go to sleep!' It was Charles, whose bed was several places down from mine. I tried to reach out; I just felt his arm with the tips of my fingers as he withdrew. He had taken a risk to come the few yards to be at my side. The boy's concern for me, even though I guessed he thought me a fool, calmed me down. I stopped crying and fell asleep.

29

ON THE FEAST of Saint Wilfred, patron saint of the college, we donned our black suits, stiff white detachable collars and black ties. The first Mass of the day was followed by a breakfast of grilled bacon. At 10.30 there was High Mass in full cloth-of-gold vestments, Father Doran celebrating in a fog of incense. We put our hearts into the glorious four-part Mass. As the choir processed out of church into the sacristy, the keyboard teacher, Mr Brennan, played a Bach fugue, with sudden crescendos reverberating in the rafters of the church. My sense of fervour was heightened by the prospect of a full day's release from Latin drill.

At lunch the nuns had spread white tablecloths and set out vases of autumn flowers and sprays of greenery. There were flowers around the statue of Saint Wilfred situated on a plinth high above the far wall of the refectory. There was roast lamb, followed by fruit pudding and custard. Father McCartie, looking congenial, came around with an enamel jug pouring an allowance of beer into the mugs of the sixth and fifth formers. Looking about me at the flushed, merry faces, I felt that I belonged. Several nuns had come to the door of the refectory to watch us. They were blushing and shyly ducking their veiled heads.

They were usually on their knees scrubbing, sleeves rolled, reddened arms up to the elbows in soapsuds; or peeling potatoes in the dark interior of the kitchens. I had never seen them outside their working element. None of them walked out in the fresh air except the retired and very elderly Mother Saint Thomas who was allowed, in token of her great age, to keep a small garden.

'Look,' said Peter Gladden, 'the witches have come to take a peek at us. Wave to them!' He gave a little wave and inclined his head.

After lunch we were divided into groups, and set off on walks in our Wellington boots and raincoats. The morning rains had cleared and the sun was out. Eventually we turned off the road beneath a popular Cotton landmark known as The Rocks. James led me up the hill to the side of the outcrop and we stepped gingerly to the edge to gain a view of the surrounding farms and moorland.

We took off our raincoats and sat side by side. James shouted into the blast: 'Don't you feel the presence of God in a place like this?' I could see the red-edged top of his copy of *The Imitation of Christ* peeping above his jacket pocket. I did not

Cotton refectory set for a feast day.

respond, but, yes, I could feel the presence of God. Then he said: 'I'm sorry about your tanning last night . . . Did it hurt?' Before I could make an answer, he said: 'I always find it best to offer up a tanning for the souls of my relatives in purgatory.' The priggishness of James's comment disturbed me. I too was beginning to think like that, even though a part of me cringed at such thoughts.

We continued our walk along a rough track until we found ourselves on the opposite side of the valley to the college. We went through a stone stile and plunged down into a wooded dell. The steep path was soft with pine needles and followed a roaring waterfall which pounded over rocks and sudden chasms. On all sides rose tall trees, casting shadows. The air smelt of damp fallen leaves. We began to climb until we arrived at a wooden bridge across the torrent where there was a shrine with a statue of the Virgin. James explained that it was known as Faber's Retreat, built by Father William Faber, the famous Victorian priest and composer of many popular Catholic hymns, including 'Faith of Our Fathers', which celebrated the English martyrs who died for their Faith at the hands of Protestant persecutors. We stood for a while in prayer at the shrine, before continuing on up the valley past the shrine to Saint Wilfred our patron, and arriving back at Little Bounds.

The day finished with Vespers and Benediction at which the choir sang Mozart's '*Ave Verum Corpus Natum*' and the college sang with great devotion the hymn by John Henry Newman, 'Lead Kindly Light'. The hymn seemed to sum up the contrast between this day of happiness and the menace 'amidst the encircling gloom' that awaited the next working day.

30

I HAD STARTED on the autobiography of Saint Thérèse of Lisieux. I learnt that she was born in Alençon, France, the youngest of five sisters who became nuns ahead of her. Entering the Carmelites aged fifteen she wrote the story of her life under obedience. After her death of tuberculosis, aged twenty-four, she became one of the most famous of modern saints. Thérèse confirmed the impression I had of my soul as a kind of inner garden or landscape. And like her, I had times when my soul felt more like a wasteland filled with rubbish than a place of beauty. There were occasions, especially during thanksgiving after Communion, when I felt no comfort or peace, only self-pity and discomfort: fear of Latin drill, fear of being sent home (and yet homesickness, too), tortured knees, blisters from my ill-fitting shoes, hunger, headache, exhaustion, my bladder full to bursting. One should pray to Our Lady in desolate periods, Thérèse advised. So I begged the Blessed Virgin to remove the rubbish from my soul. I would try to imagine a splendid tabernacle worthy of the Lord, inviting in the angels and saints to sing songs of praise to Jesus. All this I tried to do every morning, but still the discomfort and distractions, the dread of Latin, would take over my thoughts. On some mornings as

Father McCartie made the signal for us to proceed to breakfast, I would, like Thérèse, resolve to continue my thanksgiving during the day since I had performed it so poorly in church.

After pouring out my heart to Father Browne about my difficulties with Latin, he reminded me that John Vianney had struggled with his studies. And he told me about Saint Joseph of Cupertino who was obliged to take his exams for the priesthood many times before he passed them. Father Browne counselled me to think of my soul like a seedling in a nursery. Jesus allows us to bask at times in his sunshine, at other times he sends the cold waters of humiliation and suffering in order to strengthen us. We must not be cast down, he told me, by setbacks and minor discomforts.

The next time we met he talked again about Saint Thérèse's 'Little Way'. He read a passage from her writings in which she says that she saw herself as a toy for the child Jesus, a little ball of no price which he could throw on the ground, kick with his foot, or leave in a corner. Sometimes, he went on, she saw herself as a little paintbrush used for filling in the small details of a picture. Most often she was his 'Little Flower'. But there was nothing sentimental about Thérèse, he insisted: 'Saint Thérèse,' he said, 'was not a delicate flower, she was tough, tough, tough.'

As the daylight hours shortened, the college buildings became colder and darker and the valley was often shrouded in mist and rain. I found myself feeling miserable to the point of tears as I struggled with Latin, or dug into the clay of the ditches, or tried to concentrate during prayers. In Thérèse's writings I found a passage that seemed to correspond exactly with my own feelings. There were times, she wrote, when a ray of sunshine lit up the darkness and she was happy and content. But then that time of joy made the darkness even more unbearable when it returned.

Father Browne said this was a passing phase; that I should think less about myself and more about others. Thérèse, he said, showed us how to spread love within the community. She said it was natural to feel drawn to one sister in the convent, and yet go a long way around to avoid meeting another. But Our Lord wants us to love those who are less attractive to us. This coincided with Father Browne's counsel to avoid 'particular' or 'special' friendships, spending too much time with those we were inclined to like most, while neglecting the friendless and those we felt an aversion for.

So I began to ration the time I spent with James, Derek and Peter, and sought the company of Oliver Stack, whom many boys accused of being a Sanctebob. He was a freckly youth with a receding forehead and untidy hair. He had a sanctimonious way of genuflecting and crossing himself in church. He walked in a hunched, self-absorbed fashion, as if to proclaim: 'Look at me! What a holy fellow I am.' He was, to boot, a grumpy, ill-favoured boy who showed, initially, not the least interest in me.

Often Stack walked alone on Top Bounds after breakfast so I took to falling in beside him and starting up a conversation. At first he looked at me suspiciously. But it was not long before he would be expecting me. Then he took to tagging along even when I came down from Little Dorm after bed-making as if to lay claim to me.

Stack was also a member of the Workers' Union, the drain-digging team. He would wait for me outside the wash places so that we would go up to the fields together and work in the same ditch. It was during manual labour that I discovered how far I was from attaining Thérèse's ideal of the 'Little Way'.

One wet afternoon we were working together in a ditch so filled with muddy water that it almost spilt over the tops of our Wellington boots. Stack was attempting to widen the ditch and smacked the surface of the water with his spade to remove the clots of clay. Each time he did this he sprayed me with mire.

Saint Thérèse had told how a nun splashed her carelessly in the convent laundry, and how, although she hated it, she would thrust her face forward to receive the dirty water more fully, seeing an opportunity to humiliate herself. But I was less concerned about my humility than my clothes. Although we wore football shorts and shirts over our normal clothes to protect them, pulling our thick socks up to our knees, I only had one pair of second-best trousers and they were being ruined by Stack's carelessness.

I asked him, kindly I thought, to be more careful. But he splashed me even more. I pleaded with him, hoping that he was merely being thoughtless rather than aggressive. Splashing me again, he said: 'You should have more pairs of trousers. Why didn't your parents make proper provision for you when you came to Cotton? This is not a college for down-and-outs.'

Thinking of Mum and Dad and how hard they had to struggle, I was stunned for their sakes by the insult. With the next splash, which soaked my trousers across the front, it was as if a pair of soapy hands had plunged inside the back of my skull and squeezed my brain. The long-suppressed rage of my former, younger self erupted, as if I had never practised self-control. I tossed my spade over the parapet of the ditch, grabbed Stack by the scruff of the neck and brought him down sideways in the freezing muddy water, yanking him straight back on to his feet again while still holding on to him. 'Wannanother dip, you bastard?' I grunted. Then I pushed him down again so that he was sitting in the mire as if taking a bath.

As he clambered up, flaying his arms, he was shaking, his face deathly white. The rest of the work team in the ditch looked on in amazement as Stack stood up and confronted me with tightened fists. I squared up to him. 'Come on then!' I said. But he scrambled out of the ditch.

There was a cry of horror from the onlookers. He had grabbed my spade and was holding it aloft as if preparing to strike. I raised my arms to protect myself, but he threw down the spade and set off for the college, dripping mud.

By teatime, my spat with Stack and its resolution had gone around the college. As he came into the refectory there were waves of giggles. It was an infectious, nervous tittering that I had heard before at Cotton – wracking the entire community, sometimes on the most solemn occasions.

Nothing could have been further from the spiritual strategy of Thérèse, and I had gained in credibility as a strong character for all the wrong reasons. But Oliver Stack had taken a plunge in reputation and lost the only friend he had in the college. He now refused to speak to me or look at me. Again and again I approached him and told him how sorry I was. As I asked his forgiveness, Stack became ever more self-absorbed, looking upwards, myopically, his nostrils flaring. In desperation, I said: 'But, Oliver, Jesus says we must forgive one another.' Eventually he snorted: 'Shut up, you bloody Sanctebob!' Those were the only words I was to get from Stack for the rest of the term.

31

A HOMILY, known as a 'conference', was an important feature of the Sunday routine. It was delivered in the assembly hall on Sunday mornings between High Mass and lunch. I had missed the first, traditionally given by Father Doran. Thereafter the profs took it in turns. One Sunday early in the term it was delivered by Father McCartie. He started, as was the custom, by praying the Angelus. Seating himself at a table on the stage, he gave us a pep talk on the virtue of obedience and the necessity of promptly responding to the college bells as one would heed 'the voice of God'. Father McCartie delivered all this in a dry mechanical fashion. Then he talked about the importance of forming habits of 'self-regulation' since many of us would one day live as priests, probably alone, where

Cotton 'study place'.

there would be no bells, and nobody to encourage us to be prompt.

I found myself puzzling over Father McCartie. His punishments included not only beatings but making boys stand for long periods of time on the college coat of arms depicted in mosaic on the floor of the main cloister. Boys being punished in this way, sometimes ten at a time, were therefore held up to ridicule by all who passed. Father McCartie's homily revealed, I thought, what a poor opinion he had of youth. Yet it seemed to me that compared with the lads at Saints Peter and Paul in Ilford we were unusually self-disciplined. We were rarely late for any duty, and performed our various routines enthusiastically, and yet the Prefect of Discipline applied his punishments, as he had done in my case, with grim vigour, making no allowances for circumstances.

By the middle of the term I had experienced Father McCartie's classroom methods, too, since he was taking my class for Christian Doctrine. Week after week he handed out cyclostyled sheets – mainly notes and quotes on papal social teaching. There was not a single concrete example; not one historical anecdote or illustration to relieve the abstract tedium couched in virtually incomprehensible language. He did not even wish us to discover for ourselves the important highlights: they were underlined for us. He spent the period reading out his own notes in a monotonous voice. One morning, as more notes were being handed out, Charles House whispered to himself at the back of the class: 'Oh Lord, what a yawn!' Father McCartie looked up. He had heard it. We sat frozen with terror, expecting a thundering: 'My room!' Instead, the priest gave House a wintry smile as if the boy had echoed precisely his own thoughts on the matter.

As week followed week the profs continued to take turns delivering Sunday homily. Mostly they rambled, filling the period between High Mass and lunch, as if begrudging us an unscheduled slice of free time. Father Gavin gave a talk on what a splendid and maligned leader Mussolini was. Father Piercy gave a disjointed and barely audible talk on the religious history of North Staffordshire.

Towards the end of October, when the college seemed generally in a state of gloom following a week or two of bad weather, the conference was given by Father Armishaw. He bounded up the steps of the stage and sat for some time staring at us. The assembled college gazed back as the tension mounted. He seemed casually conscious of his own striking good looks.

'The first half of the first term of every new academic year,' he began, 'is always a difficult time. But I wonder whether you lot realise just how *bloody* lucky you are . . . I wonder, when I watch you sometimes, and hear you bellyaching, whether you have an inkling just how privileged you are.' His conference, it now became obvious, was another pep talk although in very different style from the others. He spoke to us directly, briefly, and in normal language.

He realised, he said, how we missed our families; how we resented rising at an unearthly hour; putting up with cold rooms, with no soft armchairs; digging ditches, cross-country running, taking cold showers, studying harder than most boys of our age, eating Cotton's 'delightful cooking'. But we had come, he said, 'to the finest school in the whole of England'. We were taught, he went on, in small classes by the best-educated, most intelligent priests in the land (he smiled at us facetiously and it got a laugh). We had a fine library 'filled to the gunwales with books'. Nor should we take for granted the beautiful surroundings. Above all we were living, he said, under the same roof as the Blessed Sacrament and taking part daily in the full ritual of the Church to the accompaniment of one of the best church choirs in England. This place, he said, had been producing great priests and bishops for two hundred years. We should thank our lucky stars and be proud and grateful to be here. 'So let's get on with it, shall we, with no more bellyaching!'

He sat for a while, staring down at us, as if watching the message sinking in. Then he rose, bounded down the stage steps, and walked swiftly from the hall. His conference had taken about five minutes, whereas the norm was a droning forty minutes or more.

As I came out on to Lower Bounds I felt a distinct sense of rising spirits among my companions. I went straight back into the church where the incense was still heavy from High Mass. Alone, kneeling before the Blessed Sacrament, I thanked God for sending me to Cotton.

32

THANKS TO Peter Gladden, I was catching up with the rest of the class by the middle of November, and even began to enjoy Latin and occasionally shine at it. The punishment tasks stopped; and the busy routine of the curriculum left me little time to brood. The worst of the darkness seemed to have lifted. Did I owe this alleviation to a deepening sense of God?

Ever since I was a child, and imagined God as a clock, I had continued to puzzle over how I thought about God; what I thought him to be. I had once imagined him as an ancient man with a beard on a throne; and I had thought of him as a sort of invisible, odourless 'gas' – the consequence of catechism classes which informed us that God was 'everywhere, even in our most secret thoughts'. When I heard the voice of Jesus in the church of Saint Augustine, it marked the beginning of a period in which I could think of God as Jesus of *The Imitation of Christ*. At Cotton I continued to imagine him as a fatherly companion, to whom I spoke at intervals of the day, and particularly, following Father Browne's encouragement, when I twice daily examined my conscience. And there were times when, as a result of the moving words of Cardinal Newman's hymn, 'Lead, kindly light', I thought of the presence of Jesus as a disembodied warm light.

As the weeks passed and I became more acquainted with the countryside around Cotton in all its moods, I began to feel a surprising new sense of the presence of Almighty God, beyond the person of Jesus. Sometimes on afternoon walks I had an impression of a vast and mighty presence in the wild landscape, the woods, the steep hills and the sky. After making my bed each morning I would go to Little Bounds and gaze down the valley. There were times when I felt that the scene was entering into my heart and expanding my soul. Sometimes I had an impression of the spirit of Almighty God in the hills and the sky that was far deeper, vaster, more real even, than my idea of the man–God Jesus.

One Thursday afternoon, after seeing Father Browne, I had an urge to walk down to Faber's Retreat in the valley by my-self. It was breaking a rule, but I reasoned that my intention was not self-indulgence but the need to experience alone that special presence in the valley that had made me tremble with excitement.

I stood inside Faber's Retreat for a long time, looking out at the late afternoon light through the trees; listening to the echoing roar of water tumbling below, I felt my spirits lift for a few moments. Then something in the dampness of the rotting leaves, and the stirring in the canopy of the trees alarmed me. I felt lonely and I shuddered.

As I walked back up the path towards Little Bounds I saw two figures among the trees. They were standing very still and close to each other: it was Charles House and the senior student Bursley. Charles looked frail and vulnerable next to the swarthy mature Bursley. When they realised who I was they turned away. I could see that they were smoking cigarettes. As I continued on up the valley, I felt a momentary spasm of jealousy for Bursley.

That evening Father Piercy showed a film: Bing Crosby, Bob Hope and Dorothy Lamour in 'Road to Rio'. Charles House came and sat next to me. He pressed his shoulder gently against mine and whispered: 'So what do you get up to down in the valley?' I was too embarrassed to say anything.

The profs arrived before the film began. They sat at the back of the hall, their legs sprawling out from under their cassocks. Father Armishaw was in their midst, wearing a cloak and puffing on a curled pipe.

At the point in the film where a group of girls begin dancing at a wedding, there was a glimpse of their bare legs, right up to their knickers, but the film suddenly cut to the next scene. Some boys at the back laughed. Charles whispered in my ear: 'Censored by Father Goebbels.'

33

IN THE LAST week of November we celebrated the Feast of Saint Cecilia, the patron saint of music. The choir sang a complicated Mass setting by Victoria which we had been practising ever since Saint Wilfred's day. After Mass Father Owen talked to us in the sacristy about our choir music. The liturgical year, he said, was Christ himself living on in his Church, reliving the shape of his life, renewing the mysteries of the redemption.

That afternoon the choir was given its annual feast served by the nuns in a drawing room in the old hall. Bacon and eggs were followed by a rich trifle topped with clotted cream. Father Doran presided along with Father Owen, and Father McCartie put in an appearance. As we continued to eat, the priests, having had their fill, leant back in their chairs and smoked, watching over us benignly. Later, in the assembly hall, the choir sang excerpts from the operettas of Gilbert and Sullivan. One of the sopranos sang 'Little Buttercup', and I took part in the singing of 'We are dainty little fairies'. The audience stamped their feet as the full choir sang excerpts from *The Pirates of Penzance* and *HMS Pinafore*.

My performance as one of the 'dainty little fairies' caused some gentle ribbing from priests and boys for several days. It was not personal, I gathered, but part of a tradition of disdain for the girlish and the feminine at Cotton. One of the Big Sixth, a lofty snaggle-toothed fellow with a great thatch of hair, stopped me on Little Bounds to say, 'You gave your dainty little fairy just the right degree of female silliness and vanity, Fru! Well done! The way you fluttered your eyelids, perfect!'

It struck me for the first time that girls and women, excluding the nuns, were as absent from our lives as current daily news. I had also noticed the practice of assigning 'silly' girls' names to some of the prettier boys in Saint Thomas's, the junior section, – such as Priscilla, Matilda, Nancy, Primrose. The fifty or so boys in 'Toss's', as it was known, were segregated from the senior school, Saint Wilfred's, under the close super-vision of Father Denis Manion. Father Manion was a balding, glum-looking priest whose face darkened whenever anybody addressed him. He seemed to acknowledge in the senior section of the college only those boys who had been in his charge in Saint Thomas's. There was no opportunity for boys in the senior school to speak to the younger, Toss's, boys and yet they were constantly in our presence, at meals and in church, where they attended morning Mass in the Lady Chapel. One day Peter Gladden said something that surprised and disturbed me.

Walking on Top Bounds, he said: 'That kid Appleton in the Lower Third, he's got a gorgeous little rump like two peaches in a brown paper bag. God! I'd dearly like to give it a smack.' He said this quite unselfconsciously. Then he changed the subject.

34

AT THE END of the month, as the days shortened and grew colder, an old Cottonian called Peter Lees was ordained priest in our sanctuary by Bishop Bright, the auxiliary bishop of the diocese. At the litany to all the saints the priest-to-be lay full-length, face down in the sanctuary. We watched enthralled as his hands were anointed with oil in the form of a cross.

After the ordination every boy in the college came up to the altar to receive Peter Lees's individual blessing. Then he came into the refectory at lunchtime to receive three cheers. Led by Father Piercy, Father Owen and the Sixth Form, we sang a moving chant in descant: *'Ad multos annos . . . Ad multos annos . . .'* 'For many years . . . For many years . . .'

After Saint Cecilia's we had been counting the days to the departure date for our brief Christmas holiday, which the boys called 'GH' – 'Going Home'. The more homesick ones would mutter to each other: 'Thirty days to GH . . . twenty-eight days to GH . . .' I had mixed feelings about GH. I had been missing the faces of Mum and Dad and my siblings, and I longed to return home to impress them with stories of life at Cotton, but I was anxious about sharing a bed again with my brother, and I was worried how I should react if my parents started fighting. Could I bring peace to the house by the power of prayer and good example?

I had been writing home at the allotted time between breakfast and High Mass on Sundays, giving glowing accounts of my activities. Each week I received a letter from Mum, listing illnesses, accidents and money problems, along with a postal order for five shillings. The money she sent each week, a significant sacrifice for her, I placed in a safe box in the bursary to pay for college bills and to buy my return ticket home on the train.

December came, the weather grew wild. Squalls of wind and rain came riding up the valley. There were times when the gales buffeted the college so strongly on its high, unprotected promontory that the beams of the roofs cracked and groaned. On the Feast of the Immaculate Conception, as if by a miracle, the weather changed. It was a still, cloudless day of pale sunshine. After working in the drainage ditches I took a bath, cold as usual, and went into church before tea. I was alone, and the light of the setting sun caught the stained-glass image of the Virgin in the Lady Chapel as if it was a pillar of fire. The image was surrounded by glowing symbols of the virtues we recited in her litany: Tower of David, Gate of Heaven, Mystical Rose, House of Gold . . . Kneeling before the window I felt as if Mary had placed a cloak of serenity and purity around my shoulders.

The wind was stirring in the bare branches of the lime trees outside. The feeling of peace was so intense that I believed Our Lady had granted me a special and personal grace on her feast day. I rose from my knees and sat gazing at the window as darkness gathered. The church was very still and the sanctuary lamp shone brightly. As I sat entranced, I heard the door of the church swinging on its hinges. The sound of slow dragged footsteps approached. Eventually the figure of the very old nun, Mother Saint Thomas, came into view supported on a stick. I had seen her at High Mass on Sundays, bent almost double. She paused to look at me for a moment where I knelt in the twilight, and smiled sweetly. Then she installed herself in a pew where she began to whisper her beads. I had seen her often, but we had never exchanged a word.

35

THE WEEK BEFORE Christmas we sat end-of-term examinations. A tense hush descended over the college. A day after the last exam the results were pinned on the noticeboard outside the refectory. My marks were average, even in Latin, and I rushed into chapel to give thanks to Saint Joseph of Cupertino. That afternoon I saw Father Browne for my last session of spiritual direction. He gave me a Christmas card with the legend in black: '*Puer natus est nobis: Filius datus est nobis.*' 'A child is born unto us: a son is given unto us.' The words were printed beneath the Gregorian chant Introit of the third Mass of Christmas Day. He counselled me to pray even more during my holiday than during the term, to attend Mass and Communion every day. He told me about the need to practise 'custody of the eyes'. On returning home I would be surrounded by lewd and suggestive images in advertisements, newspapers and magazines, as well as the sight of women who failed to dress with due modesty. 'We can control what we see,' he said. 'We can refuse to dwell on images that do not give glory to God.'

The following day was a holiday and much of the morning was spent packing our trunks and suitcases. I spent an hour in church before lunch and I saw other boys coming in to say private prayers, including Derek, James, Peter Gladden and Oliver Stack.

That afternoon we were allowed to talk in the dormitories, and we sat and lay on our beds gossiping. Father McCartie was nowhere to be seen. In the evening there was Vespers and Solemn Benediction celebrated by Father Doran. I felt especially devout as we recited the prayer known as the 'Divine Praises':

> Blessed be God.
> Blessed be His Holy Name.
> Blessed be Jesus Christ, true God and true Man . . .

Then Father Doran intoned the Te Deum followed by the Litany of the Saints. It was the last service of the year. As we walked in ranks to our supper we were conscious of enticing cooking smells coming from the kitchen and I caught a glimpse of the nuns through the open baize door. Amidst clouds of steam they were placing haunches of roast meat on to silver salvers as they prepared a Christmas feast for the profs.

After our own austere supper, just two ginger biscuits and an orange, Father Piercy, who was in possession of what looked like a glass of port, showed a film comedy, *Passport to Pimlico*, and we went up to the dormitories afterwards in a state of restrained excitement. Father McCartie did not put in an appearance. Some of the boys talked and laughed for a long time in the darkness, before falling asleep.

I lay awake, tense with anticipation at the idea of returning to the Peel. I grew tired, rehearsing all the things I wanted to tell Mum and my siblings. Before I nodded off I felt some-body's breath on my face, and a disembodied voice said: 'Fru, it's me!'

It was Charles. 'Have a lovely Christmas, Fru, and don't eat too much Christmas pudding.' Then he felt my face with gentle fingers and plucked my cheek before disappearing in the dark-ness. I lay awake for a long time, thinking about Charles, my heart pounding.

When the lights came on in the morning, it was five o'clock, and most of the boys were dressed. Charles had already gone. Carrying overnight bags (our heavy luggage was due to be sent to our destinations by lorry and rail), James and Derek and I set off for the station at Oakamoor in the freezing air before dawn under a hard starlit sky. There had been a light fall of snow and the moon was brilliant above the tops of the pine plantation across the valley. A group of older boys, tenors and basses in the choir, caught us up and overtook us. They were singing the carol 'In Dulce Jubilo', their voices carrying down the valley and re-echoing back to us.

The steep and wild country around Oakamoor and neigh-bouring Alton gave way to a tamer landscape by the time the train reached Uttoxeter. It was dawn when we arrived at the industrial outskirts of Derby. Here the London boys including Derek and O'Rourke, together with James, who lived near Reading, boarded the express train bound for Saint Pancras. Standing on the platform I watched young women coming and going, transfixed by their legs in sheer stockings and made-up faces. What strange narcissistic creatures they seemed after so many weeks without so much as a glimpse of a woman save for our well-covered 'witches'.

Staring out of the window, waiting for the train to depart from Derby station, I watched a girl come out on to the platform. She stood close to our carriage. She was about sixteen and had large dark eyes in a pale elfin face. She was slight of build and wore a well-cut navy blue coat and neat black shoes. Her dark lustrous hair was cut short and parted in the centre of her head. She seemed to me the most beautiful, delicate creature I had ever seen, and I was surprised by my sudden sense of wonder. I thought: 'I shall never forget this girl and this moment for as long as I live.'

I looked at James, who was sitting opposite. He had seen the girl, but now he had his nose in his *Imitation of Christ* and I felt a pang of guilt. The whistle blew and the train eased away, but the girl's image remained in my mind's eye.

36

MUM MET ME on the platform at Saint Pancras station and squeezed me fiercely, marvelling at how much I had grown. 'Quite the young man,' she said. I felt breathless on seeing her very own lips, her very own eyes, and hearing her distinctive voice. But her strong arms and the softness of her breasts filled me with sudden alarm as she embraced me hard with an overpowering whiff of dried lavender.

As we rode on the bus back to Ilford, at the front of the upper deck as usual, she regaled me with stories of her new job as a night-nursing orderly at Wanstead hospital. There were tales of laying out dead bodies; disagreements with ward sisters. She looked straight ahead, reliving her dramas, as we lurched along the scruffy streets of Bow, Stratford and Manor Park. I was saddened by the sight of so many drab, damp people hurrying about their worldly activities in the rain, oblivious of God. Secretly I uttered a word of praise to Jesus, and begged Mary for her help. But I was annoyed that Mum had no questions for me; that I was sitting in silence while she told one story after another.

The family was gathered for tea in the living room which

had been decorated with holly and coloured paper chains. There was a Christmas tree standing in a bucket bound with red and green crêpe paper. Dad, in his work overalls, blinked and put out his cheek for a kiss; my younger brothers stared. My sister, looking elegant, her hair perfectly coiffed, said: 'Who's this good-looking chap!' My older brother was out doing last-minute Christmas shopping.

There was a surprise visitor, sitting in Dad's chair – Grandma Cornwell, my Jewish grandmother. Since Granddad's death she had been spending Christmas in turns with each of her sons. She was an overweight bespectacled lady dressed in black, with pure white hair done up in a bun under a black straw hat. Looking a little confused, she said in her pronounced cockney: 'Bin to collidge there, Jack, 'ave yer?'

Eventually Terry, who was now working at Plessey's electronics factory, turned up with two laden shopping bags. He gave me a nod, and said sniffily: 'All right? Nice journey? Mmmm . . . Got to see to this.' Then he disappeared up to the boys' bedroom to wrap his Christmas presents. Terry was as private and well-ordered as ever.

In the crowded living room, surrounded by cockney voices, I sensed a tension pervading the household. I felt vulnerable, and my spirits, so high that morning, had plunged.

37

LATE ON CHRISTMAS EVE we walked to the Camp for an early first Mass of Christmas celebrated by Father Cooney. The arrangement relieved the growing numbers at midnight Mass in Saint Augustine's. When I arrived Father Cooney was vested, eyes fast shut in an area beyond a makeshift curtain that served as a sacristy. Two other servers were already in cassocks and cottas. When he opened his eyes he inclined his head gravely in my direction and whispered: 'Wisswiss . . .'

By the light of hissing gas lamps Father Cooney prayed the Introit of the first Mass of Christmas Day in Latin that I could understand now without the translation: '*Dominus dixit ad me: Filus meus es tu, ego hodie genui te*.' 'The Lord hath said to me: Thou art My Son, this day have I begotten Thee.'

I had hoped to engage Father Cooney in conversation about Cotton at the end of Mass, but he fixed me with a stern eye and merely said: 'Ah well, wisswiss . . . A happy and a holy Christmas to you and all your family!'

Miss Racine, who was standing in wait for me, crowed with delight as she took both my hands in hers, telling me how delighted she was to see me and how I must come to visit her.

The Cornwells walked in the frosty air past the cemetery filled with dead pets on our way back to the Peel. Dad had stoked up the fire and carved a ham for sandwiches; Grandma was already in bed. Drinking tea with a dash of whisky, excepting the little ones, we sat around the fire and exchanged presents. Terry had bought me a book about battleships; Maureen had bought me a new pen. For each member of the family I had made a set of rosary beads during Father Piercy's Thursday afternoon handicraft sessions. Terry, cheerful on his alcoholic tea, chuckled as he opened the little box containing the beads. 'Cripes!' he said. Then he looked up brightly: 'Come on then folks, who's for Rosary?' It hurt my feelings, but I laughed with the others.

Eventually we went up to bed. Grandma was already asleep in my sister's room. My sister was to sleep with Mum, and Dad was to sleep in the boys' bedroom. I was to share a bed with Terry. The bedroom was intensely cold as there was no heating upstairs. I went down on my knees before getting into bed. Terry, grumbling a little about five people taking all the oxygen out of the air, lay stiff and as far from me as he could.

Dad, who slept on a camp bed, was snoring the moment his head rested on the pillow.

I slept fitfully through what seemed an interminable night. Then, in the early hours before dawn, half-awake, half-dozing, I had a semi-conscious impression that I was stroking my penis which seemed to me in my dream state as hard and smooth as ivory. I had an irrepressible urge to stroke myself and a vivid impression of the girl on Derby station rose before me. Then I felt the pleasurable shock of release.

Climbing out of bed I padded to the door and into the bathroom, fraught with fear and curiosity. I stood for a long while in the bathroom, puzzling and thinking about the experience, which had been pleasurable in a way, and yet not entirely unexpected. I was thinking of what happened at South Kensington, and the larks of the big boys in the latrines at Saints Peter and Paul. I felt that I had done something forbidden. But what? I had no words for it. And why had the almost tangible presence of that girl been so vivid? Shivering with the cold I washed my hands and climbed back into bed. For a long time I lay curious and anxious. I slept for an hour or so; then I awoke, again needing to go to the bathroom.

What happened next was a conjunction of chance and forgetfulness. As I opened the door on to the landing, which was lit by a single low-watt bulb, I was greeted by a startling vision. Before me, swaying slightly, stood an ancient woman, half-dressed in a filthy gown which fell off her sallow shoulders exposing her breasts which sagged down on to her stomach, her eyes bloodshot, her mouth open, revealing toothless gums.

As I screamed, the old woman collapsed on the floor and let out a shriek to match my own. The little ones were screaming, my father was hollering, and Mum rushed out on to the landing.

The horrifying vision was just Grandma. She had made her way to the bathroom at the same moment as myself. She was dressed in nothing but her tattered unwashed nightgown and was unrecognisable with her hair down, her false teeth absent, and without her glasses. As Mum picked up the shocked old lady, she yelled at me: 'You blithering idiot! What did you want to do that for? Spoiling everybody's Christmas!'

Overshadowed by my screaming fit, Christmas Day began, earlier than usual, in its time-honoured way. Dad insisted on us all taking a dose of Andrew's Liver Salts, followed by a mountainous breakfast of fried eggs, bacon and sausages.

Then I set off for High Mass at Saint Augustine's on my sister's bike. I served as an acolyte on the altar, feeling troubled and exhausted, and knelt for a long time making my thanksgiving with a feverish mind. I returned home a long way round so that I could have time to think, turning over again and again the incident in the early hours which had almost been blotted out by my screaming fit. Had I committed a sin? Had I removed myself from God's grace? Must I confess before going to Holy Communion? Cycling down the length of Claybury Avenue, this much I knew, even at the age of thirteen, that a sin required intention. The problem was recapturing my precise state of mind: was I awake, or asleep? Was the act deliberate? And what was the act?

I arrived home just as my mother was serving up Christmas lunch, the consequence of weeks of saving and hoarding. Eight of us sat down to plates piled high with turkey, ham, sausages, stuffing, roast potatoes and a pyramid of Brussel sprouts. I heard Terry muttering under his breath out of Mum's hearing: 'Where's Gyp when we need him! How do we get through all this?' Terry had once been in the habit of slipping Gyp, our much missed sheepdog, handfuls of unwanted food under the table.

Mum insisted that not a scrap should be left on our plates. She was also of the school of thought that children should not speak during mealtimes. We had by this stage a small hired television, acquired in time for the Coronation of Queen Elizabeth earlier that year. The image was sickly green and magnified with a thick piece of Perspex strapped over the screen. We watched the Queen's speech, then a programme about other people celebrating Christmas around England. I worked my way through the food mountain feeling nauseous and detached. The family went to bed early and slept soundly, making up for the loss of sleep since the Mass on Christmas Eve.

The next day, Boxing Day, Mum and Dad were edgy. We were all crowded into the living room, and the windows steamed up as Mum prepared yet another huge meal. The radio was blasting the popular hit song of that Christmas: 'Doggie in the Window'. My younger brothers joined in, adding their own 'Woof! Woof!' How I missed the music of the seminary: the nightly *Salve Regina*, the measured elegance of Gregorian chant.

After lunch I walked the streets. Eventually I found myself outside the church of Our Lady of Lourdes at Wanstead, several miles from home. The church door was open and I went in to pray. I knelt for a long time, my thoughts and conscience in turmoil. Just as I was getting up to go, an elderly priest came down the aisle. 'Did you want to go to confession?' he asked.

In the confessional I tried to explain what had happened, and he spoke to me soothingly for a long time. 'Obviously you were not fully conscious of what you were doing in the early hours of the morning,' he said. There were times, he went on, when it was perfectly natural to have this experience in one's sleep. It was known, he said, as 'a wet dream'. A boy should know, he said, that it was a serious sin in the sight of God to entertain impure thoughts and deliberately to stimulate one's penis in order to 'spill one's seed or semen'. For this process of ejaculation, through God's great providence, was how human souls were brought into the world. God in his providence had given man a special pleasure in the act in order to encourage him to produce children. But the act must be done responsibly and only within marriage.

The priest, whose name was Father Hemming, asked me about myself. He became especially kindly when he learnt that I was a junior seminarian. (How strange, it now occurred to me, that semen and seminarian derived from the same Latin word: seed!) I must ask our Blessed Lady, he said, for special grace to protect me from impurity. When he finished, he said: 'Go now in the peace and the great love of Almighty God.'

I went out into the cold December air and walked all the way to Redbridge where Miss Racine lived. As I sat in her familiar cluttered room, warmed only by a paraffin stove, she asked me many questions about Cotton and listened with appreciation and fascination, I thought. In turn I listened to her religious prattle and drank her terrible tea as the fat marauding cats crouched on the kitchen surfaces. All the time, though, I was rejoicing inwardly to be reconciled with Jesus and in a state of grace.

When I returned to the Peel I came through the entrance to the sports ground feeling that my cup of happiness was full to the brim. Mum met me at the kitchen door, her face angry.

'I watched you from the window coming in through the gates,' she said. 'Oh, you're so cocky and pleased with yourself, aren't you! Did you know that you walk proudly, your head high, your shoulders pulled back as if you're so very grand? I thought that those priests would teach you some humility . . .' She stood blocking my way at the door as if she would hit me. Then she turned away. I wanted to howl with rage and humiliation.

38

BACK AT COTTON the valley was white with frost. We threw ourselves at once into work and our religious routines while trying to cope with the cold. I wore two vests under my shirt, as well as my 'junior hair shirt'.

When the snow eventually came Father Piercy appeared with two sledges he had made in his workshop, large enough to take ten boys at a time. The favoured slide was in the field between the old hall and the margins of the wood where one could see branches of larch trees weighed down by snow, brilliant in the sunshine, and hear the muffled sound of the torrent on the icy rocks.

There was something about the snow-bound valley that matched my mood. I saw the snow as the pure mantle of God, soothing, cleansing and protective, filling my spirit with acceptance and silence. Reading Saint Thérèse, I was struck by those passages which spoke of emptying one's desires, opening oneself to the person of Jesus by being abandoned, open to his presence. Saint Thérèse also made much of the call in the Gospel to die to oneself: unless the seed falls to the ground and dies, it cannot rise again and grow. Pondering these thoughts, I accepted the humiliation meted out to me by my mother. I had not been walking arrogantly into the Peel, of that I was certain. But I would accept her hurtful comment as an act of self-denial.

Meanwhile my studies had become not just less of a struggle but even absorbing and pleasurable. Our history teacher that term was Father Francis Grady, a Cambridge graduate with smooth dark hair, greying at the temples; he looked, as James insisted, not unlike Gregory Peck. He had a dignified walk, smooth mannerisms and careful speech; a way, every so often, of clearing his throat with a brief 'hmm . . . hmm' while putting a genteel fist to his mouth. He was teaching us the history of the English monasteries of the Middle Ages. He brought those communities to life: the great choirs, the libraries and the chapter houses, centres of civilisation and holiness on the high moors of the North of England. I saw myself, as I knelt in church alone, conscious of the snow-bound landscape outside, as a young monk in a powerhouse of learning and spirituality.

Meanwhile, the choir master, Father Owen, was teaching us zoology. In the very first lesson he taught us the mysteries of reproduction. Like Father Armishaw he had a motorbike, although not a fashionable or new one; he would ride off along the college lane in a heavy raincoat, wearing a peculiar Gothic-shaped helmet and goggles. The motorbike figured in his instruction. He started by saying: 'If I were to arrive in the garages and found a little motorbike one morning alongside my own, I would be most surprised.' This led to a discussion of cell separation, reproduction in plants and mammals, then, finally, in human beings. In one notable sentence, delivered in his clerical voice, he pronounced: 'The man inserts his penis into a hole in the woman and deposits his semen . . .' He did not tell us precisely which hole in the woman. Then the bell rang and he began the prayer that we said at the end of each lesson. After he had gone from the room, I heard Charles House saying in a facetious voice behind me: 'That sounds an interesting way to pass the time! When do we get started!' Part of me, the priggish seminary boy, was shocked, while part of me was mischievously amused. I was not to hear any further mention by my classmates of what Father Owen had said.

Due to the snow and ice, and my dislike of tobogganing and snow sports, I was allowed to spend my afternoons during these winter-bound days poring over my books, an old curtain wrapped around my shoulders in the music practice room underneath the stage in the assembly hall. Having no gloves, and pressing my hands into my ears, I developed suppurating chilblains on my fingers and earlobes. My feet were also

Cotton 'old hall', snow-bound.

suffering as my only shoes were cheap and made of imitation leather which was disintegrating in the snow and ice that turned to slush on the Bounds. I developed a painful form of foot rot. Following the example of Saint Thérèse, I regarded these miseries as an opportunity for self-mortification, conscious that I was becoming something of a Sanctebob.

As the term progressed the sun was permanently shrouded. Father Piercy kept the boilers going to heat the library and the church. The cold grew more intense and we wore raincoats and overcoats indoors. Pipes froze, the electricity supply failed. We were allowed to keep the windows of the dormitories closed at night, but if I breathed on my glasses as I got into bed the lenses became frosted within moments.

39

On the Sunday before Lent began, Father Armishaw gave the Sunday homily after High Mass again. He arrived in the theatre, swaddled in his heavy cloak. Lent, he announced, was an ancient 'mystery', reminding us of Our Lord's forty-day fast in the desert: it is a desert time of cleansing and preparation. He ended with a word about fasting. 'You may well think,' he said, 'that fasting during Lent makes you somehow a better person, but the practice was to deny oneself in order to give to the poor. We should know what it feels like to be poor and hungry.' He asked us to give generously for the Shrove Tuesday tradition at Cotton of collecting for the orphans of the Birmingham diocese.

The homily finished abruptly. Father Armishaw gathered the collar of his cloak close to his neck and hurried out into the snow. As we followed and ran across Lower Bounds to wait in the cloister for lunch, it occurred to me that the conference coincided with my new spiritual mood. I had found courage and strength in the sufferings of winter, and now there was Lent, in which we joined Jesus fasting in the desert. I was dying to myself, like the seed that falls to the ground, so that I could rise a new and better person.

On Shrove Tuesday we auctioned a ceremonial pancake which had been tossed three times high in the air by the school captain. The aim was to hit the ceiling and yet still have the pancake fall back into the pan. The captains of the college houses had collected money from all their boys. I had given the equivalent of two weeks' pocket money. Father McCartie conducted the auction. Our house, Challoner, won, and amidst cheers our captain received the uneatable object, which had frequently landed on the floor of the refectory. The money collected from all the houses was donated to the diocesan orphanage, Father Hudson's Homes.

I had now started reading a novel entitled *My New Curate* by Canon Sheehan, an Irish Catholic priest. It depicted the relationship between an elderly parish priest and his smart, ambitious young assistant curate. I would daydream intensely about the rural parish he described, close to the shore of the Atlantic in the West of Ireland, and peopled with simple peasant parishioners. I imagined the austere pastoral life of these priests against the background of cliffs, stormy seas and breakers, walking the muddy roads in the teeth of rain squalls to visit the poverty-stricken hovels. This seemed to me the most desirable mission that a priest could wish for. I felt that it was deepening my love of the priesthood and poverty.

40

SINCE THE BEGINNING of the term I had spent less time with James Rolle and Peter Gladden, save for brief conversations about the weather and keeping warm. Oliver Stack had come around to acknowledging my presence, but there was no attempt on my part, nor on his, to establish a closer friendship. Derek, meanwhile, seemed to have hibernated entirely into a kind of Lenten monastic silence.

Charles House, who had never mentioned the incident when he touched my face in the night, nor the occasion when I caught him smoking down the valley, was usually in the library, surreptitiously feeding himself with sweets from time to time, although it was expressly forbidden to eat in the library, let alone eat sweets in Lent.

One day when the librarian had left the room, Charles came to lean over me to see what I was reading. '*My New Curate*? . . . Very edifying, Fru,' he whispered in my ear, so close that I

Cotton boys' library.

could feel the warmth of his breath. Then he placed a sweet in its wrapper on the page before me. 'Have a bon-bon,' he said.

I looked into his face with its refined, even features. His eyes were golden brown with flecks of grey and blue.

After a few moments, he said quietly, so as not to be heard: 'John. You are very beautiful.'

I could not remember a time when anybody had looked directly into my eyes. As for telling me that I was beautiful! I could not cope with the flood of feeling and confusion that he had provoked. I looked away.

He returned to the table where he had been reading and smiled before picking up his book. I watched him for some time, wondering whether he would look up again. But he appeared absorbed. I put the sweet in my pocket. It then occurred to me that Charles was doing what I had done to Oliver Stack. He was making me an object of his charity I thought, and this token of his affection was a sign that in fact he disliked me intensely. Later I threw the sweet into a waste bin. In subsequent days, whenever I saw Charles we would exchange looks, and I would turn away embarrassed. There was something between us, and it disturbed me.

In the second week of Lent, I told Father Browne about my Canon Sheehan novel and he was disappointed. He told me that during Lent he wanted me to make sacrifices that really meant something. 'Your Canon Sheehan,' he said, 'seems to me a self-indulgence.' He wanted me to go back to Saint Thérèse.

As Lent got under way I was conscious of an underlying tension in the college. The weather had been too inclement for sports, and we had been cooped up inside the gloomy unheated buildings for days. We were giggling a lot at the least excuse. There was a spate of practical jokes which prompted paroxysms of collective nervous tittering. One night as I climbed into bed I felt a bristly object like a hedgehog. I leapt with fright, giving a great shout. It turned out to be a boot brush. All the dormitory seemed to be in the know and there were fits of giggles in the darkness, despite Father McCartie's growled warnings from the door of the laundry chute.

Then Derek, deep in his Lenten piety, became the victim of a cruel practical joke with more drastic consequences. At supper one evening we were given a slice of cheese each. One of his table companions swapped Derek's cheese for a piece of white soap. He scrutinised the object and sniffed it. But instead of leaving it on his plate, as was expected, he consumed it in one bite. He immediately began to retch and was violently sick. For several days the mere sight of Derek prompted titters and whispers of 'Cheese!'

By the end of February my chilblains had begun to give me trouble, especially on my ears. As fast as they healed they would break out again in painful, bleeding sores. One evening I had to take our Greek class exercise books to Laz's room after prep. The door was open and the old man, weary and dishevelled, was sitting in the bitter cold by his empty fire grate wearing a threadbare trench coat over his academic gown. He smiled at me wanly. As I returned down the corridor Father Armishaw came out of his room and stopped abruptly.

'Those chilblains look terrible,' he said. 'You must show them to the matron after Rosary.' Later that evening he was invigilating prep in the study place, walking up and down the long room while reading his breviary. He stopped next to me. Bending over he said gently in my ear: 'Make sure you see the matron.'

That evening I queued up outside the matron's 'dispensary' opposite the sickbay and had my chilblains treated with an evil-smelling ointment. Matron was a Belgian, her religious name Mère Saint Luc. She clucked away, reprimanding me for not coming earlier. 'You might have got blood poisoning,' she said. She ordered me to return every evening until the sores had disappeared. It was the first time I had spoken to a woman since the end of the holidays.

Even after the thaw, mid-way through the term, snow remained where it had drifted in the hollows of the fields. It was still too hard to dig drains, but there were games of hockey, and the entire college was sent out on cross-country runs almost daily right up until the beginning of Holy Week. As I became more familiar with the landscape and capable of keeping up at least with the middle of the field, I began to enjoy running, especially when we spread out and I found myself alone with my thoughts and the landscape. I pushed myself hard, day after day, conscious that I was gaining in strength and stamina.

41

ON THE MORNING of Palm Sunday there was still no sign of spring and the fields looked bleached, the sky a vault of still, cold white light. Clutching our blessed palms, we walked in procession two by two along the gravel paths at the front of the old hall. When we returned to the church, the celebrant knocked on the closed doors with the tip of the processional crucifix, re-enacting the entry of Jesus into Jerusalem. The choir sang the Gregorian chant refrain: *'Gloria, laus, et honor, tibi sit Rex Christe Redemptor . . . Hossana filio David.'* 'Glory and praise to Thee, Christ King Redeemer! . . . Hosanna Son of David.'

The next day we started end-of-term exams before going into our annual four-day retreat which began after the ritual known as *Tenebrae*, or Shadows on 'Spy Wednesday', the day Judas schemed to betray Jesus. Tapers on a fourteen-branch candlestick were quenched one by one. When the church was finally in darkness, save for the glimmer of one remaining taper placed behind the high altar, we struck our missals on the benches in memory of the earthquake before Jesus's death. The banging lasted for several minutes and my heart pounded with excitement at the strange drama.

After the service a tall, pale priest with smooth dark hair walked slowly up the aisle to take his place at a chair and table on the sanctuary. He greeted us in the semi-darkness, introducing himself as a member of the Passionist order, a religious community dedicated to preaching the passion and crucifixion of Jesus. He explained that each day of the retreat he would preach four homilies, which we should consider as 'points for meditation', or reflections to help us in our silent prayer.

The Gospel of the Mass of the day, he began, reminded us

Cotton church.

that on Wednesday of Holy Week, Judas betrayed his Lord. How could that happen? 'The answer,' said the priest in grave tones, 'was that Satan had entered his heart.' These were no idle words, he went on. We should realise that Satan, 'the Father of Lies', lay in wait especially for those young ones who were intending to be priests. There was a seminary in Rome, he went on, after a dramatic pause, where a demon had entered a young seminarian. He was an average, decent boy proceeding

119

in his studies like any boy at Cotton. He became uncontrollable, raging with the strength of ten men. Only by frequent exorcisms, said the priest, was the demon cast out. Before the Devil left him, the boy chanced to put out his hand against the panelling of the seminary refectory and the shape of that hand was burnt indelibly into the wood. 'That burn mark,' he said, in a low voice, 'remains to this day.' Then he cried out: 'Whence comes this terrible hatred of the Devil for God's chosen? It was pride that led to his bid to challenge God. The consequences of pride are terrible indeed . . .' So he went on. But I could think only of the terrible plight of the youth who through no fault of his own had been possessed. I could scarcely breathe.

When the priest had finished and retreated from the sanctuary, we sat meditating, tense and silent, on our knees for more than half an hour. Finally Father McCartie made his signal and we walked out in ranks to the refectory where we continued to sit in silence. As plates of baked beans were distributed, the school captain read out a meditation on the passion. But I hardly heard a word, nor could I eat a morsel; and I was not the only one.

42

LYING AWAKE BEFORE dawn on Maundy Thursday I felt sick to the heart at the thought that Satan could have power over a person irrespective of the state of their grace and holiness. The retreat priest had said that Satan could not permanently harm a person thus possessed; but that seemed to me a small consolation.

The day at last dawned pale and cold. After the Mass of the Last Supper, and for the rest of the retreat, we were allowed to walk in the gardens in front of the old hall and along the pathways around the church, a privilege intended to aid our meditations. There were crocuses appearing in the borders and timid shoots of daffodils on the margins of the lawns. Sitting by the statue of the Virgin I read the book I had chosen for my retreat reading, Archbishop Goodier's account of the Passion and Death of Jesus. I felt that I was reliving, vividly, immediately, the Passion of Jesus through the liturgy and in my imagination. I could see Jesus in his suffering and feel his presence.

The sound of a rattle echoing inside and outside the buildings (bells, a sign of celebration, would not be rung now until the Mass on Saturday night) announced that it was time to return to the church for the Passionist's first homily of the day. He kept us waiting for some time before he glided up the aisle. His text, taken from the day's Mass, the Mass of the Last Supper, was: 'Whosoever shall eat this bread, or drink the chalice of the Lord unworthily, shall be guilty of the body and of the blood of the Lord.' The priest said that he wanted to encourage us that day to review, year by year, all the sins of our past life from the dawning of our age of reason to this very day when Holy Mother Church remembers throughout the world those sinners who have come back to God.

After the retreat father's homily I walked to and fro on the driveway behind the church where I could be alone. I could see the distant hills beyond the valley and hear the wind in the pine trees at the top of the bank known as Peggy's Wood. A cold sun shone in the white sky. I was growing more and more agitated as I attempted to recall the principal sins of the whole of my life. The peace of mind gained during Mass, after the terrors of satanic possession before dawn, had been replaced by a compulsion to question my confession with Father Hemming in Wanstead after Christmas. Had I been strictly truthful with him about the event in the early hours of Christmas morning? Had I not, in fact, deliberately indulged in impure thoughts? Had I not touched myself deliberately? Had I tried to give Father Hemming the impression that I was only semi-conscious? Did this not mean that my confession was wilfully false? And did this not mean that all my Holy Communions had been sacrilegious ever since? 'Whosoever shall eat this bread, or drink the chalice of the Lord unworthily, shall be guilty of the body and of the blood of the Lord.' As I stalked up and down the pathway in a state of mounting anxiety, my stomach was churning.

At the priest's homily that afternoon he said nothing to allay my mental torment. He talked of the danger of being smug about the state of our souls, and of presuming that we were in a 'state of grace' when we might well be headed for hell. He told the story of Thomas à Kempis, the 'supposedly saintly' author of *The Imitation of Christ*. This man, said the priest, famous throughout the history of the Christian Church for his spiritual guidance, was considered for many years a candidate for sainthood. It was common, he went on, to exhume a candidate for sainthood in order to establish whether the corpse was incorrupt. To the dismay of the onlookers, Thomas à Kempis's corpse was found to be contorted as if he had died in terrible agony. It was obvious that he had been buried alive and had died in a frenzied attempt to claw his way from the grave. 'This supposedly holy man,' he said, 'most likely died in despair.' His beatification process was dropped and had never been resumed. 'If I tell you this, dear young brothers in Jesus Christ, it is to be ever mindful of the sin of presumption.'

After meditation, in which my brain raged with the certainty that I was damned and destined to spend eternity in Hell, I developed a sharp headache over my right eye. I hastened to the room where the retreat father was hearing confessions. I stood outside for what seemed an age. Eventually the bell rang down in the cloister for tea.

The door opened and a boy came out. The priest was about to follow him. I stood before him as if to block his way. He said: 'You are troubled, young man ... Why don't you come in.'

We sat opposite each other in rose-coloured armchairs. I began to cry, holding my painful head and rocking to and fro. The priest sat looking at me impassively.

'Well, I can't help,' he said, 'unless you tell me what's wrong.'

So it gushed out. The Christmas morning, my uncertainties, Father Hemming, my fear of being in a state of mortal sin.

He took a handkerchief from the pocket of his robe. 'Dry your eyes!' he said curtly.

As I sat trying not to cry, he launched into a lecture on masturbation, wet dreams, intentional acts and sexual fantasies. He used a lot of long, unfamiliar words about bad habits of 'concupiscence', and the vicious circle whereby sexual excitement becomes an irresistible compulsion if early restraint has not been achieved. Wet dreams, or what he called 'nocturnal emissions', were natural in a boy, he said, perhaps every ten days, or even more often. Their frequency, he said, could be reduced by avoiding deliberate indulgence in sexual thoughts and images during waking hours, abstinence from rich food in the evening, or vigorous exercise in the fresh air. He said: 'When the emission has occurred in the half-waking state it is not a mortal sin. But if you wake up it would be a mortal sin to take pleasure in it or to provoke it further.'

At this point, I was most alert. For he had now touched on the subject that was agonising me most: my culpability on Christmas morning. But I quickly lost him. Was I stupid, I thought, or was this business of masturbation, nocturnal emissions, culpability and mortal sin, an inextricable maze in which the soul could wander forever lost?

I asked: 'Father, what if I'm in a state of doubt about whether I was awake or not?'

'Why then, where there is doubt as to sin committed, one must judge by presumptions.'

I was baffled. What could that possibly mean? 'Presumptions!' And what had it to do with the 'presumption' of the man who had been condemned to hell? Why was this matter of sin and damnation so complicated, shrouded in ambiguities? But he had already launched into a lecture on how 'illicit' sexual acts could become an obsession, taking over our entire bodies; how this domination could begin remotely, in small acts, such as taking pleasure in a picture or the sight of a particular person, leading to a nocturnal emission. In other words, while we were not responsible for acts performed in our sleep, or 'twilight' state, we might well be responsible for them as a result of something we had done, or failed to do, during our waking hours. It was these waking *causes*, he said, 'that would become a grave sin, if performed in full knowledge of their outcome.'

Throughout his lecture I had a growing urge to tell him about the man at South Kensington. Why did priests speak of sin, I wondered, only as a personal fault of the penitent rather than things done to the penitent? But he gave me no opportunity to broach the matter.

'Let's be practical,' he said cheerfully at last. He was going to presume that I had committed a mortal sin on Christmas morning, and that I had not been honest with Father Hemming, which amounted to a second mortal sin – making all my Communions sacrilegious ever since. He would now give me absolution for everything in so far as it was culpable. For the future, however, I should be extra vigilant for the *causes* of nocturnal emissions.

'Practice avoidance of pleasurable tastes, and sights and sounds to build up your spiritual stamina,' he said brightly. 'Now in your youth is the time to become an athlete in purity.'

He asked me to be truly sorry for all the sins of my past life, and gave as a penance five Our Fathers and five Hail Marys. Then he gave me absolution. As he finished he said: 'You must place yourself in the safekeeping of Mary, our Mother and our refuge.'

When I got to the refectory the plates had been cleared and I had missed afternoon tea. My headache had vanished, my stomach was more settled, I knew that Jesus loved me truly. But I was conscious of a deeper anxiety that I could not put into words. The thought that I had been in a state of mortal sin all through the term left me feeling spiritually and emotionally numb, as if I was sleepwalking. And the priest had planted the seed of an idea in my mind that could grow, I felt, into something that I dared not think about. I felt a hint of that old terror of 'he who wanders through the world for the *ruin* of souls.' I went out into the cold air of Little Bounds, Goodier's book on Christ's passion under my arm, trying not to think.

We were allowed on Maundy Thursday to stay up late in order to visit the Blessed Sacrament which was kept in 'repose' in the Lady chapel. The high altar was stripped of its altar cloths and candlesticks; the tabernacle doors were wide open, signifying the coming death of Christ. The presence of Jesus in the Lady chapel signified the agony in the Garden of Gethsemane.

I spent four hours in the chapel reading Goodier, sometimes gazing up at the altar where the real presence of Jesus Christ resided within a chalice beneath a piece of gold cloth. I was imagining myself among the disciples in the Garden of Gethsemane: I could see Jesus sweating blood in his agony. How was it, I wondered, that I had never realised the savagely painful nature of seeking true holiness. How was it that I had not understood that I must make supreme sacrifices to follow him: even to the point of death. I would become an athlete for Jesus. At midnight, Father Doran appeared in a cope and took away the Blessed Sacrament to hide it within the sacristy. The church was now empty of the presence of Jesus in memory of his death.

43

THE FOLLOWING DAY, Good Friday, was a fast day. We were given only bread and tea for breakfast. A cold silent stillness descended on the valley and college grounds. In the course of the long morning, punctuated by the sound of the rattle, the retreat father gave two homilies. He no longer concentrated on our sins, and the penalties for them, but on the terrible price Jesus had paid for our salvation.

The liturgy of the day was long and sombre. Gathering in the stripped sanctuary, the celebrants sang in Gregorian chant the entire account of the Passion by St John. The choir sang the words of the crowds to a setting of Victoria. When the celebrant sang: '*Ecce Rex vester*,' 'Behold your King,' the choir responded: '*Tolle, tolle, crucifige eum*,' 'Away with him. Away with him. Crucify him.'

After this a splinter of what was claimed to be the actual wood of the original cross was venerated in a gold reliquarium. We queued in the aisle to kiss the object, while the choir sang a polyphonic setting of the Lamentations: 'My people what have I done to Thee.'

The college fell silent again as we continued to fast and to pray and read in private. At the evening homily the Passionist took us through the story of the crucifixion, asking us to smell the sweat and blood of our saviour, to hear the sound of the nails being hammered in, to see his writhing body, taste the vinegar offered on a sponge, and feel the excruciating pain of crucifixion.

That night as I lay in bed looking up at the starless night, the full significance of what the priest had said to me on Maundy Thursday at last dawned on me. I allowed myself to ponder it, and I became engulfed with misery, with despair. Even as I lay there, my penis, to my shock and dismay, was growing hard and erect. Was it possible that, as the priest had warned, every thought, word and deed, every sound, smell, taste, feeling and sight in the world, could prompt a feeling that would lead to 'irregular motions of the flesh', and must I seek out these 'causes' and eradicate them, however innocent they were? Taking the cord from my pyjamas I tied my wrists and put the slack around the back of my neck to prevent my hands straying downwards while I slept. My last thoughts were of Our Lady – Our Mother and our refuge.

44

HOLY SATURDAY, I awoke confused at first as to why my hands were tied. Then I remembered. Untying the knots, I prayed to my Guardian Angel. I tried to stop thinking about the priest's terrible counsel. Surely, I thought, the power of God's grace existed to keep me safe from sin. I got up and dressed, trying valiantly to be confident in Mary and Jesus.

As I walked in the gardens after breakfast (there was no morning Mass on Good Friday), it occurred to me that the salvation of my soul might depend upon a monastic regime of silence, self-denial and constant prayer, for the rest of my life. Was this not my true vocation? Should I not sacrifice all to seek the face of God and earn heaven?

There were many boys walking along the gravel paths at the front of the house; so I decided to make my way through Little Bounds to Upper Bounds, which appeared to be deserted. I took out my rosary and walked along the pathway above the cinder yard where there was a herbaceous border and a low stone wall. I had gone only a few paces when I heard voices. Sitting on the wall, partly obscured by a bush, I saw Charles; next to him was Bursley. They looked at me, then looked at each other. Charles smiled and raised an eyebrow. I had caught them breaking the retreat rule of silence. The growing prig in me pitied them for rejecting the spiritual opportunities of the reatreat but, again, I felt a brief pang of jealousy for Bursley.

That night many of us stayed up late, meditating in church or reading in the library until the rattle summoned us for the service of the Easter Vigil. We gathered outside the church where a brazier roared, shedding clouds of sparks in the night wind. We processed up the aisle holding our Easter candles, singing higher and higher: '*Lumen Christi: Deo Gratias!*' 'Light of Christ. Thanks be to God.' Finally the Mass of the Vigil of Easter began. The bells were rung, the palls taken away from the statues, and the choir sang a Pallestrina setting of the Gloria. After Mass we gathered to eat sandwiches and milk in the refectory; we were allowed to talk and most of us were making up for the four days we had remained silent. But I went to bed with a dark shadow over my Easter happiness.

45

EASTER SUNDAY DAWNED with warm sunshine and a spring breeze. The examination results went up on the board and showed that I had done reasonably well in all subjects. We were free through the afternoon to pack for a short holiday which would begin the following day. Many of the boys were sitting around on their beds talking quietly about incidents in the retreat. Others were walking on Top Bounds. I did not want to speak. I wanted to stay in the retreat which had been spoilt, I felt, by miseries of guilt and the ominous things that the Passionist had said.

I went into church with my copy of Saint Thérèse's auto-biography and began to read. After a while I just sat gazing up towards the tabernacle. An hour passed. From time to time the doors of the church swung open and other boys came in to pray. I noticed Derek kneeling for a long time in the Lady chapel, and I wondered whether he too had experienced torment like mine. Eventually the church was empty. I began to think of what the Passionist had told me about the incidents in my waking life that could trigger 'irregular motions of the flesh', as he called them, creating occasions of sin out of almost any act, thought, or experience. How could this be so? How could anyone avoid damnation? The agitation and panic I had experienced while walking on the path by the church on Maundy Thursday came flooding back. It had taken only seconds for me to lapse from spiritual contentment into a state of feverish anxiety, setting my pulse racing.

I rose from the pew and left the church, uncertain as to what I was going to do. Hurrying along the cloister I ran into Father Armishaw who was coming from the opposite direction, breviary in hand.

'Whoa!' he said. 'What's all this?' My face must have said it all. He barred my way. Then his expression changed to concern. That was all it took for me to start weeping.

He said: 'Come with me.'

There was a staircase by the clock cloister just beyond the infirmary. He took the stairs two at a time ahead of me, then turned along the corridor and mounted the second flight which led up to 'Creepers' where he and Laz lived.

In his room he told me to sit down in the armchair by the fireplace. 'And stop that crying, Cornwell, for God's sake ... What's wrong with you?'

As it tumbled out, I told him – and it was the first time I had told anybody – about the man at South Kensington; I recounted the sordid trail of misery that led up to the Passionist's advice given on Maundy Thursday; barely capable of speaking, I told him how miserable I was, how I was in a state of despair.

When I had done, he took off his glasses and sucked one of the ear pieces. He was silent for what seemed an age. Replacing the glasses on his nose, he said: 'To tell you the truth, I was not too happy with some of things the retreat priest said. But as for his personal advice to you, you must ignore it. D'you hear?'

As he spoke, the tone of his voice, his kindness, calmed me. He said that God did not expect the impossible of us: he loves us and wants us to be happy and to flourish. 'That Passionist I'm afraid is confused. If you believed that you were causing wet dreams by innocent actions in your waking life you would end up finding occasions of sin in everything and anything. That's foolishness as well as heresy.'

He told me that I had been suffering from 'scruples', agonies of conscience, and that many boys in seminaries experienced this, especially if they became victims of irresponsible advice. He was looking at me, as if calculating whether I had taken his advice on board. I was thinking: 'Scruples!' It was a new word to me.

At length he said softly: 'Now bugger off. And for God's sake put that bloody book away and give church a rest!'

As Father Armishaw spoke in these jaunty, vulgar tones he seemed fatherly and dependable. He soothed the turmoil in me. And he revealed something of crucial importance. It had never occurred to me throughout my boyhood that priests could disagree.

Before I left the room, he said: 'And another thing, when you go home tomorrow get out into the fresh air every day and do some exercise.'

I went down the stairs, my spirits soaring.

PART TWO

SPECIAL FRIENDSHIP

46

ON EASTER MONDAY, travelling from Derby to London, I had tea in the restaurant car with a sixth former who was taught by Father Armishaw. I asked him what he thought of the priest. 'Oh,' he said, 'Vince is the most civilised man at Cotton. Several of us go up to his room on Saturdays to listen to music and "chew the fat" as he calls it.' The student assured me that I had that to look forward to if I showed promise in Armishaw's English classes. But the sixth form seemed an age away.

In London I made the journey from the city to Barkingside on my own by tube. In my suitcase I was carrying Latin and Greek grammars, the copy of Thérèse's autobiography, trainers and running shorts.

It was the bank holiday and the family sat together for tea late in the afternoon. I was telling them about the Holy Week ceremonies, and I was conscious that I was speaking in a slightly nasal tone with an edge of Black Country no-nonsense confidence.

'Why are you talking in that funny voice?' Mum asked crossly.

'You sound like that Northerner Wilfred Pickles on the radio,' said my sister.

I felt rebellious, and determined. In the course of two terms at Cotton I was losing my cockney accent, which I had grown to despise, and now I was deliberately attempting to speak, I thought, more like Father Armishaw. Wilfred Pickles!

I had devised a holiday routine: early morning Mass, breakfast, visit to the local library where I would study Latin and Greek, then home to change for a run; then back to church for meditation and recital of the Rosary before Father Cooney shut up at five o'clock. As I put the routine into practice I was conscious that my prayers were becoming mechanical, repetitive, less interior, less troubled and self-conscious. My running and rote learning of Latin and Greek grammar helped me to avoid preoccupation with my conscience: less inclined to *scruples*, to those agonies of conscience.

Running was a means of escape from the crowded little house and its tense atmosphere. First I warmed up, jogging around the sports ground three or four times, wearing two football jerseys. Then I stripped off to my vest and headed along the avenues and streets of Barkingside, following a set route along the broadest pavements and the less busy districts. Each day I ran farther and farther. I began to run in the evenings, after dark, around the sports field. I ran until I was exhausted. I developed blisters, a painful knee, an ache in my groin. And as I ran, I found ringing constantly in my ears Doris Day's latest radio hit, 'Secret Love'.

One morning my younger brother, Michael, aged nearly eleven, scrawny and underdeveloped, asked if he could run with me. 'Why not,' I said brusquely. He was wearing sandals. We jogged together around the field easily enough since I was virtually running on the spot to allow him to keep up. Then it was time to take to the roads. Deliberately, I flew off at a sprint to lose him. At the corner of Claybury Broadway I paused to look back. He was standing on the pavement weeping. But I turned and ran on. It did not occur to me, despite all my religiosity at Cotton, that growth in the spiritual life should have included kindness to younger brothers.

I had noticed that Miss Racine was not attending early morning Mass, nor was she at the Camp on Sunday. Several times I called at her house while out running, but she did not answer the door. One afternoon I was running along the cycle track on the road that led from Redbridge to Wanstead when I overtook her pulling her trolley. She was slower than usual and she appeared to be in pain.

Something had happened. She did not greet me warmly as in the past, but began to splutter criticisms of Father Cooney. She was now attending church at Our Lady of Lourdes in Wanstead, a walk of about two miles from her house. She kept saying crossly: 'I've written to the bishop! I've written to the bishop!' It saddened me that she was so gripped by her quarrel that she had no interest in me. 'Don't go to Saint Augustine's,' she said. 'That's a bad parish, and a bad parish priest.' Her quarrel with Father Cooney had something to do with his refusal to wear the biretta, the three-cornered clerical headwear, on the sanctuary (apparently his had finally fallen to pieces). Eventually I made my excuses and ran towards Wanstead. Before turning at the George pub, I looked back to see her toiling up the hill jabbering angrily to herself.

One fine afternoon my father devised a quarter-mile eight-lane running track on the grass of the sports field in readiness for the summer athletics. He worked out the calculations from a book and marked the lanes and curves and staggered starting points with pegs and lengths of string. I stood watching him with astonishment as he bent to his task, walking to and fro, to and fro, with his stiff-legged limp. When he stopped for a cup of tea, which he drank from a flask, he explained what he was doing. I was fascinated by his ability to make such complicated calculations, and pretended that I understood completely. While we were talking he expressed admiration for my running, but he annoyed me when he suggested that I was using my arms too much.

After he had marked out the course with the whitewash applicator I had new targets as a middle-distance runner. I started to time myself over the quarter- and half-mile as well as doing my long-distance runs. One afternoon, despite his extraordinary handicap, my father raced me with his strange hoppity-skip around a quarter of a mile in his working boots, and almost beat me. He lay on the grass in his overalls looking up at the sky, his face covered in perspiration, his steel blue eyes dazed with satisfaction.

47

ONE MORNING I was running up Clissold Avenue when a boy came out from his front garden and shouted after me: 'Oi! Sissy!' He was older than me, I guessed, and fat.

I had often felt self-conscious, running in vest and shorts around the streets of Barkingside, especially when a pedestrian would smile oddly. I was enraged. All the emotions of the Lenten weeks and the retreat, the nerve-racking tensions of being at home, came to a head. I ran on a little further, and the boy called out again: 'Sissy!' Making a little loop, without breaking my run, I turned back and came running towards him at speed. He was making a peculiar face, curling up his lips, his fists clenched. Without slowing down I sprinted past giving him a resounding smack full in the face. I felt his bared teeth on my fingers. His squeal of rage echoed down the street; but I ran another loop and came up to him at speed again. This time he punched me in the head before I could get in another blow. I ran on a little, my ear throbbing with pain. Then I came running back and gave him a flying kick on the side of his knee, making him yell as he collapsed on the pavement.

At that moment, a man appeared at the front door. 'Wass all this!' he shouted.

'Dad, 'e kicked me,' whined the fat boy.

'You little bastard!' shouted the man. 'Just you come 'ere!'

The man began to chase me. An incline of about half a mile

lay ahead. He was tall, overweight like his son, and he was puffing and cursing. But he was determined.

'Geddim, Dad!' I could hear his son shouting, as he limped along behind.

We ran up Clissold Avenue, turning into Otley Drive, then down Clayhall Avenue, then around Sunrise Crescent, then through Clayhall Park, the man just ten yards or so behind me gasping and cursing all the way. The fat boy had dropped out by the time we reached Woodford Avenue. Up Woodford Avenue we went as far as Gants Hill then down Eastern Avenue. Something mischievous and dogged in me wanted to make the man suffer, to make him hurt in body and spirit, so I kept slowing down, allowing him to remain at the same distance, while keeping a reserve of energy. People were stopping in the street to watch us. Two young men, guessing what was happening, cheered me on. Finally I turned into Horns Road, having run about three miles, and I let him come within five yards of me before I increased my speed and sailed away up towards Barkingside High Street with a little bye-bye wave of my hand. Eventually I looked back. He was standing with his hands on his hips, his shoulders heaving.

On the Saturday, making my weekly confession, I told Father Cooney that I had struck someone in anger.

He looked at me curiously through the grille. 'Everything gentle,' he said. 'Always gentleness and kindness even when we are insulted ... Why would you want to go hitting anybody,' he asked, 'and you the seminary boy?'

'He called me a sissy, Father.'

'He called you what?'

'A sissy.'

'Well, next time give the fellah a tump from me as well,' he said. 'Now say three Our Fathers, and three Hail Marys ...'

Violence was in the air that holiday.

The night before I returned to Cotton, I was woken by the sound of angry voices in the living room below. Mum and

Dad were quarrelling about money. It was one of those familiar circuitous rows which could have only one resolution. There was a bill which she could not pay, and somehow it was Dad's fault. His wages could not cover the household expenses, she was saying, and he had been spending money on himself going to football matches and treating himself. Dad was hotly denying everything, telling her that she should put money aside for the bills. But the more he argued back the more shrill she became. Then came the sound of a smack and a screech, and a chair overturning, followed by the full-scale rumpus: grunts, clouts, bangs, insults. My brother Terry, who had to get up at six in the morning, stirred and cursed: 'Oh God! Not again.' He put a pillow over his head. The little ones were now awake and whimpering and I could hear my sister weeping on the landing.

In the end I went down the stairs and entered the sitting room. Dad had Mum by the hair trying to pull her to the ground, while she was punching and kicking him. They were both yelling and screaming at each other.

'Stop this at once!' I bellowed at the top of my voice, emulating the accents of Father Armishaw.

They stopped. Mum was staring at me, her eyes starting out of her head as if she had been disembowelled. 'How dare you! Who do you think you are! Get back to bed! It's your fault I'm in this mess. I've had to buy new shirts and shoes for you to go back to that college. Get up to bed before I give you a bloody good hiding . . .'

They had stopped fighting long enough to hold a truce for the rest of the night.

48

As the train steamed along the valley of the Churnet following the flow of the river towards Oakamoor, I was astonished at the transformation of the countryside by the arrival of early summer. I sat next to James Rolle with the window down, breathing in the scents of the meadows and the river; gazing on the horse chestnut trees in full red and cream blossom, and the white hawthorn hedgerows brilliant as wedding dresses. In the luggage rack above my head were the items I had taken home at Easter as well as white cricket pants and cricket boots, donated by my elder brother who had grown out of them, and a new pair of swimming trunks.

At night prayers I was full of resolutions to apply myself more closely to my studies, to read more, and to make more friendships. As I came out of church in ranks at the end of prayers, I saw Father Armishaw reading his breviary. He was bathed in rich orange evening light that flooded into the back of the church from the west window. The very sight of him, sitting in a relaxed posture, one hand raised to rest his chin, filled me with relief.

I lay awake for hours listening to nightjars and owls in the woods, breathing in the cold sweet air from the dormer windows. The next morning I woke to the sound of the dawn chorus in the valley. Looking out of the window I stood entranced by the sight of the early sun lighting up the distant hills. I had been assigned to serve the Mass of Father Owen, and I knelt almost trembling with happiness beneath the floodlit stained glass of Saint Francis. The great doors were open at the west end of the church, creating a Gothic-framed vision of the steep fields on the far side of the valley. Every window in the college revealed a perspective of abundant dappled greenery and blossom, and the promise of hazy distant prospects.

Several days into the summer term Father Piercy entered the refectory to announce that the swimming pool was ready. The lower and upper fourth years were allowed up for a swim after tea. The pool was a concrete tank fed by a stream that gushed down from Peggy's Wood.

The dark green water was stunningly cold. Boys were diving in from a crude board, and the air was filled with the echo of their shouts and laughter. Floating on my back I looked up at the great elms rising on every side of the pool. I had never been so happy in my life.

As the weather grew warmer, the daily swim became a routine of exquisite pleasure. Afterwards I would go to the library to read Hilaire Belloc's *Path to Rome*. I imagined his descriptions of the French valleys as if they were part of our own landscape at Cotton. I enjoyed the rhythm of his prose and the bullish confidence of his Catholic certitudes. I had stopped reading Thérèse of Lisieux and *The Imitation of Christ* and I was spending time privately reciting the psalms of the Little Office of the Virgin. I felt as if I was living on the surface of Cotton's routines, sustained like a child by the hands of Jesus and Mary.

I decided not to return to Father Browne for confession and spiritual direction for a time. I went instead to Father Owen, who heard confessions in the sacristy during Rosary on Wednesday evenings and spoke briefly and with detached reassurance. Less self-centered, and prone to those scruples, I felt that I was becoming like many of my more contented companions. I was taking myself less seriously.

As the days lengthened I was spending time after Rosary in the cricket nets with James Rolle. But I found that as a batsman I was taking more balls on my knuckles than on the bat. My defective eye was letting me down. I cracked two fingers in the third week of term during a Sunday cricket match. I was not wearing protective gloves and a huge-shouldered boy called Stubeck hurled a ball at me which I took full on my left hand.

As Mère Saint Luc, the matron, bound the fingers she told me that I was off cricket for a week.

And that was how I came to fall under the spell of Charles House who had lurked at the edge of my consciousness ever since the day he had bent over me in the library during Lent and told me that I was beautiful. Why was it that I had thought of his face, close to mine, whenever I heard the refrain from Doris Day's 'Secret Love'?

It was a blazing Wednesday afternoon on which we had a half-day holiday for cricket. I had been lying on my stomach, leaning on my elbows in the long grass below the seniors' cricket pitch, watching a match against a visiting team. Charles appeared walking up from a lower field, where he had been playing for the under-fourteens team. He was wearing crisp white cricket pants and a short-sleeved Aertex shirt. His sports clothes were of the best quality, and his boots were of a fine creamy kid leather. He lay next to me, stretching out his arms which were already lightly suntanned, smooth and delicate like a girl's. He was chewing on a stalk of grass. 'I was bowled out for a duck,' he said. Then he looked me full in the face, very closely.

'Poor old Fru!' he whispered. 'How's the broken fingers?' He had a flirtatious way of glancing to one side before looking at one directly. He talked for a while about the match; in my confusion and excitement at his proximity – his hip was gently pressed against mine – I hardly understood what he said, except that it was funny and soothing.

Then he said: 'Shut your eyes, Fru.'

I shut them, and a moment later I felt his lips touching mine.

When I opened my eyes, my heart racing, he was lying on his back, his head in the grass. His lips were parted, his teeth pure white and even; his dancing blue eyes were laughing.

'Oh, my God,' he said. 'What have I done, Fru! What on earth have I done!'

I was looking at him, breathing deeply as if he had punched me hard in the solar plexus.

He said softly: 'Come on, Fru. Give me a kiss.'

And I did: lightly on his flushed cheek. And I found my soul melting at the smell of his hair and breath which seemed to me sweet as the early summer grass. As I looked at him, a few inches from his face, he was transfigured into the most beautiful creature in the world. His features were delicate, perfect, thrilling.

I knew that I had done something forbidden, but it did not occur to me that I had committed a sexual sin. Homosexuality meant no more to me in those days than a tendency for boys and men to behave like women – 'sissies'. I was intoxicated, obsessed, prostrate with adoration.

49

FROM THAT MOMENT in the long grass I was thrown into a minute-by-minute agony of suspense. I was thinking of him all day long and half the night. It was as if the earth would open up and I would plunge into an abyss unless I was with him. I contrived to be with him whenever there was a break in the routine; and he, in turn, seemed to want to be with me too. My infatuation for Charles was from the start inseparable from my feelings about Cotton's enchanted valley in those early summer weeks. Through the open windows came the scent of newly mown hay in the meadows below the college, and scents of flowers from the gardens before the old hall. When we were together our conversation was banal. We would talk about cricket, or make wry comments about Father Gavin or one of the other priests. Apart from those compulsive first kisses I felt no desire to touch him or kiss him again. Nor did

Cotton 'rocks', popular on walks.

he touch me either, or express endearments. Only the slightest expression in his eyes when we were not observed confirmed that he returned my adoration.

The peak of my bliss during those early days was the afternoon Charles and I came to spend two whole hours together lying side by side. Our class was sent on a walk across fields to a hidden dell where the turf was cropped down by sheep to a smooth lawn on the banks of a fast-running brook. The sixth former wanted to sit beneath the shade of a tree to study a textbook for his exams. The rest of us were allowed to laze in the sun. Charles and I lay on the warm turf out of sight. At one point, throwing blades of grass gently towards my chest, he said: 'John, I love you so much.' When he said it, I thought I was going to die of happiness. And yet the sense of delight was so excessive that I felt a momentary chill, as if the sun had darkened for a few seconds. I felt overwhelmed. How had I come to deserve such love? I was not good-looking, or funny, or interesting. And it was Charles, the most perfect, most adorable human being on earth, who was saying this.

'Why?' I asked him, trembling.

'Because,' he said, laughing, 'you warm the cockles of my heart.'

As we walked back to the college in the heat of the afternoon, he just once bumped lazily against me with his shoulder. I thought that I would never forget the pressure of his beautiful shoulder against my arm. After tea we sat in the library at the same table. The windows were open, letting in the warm quiet evening air. I was happy, and yet from that moment I began to feel a sense of danger. I had dim and ominous memories of perfect summer days in London towards the end of the war, when death could come silently at any moment from a cloudless sky.

50

CHARLES WAS NO longer consorting with Bursley, who would sometimes watch us miserably from afar. One day Bursley came and joined us on Top Bounds as we were sauntering together after breakfast. Charles said to him: 'Get lost!' Bursley turned away wordlessly. I felt deeply for him, and it filled me with consternation that Charles could treat him like that. Will he, I wondered, say that to me one day? It was unthinkable.

James, Derek and Peter were all too aware of my attachment. I felt no embarrassment; I felt immensely proud. Standing in ranks preparing to march into church for Sunday Compline, Oliver Stack murmured in my ear: 'Are you aware that we are not meant to indulge in special friendships?'

'Get lost, Stack!' I said.

I was conscious of my fall from grace, but I was living just for the moment. The point of life was to be with Charles, to be thinking about him every waking moment. I was conscious of him as I knelt saying the Rosary after supper; even as I went up to receive Communion during Mass. We were separated by several desks in class, but we would exchange looks occasionally through the lesson. When I sang in choir I could look up from my music score to see him in the front row of the pews. At night I lay in bed looking up at the sky through the dormer window, thinking of his beautiful face, his particular mannerisms, his way of turning and looking, conscious that he was just a few feet away in the darkness.

How I would have loved to climb into bed with him. I just wanted to be with him.

51

THE SPELL BROKE on the Feast of the Ascension. After a glorious High Mass, the choir set off in a bus for the annual treat at Dovedale. We passed through the town of Ashbourne singing 'Faith of Our Fathers' at the tops of our voices in the hope that passing Protestants would get the full force of our Catholic convictions.

Lunch was laid out in readiness at the Izaak Walton Hotel which stood at the entrance to the famous gorge with its high rocks and rapids. After feasting ourselves on roast chicken and vegetables followed by 'cabinet pudding' and custard, we were allowed to roam free, while the priests reclined in armchairs, their jackets unbuttoned, smoking cigars. There was a tradition that after lunch the sopranos and altos raced to the top of Thorpe Cloud, the hill overlooking the river. I sprinted off with the first five. We crossed the rushing waters on stepping stones, and approached the flanks of the hill through a stone stile. Halfway up, I was fit to vomit, and stopped. I sat on the side of the hill. Looking about me I felt overwhelmed by the immense vistas on every side. I had never stood so high, nor seen so far, nor felt so small in the vast grandeur of the landscape. There was just one person missing: Charles.

I sat there for a time, gazing at the landscape. Bursley and another fifth former came into view; Bursley said something to his companion and came over to me.

'This thing with you and Charles,' he said in a low voice, 'it won't last, you know.' Without waiting for an answer he went to join the other boy.

I knew that Bursley was right. What Charles was doing to me was what he had done to Bursley. It was what Charles did; and I vomited. When the choir returned from Dovedale, Charles was sitting on the wall that bordered Top Bounds, waiting for me.

'I missed you,' I said, my heart pounding.

'I missed you, too,' he said.

52

CHARLES WENT COOL on me slowly, very slowly, every small token of his rejection an exquisite torture. It began when he asked me to come for a smoke down in the valley. I told him that smoking made me feel sick. In fact, I was afraid of being found out. He pulled a face, and whispered: 'Sanctebob!' Then he said something that filled me with anxiety: 'The rules in this place,' he said, 'are ridiculous . . . I'll find someone else to come with me.'

There was no dramatic falling out; just a long withdrawal of his presence. Instead of being in our usual places at our usual times, he was increasingly absent.

One Sunday evening as we gathered for a film in the assembly hall, I saved a seat for him. He came in just before the lights went out. He looked at me directly for a moment, then went off to sit with Bursley, smiling amiably as he greeted him. I felt a pang of sorrow like bereavement. That night I did not sleep; my brain raged until dawn.

For days he blew hot and cold. There were occasions when he seemed to send small signals of affection just as before; but these tokens were as agonising as his rejection. One day when we were walking on Top Bounds together after breakfast, he stopped in his tracks. He said: 'Oh, Fru, you do know I love you, don't you!'

I was so miserable, so confused, I wanted to scream: 'No, Charles, I don't know!' I looked away, fit to cry.

For three days after this, he appeared to be ignoring me. And all the while the term was passing in a succession of painfully lovely days amidst the scents and brilliant foliage of our valley retreat.

How much time had I spent with Charles when I should have been studying. How much of my prayer life had been wasted in distracted, lovesick ponderings. What of my commitment to bask in the presence of Jesus my Lord and true Father. For how many hours had I walked up and down the cloisters and across the Bounds in the hope of 'bumping' into Charles when he had gone absent.

Two-thirds of the term had vanished when I was summoned to Father Gavin's room during prep one evening. He was sitting at his desk wearing heavy reading glasses, his face solemn. He did not invite me to sit down. He had a selection of my exercise books before him.

'Are you determined to be put on a train home?' he asked coldly. My work in every subject was in decline, he said, and the effort the staff had made with me had been in vain. The promise I had shown at Easter was an illusion. I began to weep.

Father Gavin was unmoved: his head was cocked to one side, his mouth pursed with indignation. 'Crying won't do any good,' he said.

I went to pray before the Blessed Sacrament; the doors were open and the church was filled with the scent of honeysuckle. I poured out my heart to Jesus. As I prayed, I realised that I had not come before Him for help to make a free decision. I knew that my love for Charles was utterly without a future. The choice was between deliberately shutting the door on him, or spending the rest of the term mooning around at our meeting places. That latter path, I now knew, would not win Charles back, and it would lead to expulsion. The interview with Father Gavin had frightened me. In all the weeks of infatuation I had not stopped to consider the consequences for my future and for my soul.

After Rosary I went to confession to Father Owen. I told him that I had given in to my feelings for another boy, that I was now anxious that my attachment had been sinful. He was brief and firm. He wanted to know whether we had committed any sexual acts together. I was not sure what that meant, but I told him that beyond one kiss we had never touched each other.

He said in a calm voice that it was only natural to form attachments. But it was not appropriate to give in to feelings of affection for someone of the same sex. 'What you must do,' he said, 'is take these strong feelings and channel them towards Our Blessed Lady. There is a word for this: *sublimation*, the purification of our feelings in our love for Mary.' Then he told me to say three Hail Marys for my penance.

That evening I began a regime that would continue to the end of the term a month hence. I set up my hidden workplace once more in one of the music practice rooms under the stage. I was determined that I would devote every free moment to study.

I skipped choir practice, affecting a sore throat. But after a few days I was dismissed from the choir anyway by Father Owen as having reached what he called 'my grand climacteric'. 'We'll see you back here when you're ready to go into the tenors or basses,' he said. It was remarkable, it seemed to me, that he could speak to me as if my confidences in confession had never been.

I got through cloister Rosary in two minutes after supper so that I could spend evening recreation under the stage. I spent the spiritual reading period with my head in a textbook. I shot off my weekly letters home in several minutes instead of the usual half-hour. I gave up swimming, and spent no more than three minutes eating breakfast.

As I plunged into studying, my heart never ceased to ache for the presence of Charles. He left a note in my desk, asking why I was avoiding him. I did not respond. I was conscious of him sometimes, looking at me reproachfully; but I steeled myself against the temptation to approach him. Then he left a note in my desk asking me to meet him in the valley near the shrine to Saint Wilfred. As I read it, I remembered him standing among the trees with Bursley. I tore up the note.

Finally he found me in my hideaway. He stood at the door looking at me where I sat among my books, using the closed piano lid as a desk. 'So, here you are, Fru!'

'Here I am,' I said coldly. 'I'm working, Charles, so leave me alone.'

'Come on, Fru,' he whispered. 'Let's make up. You know I love you.'

He was wearing an appealing smile. I adored him, soul and body. I felt as if I was murdering my own soul when, conscious that my eyes were blazing, fists clenched, I said: 'Get lost, Charles, and I mean it.'

He was not frightened of me. He just nodded and left.

That evening I knelt before the triptych of the Annunciation in the Lady chapel and tried to direct all my feelings for Charles towards Our Lady. After fifteen minutes I felt a headache coming on, so I rose and left the church.

53

DURING THE REMAINING days of the summer term I discovered that, summoning my determination, making what I called 'a *fiat*', I could study to good effect even in the midst of love-lorn misery. I could work well even as I pined. Yet I found it difficult to concentrate on my prayers. In church I found myself merely uttering the sounds, while my mind was on Charles. Whenever I attempted to meditate, and to 'sublimate,' I found myself thinking about him. When I said the Rosary or attended Mass, I could not concentrate on the mysteries and the sacred words. In church I laboured to keep my mind on the rituals, while every thought and image was of Charles.

This was a fresh cause for anxiety. We had been studying prayer and liturgy in Christian doctrine classes, with special reference to the papal document, *Mediator Dei*. The Holy Father had written that it was not enough merely to utter the words of a prayer. We should mean what we say. The 'interior' expression is as important, he had declared, as the 'exterior' expression.

Was I losing, I wondered, my vocation? Even as I pondered this, it occurred to me that staying at Cotton was the most important thing in my life. My vocation, the idea that I would one day take a piece of bread into my hands and bring God down on to this earth, was so far in the future, that it had no power to motivate me decisively. I was living intensely in the present. And if I had been asked to choose between Charles and the distant prospect of being ordained, if I had been asked to choose even between Charles and God himself, I would have chosen Charles. But leaving Cotton was not an option. Cotton was where I belonged now.

When I saw Charles pairing off with another boy called

Staines, when I caught glimpses of the two of them exchanging clandestine looks, I knew for certain, even as it scourged my heart with jealousy, that I would not now weaken. But I was also sustained by another influence, always present but hardly noticed.

The day after Father Gavin's pep talk, Father Armishaw sent for me. He was sitting with the door and the window open. He was playing a piece of piano music on his gramophone and smoking a cigarette. Looking towards the gramophone he said: 'Listen to that, Cornwell.' He had never called me 'Fru' like the rest of the staff and boys. 'Isn't that a beautiful fugue! Do you know what a fugue is? . . . Never mind . . .'

I listened, and I liked it. I felt secure sitting in the priest's room with its rows and rows of books and splendid views down the valley. My eye ran along the book shelves. Among the authors were names and titles that were strange to me then and therefore unmemorable; but I was conscious that they had nothing to do with the sacred, with Catholicism, with religion. When the music came to an end, he said abruptly: 'How goes it?'

I was wondering whether to speak about Charles. But instinctively I kept silent.

'No more *scruples* this term? No more agonies of conscience?'

I shook my head.

'Right as a ribstone pippin?' He paused as if he was about to say something else, but he left it hanging in the air.

We sat in silence for a few moments more.

'And what about the man in South Kensington?'

I shook my head again. Silence.

Then I felt compelled to ask him the question that loomed uppermost in my mind. 'Is it a sin, sir, if you don't concentrate properly on your prayers; do we receive grace if we can't concentrate on the Mass, if we find it impossible to pray even at Holy Communion?'

'Are you trying to concentrate?'

'Yes.'

'Then the trying is what matters ... God expects you to pray with your heart and mind as well as your lips and body. But there's something else. There are times when you acquire grace just by going through the motions ...' He gave me a strange smile: 'One day you'll understand, but perhaps not today.'

'Do you concentrate on every word of the liturgy and the divine office, sir?'

'I certainly don't. But you tell God that you want to concentrate, and leave the rest up to Him.'

'But, sir ... do you always concentrate when you read your books, your poetry and novels?'

He laughed. 'Aha! I have to say that I do ... but that's different.'

'How is it different, sir?'

He got up from his chair and stubbed out the cigarette. 'Cornwell, do something for me, will you! Scram!'

Before the last day of term I went to confession to Father Owen in his room. He was brief as usual and recommended that I say my prayers each day at regular times. Swinging around to his bookcase, he plucked a book from the shelf. 'I've something for you to take away for the summer break,' he said. It was *The Devout Life* by Saint Francis de Sales.

54

BACK AT THE Peel the summer sports activities were in full swing. My father was working from dawn till dark most days, while Mum was running the club-room canteen, selling her Spam sandwiches and rock cakes. My sister, the convent-school girl, took care of the house at weekends; cleaning every room, making beds, washing and ironing, while looking after my younger brothers. Jimmy, a cheerful little lad, sucked his thumb while living out his horse-riding fantasies. He could go nowhere, even a few yards, without mounting his imaginary horse, trotting forward or galloping, one hand on the reins, making a clopping sound with his tongue. Michael, small for his age, spent hours drawing elaborate castles with intricate defences: moats, battlements, vats of boiling oil to inflict mischief on invaders. It was if he had embarked on a massive imaginative strategy of defence against the entire malefic world, starting with the Peel.

My sister was a surrogate mother to my younger brothers, and she did it without complaint. But I sometimes caught her standing at the sink, looking through the window towards the gates, just as I had seen my mother do. That summer I heard Maureen singing 'Mr Sandman' at the sink, over and over again.

My eldest brother, Terry, went to night school several evenings a week as part of his training to become a draughtsman. He was obliged to work on Saturday mornings at Plessey's factory, and on Saturday afternoons and Sundays he was out all day playing cricket.

I was to help Dad in between my home routine of early morning Mass, running, and stints in the local library. I saw at first hand now the application and expertise he put into the care of his pitches, the tennis courts, the running track, and the gardens at the entrance to the sports ground. His centre of operations was a storeroom and adjoining garage which housed his mowers, rollers, spikers, whitewash applicators and tractors, all of which he serviced himself. On a shelf in the storeroom were his seed catalogues and manuals on the proper care of the cricket 'tables'.

He worked mainly in silence, giving me brief instructions from time to time. But when we took a break to drink tea from his flask, he would tell me stories about his struggles as a grounds keeper. 'Believe you *me*, son, when I first came to this place,' he told me one day, 'it wasn't fit for a fairground. The plantains were big as cabbages. As for the machinery, it was only fit for a museum . . .' He told me how the land was reclaimed swamp, 'full of tetanus', and how step by step he rescued the soil and the grasses from dereliction, and upgraded his machines, doing it all by himself with no help.

I enjoyed working with Dad, but I noticed that he was blinking more than usual as the day wore on. I also saw him on several occasions staring with a faraway look in the middle of the cricket table for a minute or so. As he shaved in the morning, he would say over and over: 'Oh dear! . . . Oh dear! . . . Oh dear! . . .' I thought he was merely fatigued. Like Mum he was working seven days a week, sometimes until after ten at night. In addition to working on the sports ground he was doing odd jobs as a gardener out in the wealthy suburbs. His clients used to come and pick him up in their cars, and sometimes I accompanied him. We would mow lawns, cut edges, weed, cut back, dead-head flowers, tidy around. Then we would be driven back to the Peel after dark, a few extra shillings in his pocket, one of which he would give to me. 'Don't spend it all at once!' he would say with a wink.

I first understood that Dad was in a bad way in his mind when he went missing for two whole days in the middle of a working week. Mum, who was on worse terms than usual with him, and out all night herself working in the hospital, remarked that she hoped she had 'seen the last of him'. A strange hope, as our house and her canteen business went with his job. But such was her exasperation with him, and her desperation for a change of her fortunes. She was convinced that he was holding her back.

On the evening of the second day, when he had still not appeared, it occurred to me to look for him in the back section of the shed where he kept his tractor. There I found him in the failing light, sitting on a pile of filthy sacks, sobbing. He had lost a tool that was essential for his work and seemed convinced that the end of his world had come. He dried his eyes, and I managed to coax him back into the house. I put my arm around his shoulders and told him how much I loved him. I was conscious of a sense of personal power: the power of a son who has outstripped his father; who aspired to be father to the man: Father John.

The next day instead of working he sat in his armchair, rocking, sighing and screwing up his eyes, mournfully humming to himself Mario Lanza's song, 'Be My Love'. It was unlike him to neglect his work.

I went with him to our local doctor. When he came out he was sweating profusely and shaking. I asked him what the matter was.

'What's the matter? I've got to see a trick cyclist, that's what the matter is. But believe you *me*, son, they won't get me into that Claybury there.'

The nature of my father's condition, which turned out to be depression, and a form of epilepsy known as *petit mal*, became apparent in the following weeks as he started to make regular visits to Saint Clement's hospital, the psychiatric unit in Bow Road. Mum attempted to explain his condition to us, as it had been relayed to her by a consultant psychiatrist. Dad suffered from occasional seizures in the brain which lasted no longer than a few seconds but which left him emotionally upset.

We did not know that Dad was only at the beginning of his tribulations. Mum said little, but she appeared to be watching him carefully. She said out of his hearing that the diagnosis of epilepsy explained many things, especially his 'filthy moods' and, as she pronounced it, in her occasional aptitude for cockney malapropism, 'his *panaroia*'.

He was on various medications which slowed him down. He continued to work, but he easily became exhausted and everything seemed to take him longer. A jolly young man on

vacation from Exeter University was employed by the secretary
of the charity that owned the playing fields to help Dad. As
the summer wore on, the pitches and tennis courts were beginning to look ragged and worn. The spores and fungi were
getting the upper hand. Marauding pests, wilts and slugs were
beginning to have their way.

55

IN THE SECOND week of September, we took a family summer
holiday. We stayed for a week free of charge in a house owned
by a Quaker charity at Cliftonville by the sea in Kent. The
terraced holiday house in a road near the cliff tops smelt
strangely but not unpleasantly of damp and the quantities of
aged cheap novels and travel books that lined the shelves in
the sitting room. I had a tiny bedroom to myself with bars
on the windows. After we had settled in, I lay on the bed, and
for the first time opened the book Father Owen had lent me:
The Devout Life by Francis de Sales.

The book had been written for the spiritual guidance of a
lay noblewoman. But his instructions were intended for people
in all circumstances of life. Francis declared that there was no
point in people fasting and being teetotal if they 'drink deep
in their neighbours' blood with detraction'. Nor was there any
point in giving to charity while refusing to forgive those who
had offended you. To be good, he wrote in that first chapter,
one needed charity; but to be devout one needed to practise
charity cheerfully, and constantly.

I found *The Devout Life* appealing for its analogies from the
natural history of animals, birds, insects, plants and flowers.
There was no hint of mystical spirituality in his writings, and
he repeatedly counselled normality and simple routines. He

Mum at Cliftonville with Jimmy riding piggy-back.

wrote that religious people often appeared gloomy and serious; but a truly devout person, he insisted, was cheerful and agreeable.

It rained frequently at Cliftonville, and cold winds laced with flying salt spray whipped in from the Channel and the North Sea. Our attempts to enjoy ourselves on the beach below the cliffs were doomed. We sat in our deck-chairs swaddled in raincoats. Looking up at the lowering skies Mum grumbled: 'I'm never allowed to enjoy a decent holiday. What terrible wickedness have I done to deserve this!'

My younger brothers ran in and out of the sea, their teeth chattering, their hands and limbs corpse-white. They ate their ice creams crouching behind the deck-chairs, hunched and shivering. I attended Mass and prayed in the Catholic church near the cliff tops. I went back in the afternoon to read *The Devout Life* and recite the Rosary.

One day I walked around Dreamland at Margate, the nearby popular seaside town, appalled by the vulgarity of the side-shows and raucous music, despising the scantily clad girls with their goose-bump flesh and silly hats proclaiming: 'Kiss Me Quick'. The revolting smell of hot dogs and candy floss, screeching bands of teenagers, disgusted me. In preference I took to wandering the cliff-top paths west of Cliftonville, walking as far as Broadstairs around the North Foreland, breathing in the ozone and smell of seaweed, looking out towards the broad expanses of the wastes of grey sea.

One night before we left for London, Dad drank several bottles of beer in the kitchen. Once tipsy he told stories about his heroic youth on the streets of Custom House and did an imitation of Charlie Chaplin's splayed shuffle, with its teetering turn on one foot. He seemed to be making a joke of his own painful disability. Mum, who had had a couple of glasses of Scotch and ginger wine, 'Whisky Macs', held herself tight and laughed shrilly at his antics. It made me happy to see them laughing together. I drank a couple of glasses of bottled Guinness.

That night, in the early hours, I woke up in the midst of a wet dream. The next day, Saturday, found me in a state of consternation. We were due to depart for London after lunch, and on Tuesday I was bound for Cotton. There were confessions in Cliftonville's Catholic church during the mid-morning. As I entered the box I was relieved that the priest did not know me. He was a small pale man with glasses, and he seemed in a hurry. I stumbled over trying to explain my sin. He looked up, and said abruptly: 'How many times did this happen?'

'Just once, Father.'

'Well, you don't have to go into all that detail. All you have to say is that you committed a sexual sin by yourself on one occasion. In future that's all you have to say. Now say three Our Fathers and five Hail Marys. Go in peace and sin no more.' The grille trap came down with a petulant bang.

56

THE BUS GROANED up the steep winding road from Oakamoor, packed with noisy returning boys from the station.
When I saw the familiar shape of the college looming through
the evening mist on its isolated promontory I felt that I was
coming home. I was no longer the boy who had arrived from
London's East End a year earlier.

Along with the rest of my year I had moved further back in
the main body of the church to make way for a new lower
fourth. As the school captain led us in prayer from the back, I
realised how deeply Cotton was eating into my soul. I had
returned to what was truly me. As I placed myself in the
presence of Almighty God during night prayers, as I sang the
Salve Regina, I felt that I was being drawn into the ranks of
the chosen men who now, and throughout the ages, served
Holy Mother Church.

The following day, James and Derek, who had travelled
with me from London, and Peter who had returned from
Wolverhampton, waited for me by the noticeboards so that we
could take a morning constitutional on Top Bounds. Then I
saw Charles. He was standing at the bottom of the Bounds
steps talking animatedly with Staines and Bursley, making
them laugh. Charles's hair was a little bleached, his face lightly
tanned. Our eyes met for a moment and I trembled.

As the college swung into its routines I found myself observing our priests. I was struck for the first time by their poverty
and discipline. The profs, all ten of them, were wedded to their
routines, and lacking in 'attachments' save for their enthusiasm
for smoking. They possessed little, other than their means of
transport – mostly ageing motorbikes. Their beds and desks,
the chairs they sat in, were the property of the college, and
hence the Church. Only Father Armishaw stood out from the

rest because of his aptitude for engaging boys, his occasional vulgarities, his books and his collections of classical records, his flying jacket and that gleaming new motorbike. And yet, Father Armishaw, as a priest, was no less perfectly in tune with the others, excercising his priesthood on the surface, without signs of inferiority. Our priests appeared content to perform the externals of the religious life. As I watched them reading their breviaries, pacing up and down the gravel paths, flicking over the pages, adjusting the silk tags, there was no hint of fervour. Their Masses were said with almost perfunctory precision with no hint of devout interiority.

I had found confirmation of this mechanical approach to the religious life in Francis de Sales. He had a compelling chapter titled 'Spiritual and Sensible Consolation', in which he vehemently rejected all emotion in the growth of the spiritual life. 'Weeping and tenderness of heart' are but 'snares of the Devil', wrote the saint, for being transitory they are not to be trusted. In his characteristic employment of metaphors from natural history he wrote that tears of emotion produce toadstools and fungi, not true flowers grown from seed. True devotion, wrote Francis de Sales, is just to do our duty 'promptly, resolutely and energetically'.

The rhythm of priestly life at Cotton had echoes of just such military efficiency, and the unquestioned protector of Cotton's clerical discipline was the Very Reverend Wilfred Doran. Father Doran was a lean, colourless, well-ordered man. The smoothness of his pale hair, the correctness of his manner of speaking, the precision of his Roman collar, the starch of his white shirt cuffs, were the epitome of Catholic clericalism. He kept us permanently poised as if we were all standing on our polished toecaps.

Sometimes I watched him from the cloisters, walking the sweep drive in front of the old hall with the archbishop, His Grace Francis Grimshaw. Occasionally they would turn their heads towards each other, deep in conversation. Then it struck me that Father Doran was endowed with an authority that connected through the archbishop and the cardinal in Westminster right up to the pope in Rome: His Holiness the Supreme Pontiff, Pope Pius XII, cleric of all clerics, whose photograph with those huge dark eyes, set in an ascetic face, gazed down upon us in clock cloister.

We were told repeatedly that His Holiness the Pope in Rome was the 'servant of the servants of God'. But we were under no illusions as to the strict order of authority that ascended up to the papal pinnacle in Rome. Despite our aspirations to be *servants* of God, we were conscious of the special charism of our calling. When I thought now of lay people, the laity, and female laity in particular, I was thinking of 'them' rather than of 'us'.

57

IN ACCORDANCE WITH tradition, the first Sunday homily of term was given by Father Doran. He appeared before us impassive, unsmiling. It was a pep talk for the slackers. 'Father Gavin,' he said at one point, 'tells me that the fifth form can take an *à la carte* approach to their choice of subjects for their public examinations this year. Well, I don't know about *à la carte*, but some of you are going to be *in the cart* if you don't apply yourselves.' That is how he spoke.

Turning to discipline in the college, he addressed the matter of boys neglecting to rise the instant the first bell rang at 6.20 a.m. 'I have received a request for an occasional *sleep-in*,' he said. 'Well, all of you here have the opportunity to sleep *in* for at least eight hours every night. What would you have me do? Allow you to sleep for ten hours? Eleven hours? I am reliably informed by medical experts that the sleep requirements for healthy living are as follows: an adult requires seven hours, a boy eight hours, a baby nine hours, and a *pig* requires *ten* hours.' So he continued, speaking a little to the side of his mouth, his lips drawn down, delivering his withering reproofs.

As we filed out of the assembly hall I found myself behind Charles. He was quietly entertaining Staines with an imitation of Father Doran's manner of speaking. Much as I felt Father Doran had been severe and sarcastic, it pained me to hear Charles House sneering at our superior within minutes of leaving the hall.

As the new academic year progressed, Charles's circumstance as a seminarian became ever more extraordinary. During Mass I saw him reading a novel, or chatting to his neighbour when the choir was singing. He missed Rosary, his lips did not move when we said public prayers, and he laughed openly at students who appeared pious. He was contemptuous of Cotton. One day, waiting for Father Piercy to arrive for a maths lesson, he commented that the priest was not qualified to teach the subject. 'You should be grateful,' James said tartly, 'to be attending the best Catholic school in England.' House turned on him, sneeringly: 'Don't be absurd! Ampleforth, Downside, Stonyhurst, are all ten times better than this place.'

'Then why,' James said hotly, 'did you not go to one of them?'

'Perhaps I will.'

James said to me afterwards: 'What is House doing here? He's so vain. And his special friendships!' He looked at me accusingly for a moment, then went on to speak of the bad effect Charles was having on the college. 'He exploits every little weakness in people and he sucks up to the profs. He is sly beyond belief.'

Like me, Charles had caught up with the rest of our year in Latin. He continued to be popular with the profs who came in contact with him, especially Father Doran who was taking the upper fourth for English. He was breaking Bounds every morning, and in so slick a manner that Father McCartie and the big sixth had consistently failed to catch him. James and I, though, had seen him, accompanied by Bursley and Staines, slipping out of Little Bounds and down the steep path between the trees into the valley for what we guessed was their morning cigarette. On one occasion we saw two more boys following them. Meanwhile, Father Doran, normally so knowing about boyish wiles, was increasingly indulgent towards Charles. Charles's weekly essay, suspiciously sophisticated beyond his years, was invariably the one to be read out, and he was always first to be called upon for his opinion. He even recycled Father Doran's brand of cynicism.

'Give me,' Father Doran asked the class, 'a sentence containing the phrase "a contradiction in terms".'

'A contradiction in terms,' quipped Charles, 'is a prompt schoolboy.'

Father Doran chuckled indulgently, apparently unaware, as James commented, that he had been laughing at one of his own jokes. 'And how is it,' James went on, 'that Father Doran failed to recognise the source of House's essay on proverb making, lifted wholesale from the first chapter of Belloc's *Path to Rome*?' Charles, James was intimating, was guilty of something more than plagiarism. Father Doran, our superior, was being suborned and undermined by the insidious charm of Charles House. Charles was a threat to everything Cotton stood for.

58

THE TERM HAD once again reached that point when autumn was about to pass into early winter, when Charles suddenly disappeared from the college. I first heard the news, arriving in the refectory from prayers before lunch. Without informing anybody, Charles, Staines and Bursley had disappeared, to-gether with two further members of the second year fifth: all of them church students. Enquiries in Oakamoor had apparently established that they had taken a mid-morning train to Uttoxeter.

Every term there were boys who 'did a bunk' as it was called, but they were usually isolated, homesick individuals who had found the regime too harsh to bear. Poor grubby O'Rourke had set off earlier in the term, walking aimlessly towards Cheadle. He had been picked up by the bursar, then sent home formally a few days later. It was unusual for boys like Charles and Bursley to leave unless they had been 'sacked'. As James Rolle explained, the voluntary departure of five church students in one day would reflect badly on Father Doran in the eyes of the archbishop.

After supper that evening, the college was summoned to the assembly hall. The school captain made us sit in silence, which we did for a full quarter of an hour, the tension building. Then Father Doran appeared. Instead of sitting up on the stage as he would for the Sunday homily, he chose to stand before us at ground level. He started in a quiet, even voice. He confirmed that a group of boys had left the college without permission. Now he wanted to talk to us about the nature of a priestly vocation.

'It was for you, and only for you, to apply to your bishop to be accepted as seminarians. You heard your vocation in your hearts. But once your bishop accepted you to be educated by the diocese for the priesthood, then your situation changed.'

The judgement as to whether we had vocations, he was saying, was a matter not only for us individually but for the Church. It was the Church that called us to the priesthood, not our interior voices, and it was for the Church in the person of our religious superior to release us from our vocations. The obligation for a boy to consult with his superior before leaving the seminary, he went on, was not trivial. 'Over the years there have been boys who left this place without consultation. In every case the consequences have been devastating, even fatal.'

He now set before us the fates, one by one, of those who had abandoned their vocations down the years without seeking permission. There was the boy who left one year and developed a brain tumour the next. The youth who absconded and was killed weeks later riding a bicycle. The boy who went mad and was locked up in a lunatic asylum.

Before he finished he said in a low voice: 'I need hardly tell you the moral of this desertion today: the influence of bad company; the forming of cliques and undesirable particular friendships. Avoid those companions who would attempt to draw you into secret meeting places and conspiracies to break the rules of the house. Of these fellows who have left us today, I fear for them from the bottom of my heart.'

59

I WAS TROUBLED by Charles's departure and Father Doran's talk. It made me more aware of a shadowy corner of anxiety in my soul. Charles had awakened me to intense and irresistible feelings. I had felt intensely, ecstatically alive. Now that he had gone, I began to wonder about my ability to resist the temptation to give in to those feelings, should they occur again.

The answer, as it had been suggested in spiritual direction, was the avoidance of 'special friendships'. But I remained anxious. At my next visit to Father Owen, I raised my fears with him. Once again, he talked about 'sublimation'. His voice filled uncharacteristically with emotion as he said: 'If it happens again, pour all your unbidden feelings, the stew pot of your passions, into your love of Our Blessed Lady. Transform those unbidden feelings by offering them to her, who is your true

mother and the only intimate human being in your life.' He
gave me a card with a prayer called the *Memorare*. He assured
me that this prayer had 'extraordinary efficacy' over every need
in our lives:

> Remember, O most loving Virgin Mary, that it is a thing
> unheard of, that anyone ever had recourse to your protec-
> tion, implored your help, or sought your intercession,
> and was left forsaken. Filled therefore with confidence in
> your goodness I fly to you, O Mother, Virgin of virgins.
> To you I come, before you I stand, a sorrowful sinner.
> Despise not my poor words, O Mother of the Word of
> God, but graciously hear and grant my prayer.

Something about the prayer worried me. *Memorare*: remember! It assumed, absurdly, that the Virgin Mary, like some absent-
minded flibbertigibbet, was likely to forget my needs unless
reminded. Yet perhaps the petition was no more than an
acknowledgement of our own childlike insignificance, our need
to plead with a mother who knew our needs only too well.
But no sooner had I eliminated this difficulty than it began to
dawn on me, in a niggling, insistent scruple, that our spiritual
lives involved not real feelings for real persons, but invented
feelings for imaginary persons. The reflection disturbed me so
much that I wondered whether it was not a whispered suggestion of the Devil himself, the Father of Lies. For if we were
inventing our joys and our struggles, our light and our darkness, if we were inventing our relationships with Jesus and
Mary, were we not therefore dwelling in a world of make-
believe? Against this creeping temptation to Faith I argued
with myself that there was nothing necessarily wrong with
imagining the world of the spirit. After all, the spiritual, the
supernatural, lay beyond the veil of mere appearances. There
was a sense in which our imaginings were a means of con-
necting with a deeper reality than this world of passing vanities.
And yet, and yet. On the night that I had been beaten for

studying under the bedclothes it had not been the Virgin Mary nor my Guardian Angel who came to comfort me, but Charles, the cynical, vain, absconding Charles. More than this, for all his capriciousness Charles had made me feel with an intensity that had devoured me. For the first time in my life I had been utterly besotted with another human being. I had been kissed, and had kissed in return. Being with Charles, short-lived as it was, had been worth every single passing moment. According to Father Owen, though, I should have taken those intense feelings and directed them towards Our Lady.

I surely spent a great deal of my everyday life speaking to Our Lady! I prayed to her constantly and fervently, with frequent invocations and routine prayers such as the Angelus, the Rosary, and the nightly Salve Regina. Yet Mary was, I had to admit, a figment, an amalgam of all the images of the Virgin I had venerated through my life, from the statue on my mother's dressing table, to the image of Our Lady of Fatima in Saint Augustine's, Barkingside, to the stained-glass Immaculate Conception in the church at Cotton.

My relationship with the person of the Virgin Mary, as it happened, had been subject to a gradual and troubling transformation. Since I came to Cotton I had begun to experience a confused, disturbing association between the Virgin Mary and my own mother. I could not think of my mother without remembering her violent, sometimes gratuitous, beatings, her rash and hurtful comments. Hence I could not think of her as associated with the Mother of God and vice versa. Yet the association had been encouraged by the awestruck reverence expressed for 'motherhood' by the profs and many of the boys. Devotion to the Mother God coalescing with love of our natural mothers was quietly and constantly fostered. The profs spoke of 'your esteemed mothers', and they made it known that like most diocesan priests they spent their free days or afternoons travelling considerable distances across the diocese to visit their own 'dear mothers'. Many of the boys received lengthy letters from their mothers each week as well as parcels containing items of clothing in which treats had been hidden.

There was a spiritual counsel that swept aside all these anxieties. Was it not better to quash all emotions entirely, the better to avoid the quagmire of feelings? Saint Francis de Sales did not write of sublimation. If we would promote 'perseverance' in the religious life, he advised, we should distrust and reject all feelings, even in our everyday prayer. But then I asked myself: would I have the strength to resist an upsurge of feeling for another person, another infatuation, if it should occur again? I would build up the strength of resistance, I told myself, by rejecting and distrusting all feelings, even spiritual feelings. I would resist feelings: resist, resist, resist.

60

THERE WAS, as it happened, a perennial and licit distraction that stirred the emotions of many boys at Cotton. As the autumn days shortened an elite set of rugby-football players, boots well-oiled, sports gear crisply laundered, became the focus of our attention as they ran self-consciously up to top field for coaching sessions. They were not necessarily the most athletic of their peers; but they had been selected early and coached to a high level of skill from the age of eleven. The best of them became the unique corps that formed the 'first fifteen' team chosen to play in away matches against other Catholic colleges around the Midlands. Those who had come late to Cotton, and from schools which had no tradition of rugby, like mine, were seldom considered for training: our role was to watch, to admire and to eat our hearts out.

The rugby gods made an easy fit with the wholesome, manly, clerical culture of the Cotton priests. Most of the profs had made it into the first fifteen team as boys, and enthusiastically coached their successors, refereeing games and accompanying away matches with Father Gavin, who had played rugby for Ireland (a fact deplored at the time, we had been told, by Archbishop McQuaid of Dublin). Our priests were eager even in the midst of class to be diverted into discussion of tactics and highlights of big matches.

Special treats, bacon-and-egg teas, and pub visits, figured large for the rugby gods. I heard a prim sixth former speaking with glittering eyes at table one day about the highlight of an away match in Burton upon Trent. 'We won by a single point. We were late back but we pleaded with Father Gavin to stop at a pub before we reached Cotton. So he asked the driver to stop at the Cricketers Arms. Over our beer he relived every pass, every scrum, every tackle. By the time we got on the bus we had replenished our glasses three times! Three times!'

One notable exception to the hallowing of rugby football was Father Armishaw who, Peter Gladden told me, loathed the game as much as he deplored the 'mindless blather of the rugger morons'. Even so, Gladden went on, Armishaw was capable of boasting on occasion about his own boyhood triumphs and how in one ferocious match he had saved the day against the 'mollycoddled sissies at Ratcliffe College'.

I had no prospects of being a rugby god, and I resented my sneaking feelings of envy. I thought many of them soft, compared with the toughs at Saints Peter and Paul in Ilford, even though they could handle a ball. I sometimes fantasised how I would tackle such a one and such a one in boxing gloves. Yet there was another agreeable alternative to rugby which promised to allay my fear of monotony.

Country walks were not new for Cotton boys, but they had traditionally been desultory strolls, supervised by a reluctant sixth former. In the year I arrived at Cotton Father Doran had appointed a sixth former called Michael Swan as 'head of walks'. Swan was a gangly youth with a reputation for high intelligence and studiousness. He was about six foot five and his clothes were too small for him. He wore very large, thick-lensed spectacles patched together with sticky tape. It was said of him that Father Doran allowed him to read the previous day's *Times* fourth leader so that he could translate it into Latin, employing a different style to order – Cicero today, Tacitus tomorrow, Plautus the next. He was lofty in every sense of the word.

I opted to go on Swan walks which were taken at a cracking pace for ten or twelve miles. The aim was not so much vigorous exercise as scenic variety. Swan led from the front with Ordnance Survey maps, dictating the speed and the direction which was at times complicated when we struck across open country. Sometimes we were so late back we staggered on to Top Bounds after dark, having missed tea.

Usually we walked in twos and threes, but I walked alone. I became lost in my thoughts as we trudged through woods and secluded dells, and over hillsides. As I walked it filled me with delight to look from high ground towards a distant prospect, fading into green mistiness. I loved to see the rapidly changing contrasts of cloudscapes and weather, especially when the summits were in shadow, while the valleys shone bright and clear after a passing shower of rain. What I treasured most were wooded dells, deep green in the early winter weeks. We would grow quiet as we entered these mysterious sanctuaries with their heady scent of pine needles and the echo of rushing waters. Best of all was the ascent of our own valley on the last leg home, following the steep, foaming torrent until we reached Faber's Retreat where I would make a silent prayer.

When we arrived back at the college after a long walk, I was excited by the contrasting ambiance: our sacred and civilised enclave in its wild and remote setting. I would go straight to the church to pray before the Blessed Sacrament, conscious of the wind in the lime avenue outside and the grousing crows as they returned to roost in the elms around the swimming pool. Walking the countryside around Cotton seemed to deepen my sense of the sublime in the world, and in the real presence of God in the Eucharist.

One of the keen walkers was a boy called Paul Moreland. Moreland had a reputation for being a swot and an oddity. He was seldom visible around the college. He had a womanish beauty: a large head and thick charcoal-black hair, full lips, a wide mouth. His sapphire blue eyes fixed on people with crazy, unfocused intensity. There was something radiant about the expanse of his pale forehead and his thick arched eyebrows. His cheeks were of a high colour, as if feverish. He generally walked alone with rapid short steps and a slight limp, as if he had one leg slightly shorter than the other. There were hints of my father's affliction in him. Sometimes I saw him in earnest conversation with Swan; which was unusual, for Swan did not regard other boys as his equal. He and Swan would quarrel loudly, attempting to shout each other down. Once I heard them shouting at each other in what I thought to be German, before they both burst out laughing. But mostly Moreland was a loner.

One day, on a rest during our walk, Moreland came over to where I was sitting on a drystone wall. I was looking out towards a lantern sky created by a break in the clouds towards the Weaver Hills. He stood between me and my view, looking intently into my eyes.

'Has anybody ever told you,' he said eventually, 'that you have a beatific aura?'

I had never heard the word 'beatific' pronounced, and I thought he had said 'terrific'.

So I said: 'What do you mean, "terrific aura"?'

He laughed, a delightful sincere laugh, and his face lit up. 'No, no, no, Fru: *beatific, beati-fic*.' He twice imploded the 'b' with his full lips, and made a flowing circle with one hand around my head like a magician. 'I can almost touch it,' he said. 'You are a blessed person, Fru. A holy person.' Then he walked away.

His remark, which I took to be wholly sincere, disturbed and excited me. Moreland struck me as an extraordinary spirit.

We seldom met a soul on our walks, still less a passing vehicle. But one afternoon as we trudged uphill towards a place called Waterhouses, a grimy village close to a quarry that had eaten deeply into the neighbouring hill, we passed a crocodile of about forty girls, walking two by two. They were from a nearby reform school for young female criminals. Their hair was uniformly cut short and they were dressed in grey raincoats, long grey stockings and sturdy black shoes. There were four burly female minders in attendance. I saw a comic parallel between our predicaments as we passed each other: like members of two juvenile monastic orders. I was fascinated by them. Some appeared embarrassed, as if ashamed to be seen in public; others had defiant expressions. Then one shouted at me: 'Who are you looking at? Cunt!' In my bad-boy days I would have had a ready answer, reflecting on the misfortune of her ill-favoured looks. But I exercised custody of my tongue and, too late, custody of the eyes.

61

IF I HAD a special friendship in the aftermath of Charles, it was one that carried not the slightest danger of romance or unruly passions, except nervous, painful laughter. It was innocent to the point of being childlike. Ever since Father Doran's talk after the departure of Charles and the others I had become more friendly with Derek Hanson. Derek had a comical Irish face: ruddy complexion, wild blue-grey eyes, cheeks and forehead ravaged with acne. He was timid by nature, a great hater of sports, and at heart very serious and dedicated to his vocation. Yet he had a nervous quirky sense of humour and would erupt in hysterical paroxysms of giggles at a word or a look, his whole body and his potato-shaped head shaking.

Walking up and down Top Bounds after breakfast together, and only when alone, we invented a private language game. We adopted pious facial expressions while uttering homiletic phrases in solemn, stately tones. Mostly we stole the phrases from books of ascetical theology in the library, and learnt them by heart for the purpose.

'Cornwell, you will avoid vain curiosity . . .' Derek would start.

'Hanson, if it be lawful and expedient to speak, speak only of such things as will edify . . .'

'Cornwell, let curiosity alone, and read such books as turn the heart to compunction, rather than entertain the mind . . .'

'Hanson, refrain from superfluous talk and idle visits . . .'

As we came out with these ludicrous imperatives we would attempt to outstare each other with baleful looks. The game was to make the other laugh first. When the dam burst we would become helpless, incapable of breathing, howling with laughter as we staggered along Top Bounds.

Other boys sometimes watched us curiously. Sometimes a boy would come over to join us. But Derek had developed a defence mechanism against intrusion, which was also part of the game. The moment we looked like being approached he would say under his breath: 'Let's be serious.'

Then Derek would begin to talk about a saint called Rupert.

'Saint Rupert,' he would say, now including the newcomer, 'was the bishop of Worms . . . he had a sister called Ermintrude . . . his coat of arms was a barrel of salt, and many churches near Salzburg which, incidentally, is a district famous for its salt mines, are dedicated to him . . .'

It was my task now to say: 'Is that so? That's so interesting, Hanson . . . do tell me more . . .' Sometimes I was so overcome that I would make my excuses and dash from Top Bounds before collapsing.

We never met or spoke from after lunch onwards, and it would have been unthinkable for us to catch each other's eyes in church or during mealtimes. Our friendship had rules and we kept to them religiously.

There was another diversion that was to bring me into brief contact again with Paul Moreland. After his Sunday homily, Father Grady, the priest with Gregory Peck looks and a nervous little cough, announced that a layman was coming to speak to us about a movement known as the League of Christ the King: LOCK. The League, he told us, was a means of spreading Catholic action at 'grass roots' among the young while promoting our prayer life and loyalty to the Pope. Anyone who wanted to learn more should come to his room after Rosary the next day.

The balding young man who was ensconced in one of the visitors' rooms had a hole in one sock. James, who had encouraged me to come along, was there, and so was Derek. Father Grady made his excuses, explaining that this was something we had to decide for ourselves. Just as we were about to begin, Paul Moreland slipped into the room.

The young man said that Communists were attacking Christianity not only behind the Iron Curtain but in the free world, seeking young recruits in schools and in the workplace. LOCK advocated the formation of cells in English schools to spread Catholic activism. We should be 'watchmen' against the dangers to come. He stressed this word 'watchmen' a number of times. The motto of the movement, he said, was '*Pro eis sanctifico meipsum*', 'I sanctify myself for others.'

As he spoke, I had the impression that he was enthusing us all, except Paul Moreland who looked bemused and occasionally frowned and shook his head. When the man invited questions, James Rolle asked whether it was considered right to actively seek recruits in the college. The visitor was all for active recruitment. Derek, blushing self-consciously, wanted to know whether one could be thrown out of the league for failing

Father Frank Grady.

to live up to its ideals. 'Oh, yes,' said the man. 'High standards, set by you and the movement, must be met.'

Moreland began to speak. He said that the Church already had its cells, which were called parishes. LOCK, he went on, his face bright with emotion, seemed to him a threat to Catholic parish life. As for bringing the league into Cotton: would it not threaten our community, creating divisions among us?

Then he stood up. 'It was so nice to meet you,' he said, holding out his hand to be shaken. 'But I do not think that I want to join this movement.' And he left the room. The visitor sat silent, evidently ruffled. I felt sorry for him, as did the others I thought. So we professed ourselves interested in forming a cell of LOCK. When Father Grady returned he seemed pleased. We could use his room on Sunday evenings after supper, he said, as he would be away most weekends travelling the diocese promoting vocations to the priesthood.

Afterwards I asked James what he thought of Moreland. 'Moreland is clever,' he said, 'but Moreland, I hate to say this, is as nutty as a fruit cake as well as singular. He has visions, you know.'

When LOCK got going at Cotton, the movement developed two cells: one named after Dominic Savio (the saintly seminary boy of Turin), the other after Aloysius Gonzaga (the saintly Jesuit youth) both of whom died young. I was in the Savio group which turned out to be more conservative than the Gonzaga group. The two groups soon clashed and for a time the separate members refused to speak to each other. My decision to join LOCK stemmed from a hunger for something different, something zealous: what could be more brave than combating the Communists! Yet like some of the others, I was less interested in the religious dimension than being a member of a club with the prospect of sitting by Father Grady's fireside on Sunday nights as winter drew in.

One day Paul Moreland came up to me on a walk. 'I've been thinking about LOCK and you watchmen,' he said. I stared at him. Then, his voice rising, he cried out: 'Saint Gregory the Great says who do you think you are, pretending to be a watchman when you don't stand on the hilltops of action but cringe in the valleys of weakness. If you love God, says Saint Gregory, he will give you all the power you need to conquer your enemies.'

Before I could say anything, he grabbed me around the neck in a kind of embrace. 'You don't want LOCK, Fru. This is what you need – a head lock!' For a boy I took to be 'womanish', he was amazingly strong. For a moment I felt his cold cheek pressed against mine. Then he released me and walked off. The incident, it occurred to me, showed that Moreland, for all his erudition and brilliance, was still just a boy.

Somebody nearby who had watched the encounter, touched his temple with his forefinger. 'Moreland is completely mad,' he said. 'I hope you realise that, Fru.' But with a stomach-churning feeling I could have knelt at Moreland's feet.

62

WHEN I RETURNED to Peel for the Christmas holiday, it was to find that Dad was in hospital. There had been crying fits and more disappearances. Now he was being treated as an in-patient at Saint Clement's hospital.

I took the bus to see him. As I approached the hospital, set back behind a wall and railings on the Bow Road, I could hear shouts coming from the windows. He had got his wish not to be committed to the dreaded Claybury; but Saint Clement's could hardly have been better. Dad was in a lock-up ward which stank of urine, cheap cigarettes and an acrid smell like burning paraffin oil; in time I would learn that the substance was paraldehyde, a standard sedative in those days for disturbed mental patients.

Dad had lost weight; his hands shook, and he was crying. His blinking had transformed into a hideous tic: his whole face was contracting every so often to a concertina-like spasm. He spoke to me in a day room. The seats of the armchairs, placed in a semicircle and screwed to the floor, were covered in rubber mats. Most of his companions on the ward were sitting with blank faces, but two or three were pacing about agitatedly, talking to themselves or hollering up at the barred windows. Dad pointed to the patient next to him whose head was bandaged. He told me that the man had recently undergone a brain operation to quieten him down. 'I hope they're not going to do that operation on me, son,' he said.

I took his hands in mine and told him that I would pray for him; but he seemed not to hear. 'Believe you *me*, son,' he said, 'this place will be the end of me!' It was not much of a conversation. He was absorbed in himself and his conviction that Mum had been telling tales about him behind his back to the 'trick cyclist' to keep him committed against his will. He kept saying over and over again: 'I'm not mad, son . . . I'm not barmy, I promise . . .'

Before I left I talked to a nurse, a young man in a grubby white uniform. He was a trifle unshaven. He told me in a strong Welsh accent that Dad was undergoing a therapy known as 'modified insulin', which he pronounced with elaborate precision. The 'administration of insulin', he explained, caused a shock to the system, rather like electric shock treatment, but less drastic. He said that it was sometimes beneficial, but nobody really knew why. He seemed to have psychiatric knowledge of and sympathy for Dad; but there was something sly about him, I thought.

When I came out on to the Bow Road, it was getting dark and a grey-green 'pea-soup' fog had descended. The late afternoon traffic was at a standstill and people were hurrying along the pavements with the last of their Christmas shopping. I walked to Mile End station to take the Central Line tube back to Gants Hill. As I walked, I wept for Dad and all he was going through in that gloomy building in the midst of that dark, dark, damp city where God, it seemed to me, was entirely absent. Was it possible, I wondered, that he could be given a brain operation against his will?

On Christmas Eve we went to Midnight Mass at the Camp. I spoke to Father Cooney, interrupting his pre-Mass meditation behind the curtain. I asked him to say a special prayer for my father. He looked up and nodded gravely. He said: 'Is he not coming to Mass?' Then he seemed to understand: 'Wisswiss . . . to be sure . . . to be sure.' And that was all. He was looking a lot older.

63

CHRISTMAS PASSED WITH the Cornwells stuffing themselves on the usual heaped plates of overcooked meat and soggy vegetables. The atmosphere was sombre, and there was a feeling that we were all retreating into our separate worlds. Mum had taken up ballroom dancing and stayed up late making flounced taffeta dresses covered in sequins.

After Christmas I was to learn that she had a dancing partner, an innocent arrangement, as we understood it. He was a married man called Arthur, whose wife was happy for him to squire Mum on the dance floor of the Majestic ballroom at Woodford once a week.

Mum had taken on more work outside of her hospital and clubhouse chores. She was washing the football gear of two teams each week, boiling mud-encrusted shirts, shorts and socks in buckets on the gas stove and drying them out before a coke fire before ironing them.

My sister, still at the convent school, talked repeatedly and at length about her companions and the nuns, some of whom, she assured me, were 'titled ladies.' She was ever more elegant and starched and would spend the best part of an hour brushing her felt school hat and polishing its badge, the motto of which was '*Serviam*'. (Let me serve.) She spent hours in the bathroom in the morning, which caused problems in the overcrowded household. The cry: 'Are you still in there!' punctuated the mornings as we boys queued up for our turn.

My younger brother, Michael, had won a scholarship to the Jesuit college in Stamford Hill, north London, and was absorbed in the graft of a grammar school education. The meticulous care he had squandered on his plans for ingenious mantraps, battlements and fortifications was now focused on Latin and algebra. He worked with impressive concentration at a corner of the kitchen table oblivious of the other lives and concerns around him, and even the blare of the television set to which my youngest brother, Jimmy, was permanently glued. During intervals in television watching, Jimmy could regurgitate whole programme sections with remarkable accuracy, acting all the parts. There was more than a touch of genius in the way he could do this.

My eldest brother, Terry, now eighteen, had become an aficionado of jazz. He went regularly to the Royal Festival Hall to listen to 'jam sessions', and requisitioned the clubhouse to himself late on weekday evenings when he would take a shower and play records on the cafeteria radiogram. He was into British renderings of American trad and modern jazz players: Chris Barber, Humphrey Lyttleton, Ken Colyer. He invited me over to the clubroom to listen to his records, but being schooled on Palestrina, Victoria, Byrd and Gregorian chant, I found jazz too jauntily crass and secular for my liking. I could not hide my feelings of distaste, to Terry's disdainful amusement. Every day at home I was missing the grace and elegance of the sacred music at Cotton.

I went to see my father again and he cried all through the visit. When I got up to go he tried to hang on to me like a terrified child. The nurse had to restrain him. He seemed to enjoy manhandling Dad. When I came out of the hospital I ran and alternately walked at the pace of a Swan walk all the way in freezing rain to Stratford East, then through Leyton and Leytonstone to Wanstead. As I walked I prayed the Rosary with my hand inside my raincoat pocket. When I reached Wanstead I tried to enter Our Lady of Lourdes church but it was locked. I stood with my forehead pressing against the door of the church, crying with frustration. By the time I got home it was dark.

My mother was furious that I had been out for so long, and that I was soaked. She was anxiously curious about how I had found Dad and what had passed between us. As I described his state I could not betray my pity and affection for him, and she grew fretful. We quarrelled. She was insistent that his problem was weakness of character. I was equally insistent that he was ill and in need of loving kindness. It ended with her slapping me around the face and calling me with a characteristic malapropism a 'sancti-nomious creeping Jesus'. When I corrected her, I got another whack – harder than the first.

I was counting the days before my return to Cotton. Every day, despite frost, fog and freezing winds and rain, I went out running; pounding the streets of Barkingside when I was not on my knees in church or in the library. One morning Mum passed me an envelope which had arrived from Cotton. It contained my college report. I already knew my marks, as they had gone up on the board before the end of term; the report also contained the profs' comments. To my dismay I saw that Father Manion, who taught me botany, had written just one word against my performance: 'Poor.' As I had come equal first with my 90 out of 100, I could only guess that he had written his comment before the results. I had worked hard and, I thought, intelligently throughout the term.

From my very occasional exchanges with him in botany class I had got the impression that the priest loathed me. Whenever I had spoken to him in class he would turn to one side and speak to the window or the wall. Why was it, I wondered, that Father Manion disliked me?

In my last days before returning to Cotton, I sat in the kitchen watching my mother pummelling and squeezing the mud out of the football shirts, shorts and socks, as she sang to herself Eddie Fisher's 'I Need your Love'. Despite the anger in her heart, she hungered for someone's touch, for someone's love.

64

WITHIN DAYS OF arriving back in the ice-bound college, my body seemed to be rebelling as if it no longer belonged to me. I only had to think about the possibility of an erection and my penis stood up. The Passionist retreat priest had called it 'irregular motions of the flesh'. How was I to offer an erect penis to Our Blessed Lady! What was wrong with me? I found myself trapped in a tyranny of fantasy-plagued days and semen-ridden dormitory nights. Sexual temptations were demanding every iota of my embattled self-control. Images that had once been innocent now assumed wayward scope for eroticism. Turning the pages of an old *Illustrated London News* in the library, already purged of provocative female pictures by Father Doran's scissors, I came upon a picture of our young Queen Elizabeth II. Deprived of the sight of the female anatomy, I found that the young Queen's sheer nylon-stockinged legs showing below the modest hem of her well-cut winter coat, emphasising her hips, waist and pretty bosom, prompted stirrings of lust. How often I returned to that page, to gawp lecherously at those short shapely legs and ankles, the majestic young bosom. On another occasion, flicking through a complete edition of Shakespeare, I lighted upon the poem entitled 'The Rape of Lucrece' and began to read with mounting curiosity and excitement right up to the moment when 'Pure chastity is rifled of her store'. Frozen with guilt I continued to read of the mounting waves of Tarquin's remorse for a deed of violent lust that I had employed as a stimulus for my own shameful fantasies.

Back came the scruples. Instead of taking my problems to Father Owen, or to Father Browne, I was caught in a cycle of sin–confession–sin–confession sustained by our opportunity for daily confession. I had seen other boys, with haunted faces, queuing for confession day after day. Now I understood the impetus for such daily penitence. It was not just the terror of being taken unawares in sudden death, to be hurled down to hell for all eternity; more real and immediate was the shame of being observed to abstain from the Eucharist at Mass. For it was inconceivable that one should receive the sacrament in a state of mortal sin, since 'he that eats this body and drinks this blood unworthily eats and drinks to his own damnation...' So I became one of the frequent penitents: those boys with hunched shoulders and anguished faces who waited behind to confess after Rosary.

One evening, after I had unburdened myself of the sullied laundry of my soul, Father Piercy, the confessor on duty, said in his clipped nasal voice: 'How can you expect the grace of Almighty God to be bestowed upon this house when you commit such grave sins?' Fresh reasons for guilt and plummeting self-worth. He gave me a hefty penance – the entire Sorrowful Mysteries of the Rosary – and told me to go away and sin no more. Easier said than done. As I knelt in the Lady chapel I was in a state of shocked anxiety. Could my actions result in the college being burnt to the ground or devoured in a landslide from top field?

65

WITH THE ADVENT of ever more savage weather, the icicles hung full twenty feet from the eaves, pipes burst, our washing and drinking water often stood frozen in the pipes. My struggles increased until I arrived at a new stage of scruples, complicated by what I believed to be a supernatural sign involving the sanctuary lamp, the oil lamp that hung from the rafters before the Blessed Sacrament on the high altar.

One evening as I stayed behind after Rosary to confess the usual sins, I saw that the sanctuary lamp was unlit; it was swinging dead with a slight motion in a freezing draught. Then it occurred to me that God had sent me a personal message. The cold dead lamp revealed the state of my soul which was dead to God's grace. As I came out of the sacristy, shriven and in a state of grace, going down on my knees to pray my penance I saw to my troubled joy that the sanctuary lamp was once again shining brightly and steadily. I might have assumed that the sacristan had relit the lamp, but instead I saw it as an infallible sign from God.

I now became obsessed with the state of the sanctuary lamp which seemed to match the state of my never-ending scruples. I took to visiting the church again and again to check the lamp. Most days I found it flickering violently, agitated by the currents of freezing air that streamed down the spiral stairway from the steeple. The flickering sanctuary lamp surely meant that my soul was neither permanently dead, nor fully alive: but in a state of imminent peril.

66

STUDYING LONG HOURS in the music practice room, I had continued to expand my capacity to learn copious texts by heart, which I narcissistically demonstrated at every opportunity. When the leading actor in the Challoner House play went down with the flu two days before the performance, Father Grady, the housemaster, put it to the house captain that I should be invited to learn the part. The play, by Agatha Christie, was *Ten Little Nigger Boys*. The vacant part was the judge, who turned out to be the murderer. The house captain had serious doubts about my acting ability and my vocal range.

'Has your voice broken, Fru?' he asked. 'This character is an old man, you know.' My voice was cracked rather than broken, but I could force it down to a rich bass, my now prominent Adam's apple quivering (an additional sign, I was convinced, of my rocketing concupiscence). I flicked through the pages. 'Yes,' I said, 'I can do this.' So I was given permission to skip lessons and spend the day learning the part.

In the afternoon we had a dress rehearsal, when it was assumed that I would still be reading the part from the book. But I had my part learnt by two o'clock and got through the rehearsal faultlessly.

On the night of the performance there was a preliminary hitch. When the curtain came up, the entire college in attendance, I came on to the stage and began shaking uncontrollably in the grip of stage fright. The house captain, who had the heroic lead role, said under his breath: 'Get a grip on yourself, you idiot!' I got a grip. Then I postured and strutted and preened. The judge being utterly crazed in the final scene, I let myself go in a burst of flamboyant mouth-frothing overacting.

I basked in the praise of several of the profs, and a wide circle of boys who had never spoken to me before. Father Armishaw came up after the show to give me a gruff: 'Well done, Cornwell!' But the most unusual approach was from Paul Moreland who had not spoken to me since the previous term.

I was almost asleep after lights out when I was conscious of someone sitting down on the bed and shining a torch in my face. 'Fru, wake up, it's Moreland!' said the disembodied voice, loud enough to wake the whole dorm. 'That was a superb piece of acting,' he went on. 'You're extremely gifted and your voice was marvellous. I especially liked the way you built your character, and the nuances of your gestures. The way you even expressed tension and impatience with the toe of your shoe. You're an absolute natural. There's something of Laurence Olivier in your voice. I just had to thank you.' And with this he gently pinched my nose and ruffled my hair, the way a boisterous uncle might do with a young nephew.

After he had gone, I heard someone mutter: 'That Moreland is completely bonkers.' A few moments later the dark shadow of Father McCartie appeared, mooching stealthily along the linoleum in his carpet slippers.

But Moreland's enthusiasm had touched me and made me feel good about myself. And I had not thought about my scruples for two whole days.

67

THEN IT WAS Lent again; and with the penitential season the sexual demons were plaguing my soul and body as never before. My sole consolation was recognising in the depths of night the rhythmic groan of springs elsewhere in the dorm, confirming that I was hardly alone in my solitary afflictions.

In my struggles to bring my body under subjection, I began to wear once again that rough woollen jersey next to my skin and I bound my upper arm with a piece of wire with a spike, hidden under my shirt. At night, after lights out, I tied my wrists with a pyjama cord to the bedhead, as I had done a year earlier on Good Friday. I gave up every item of food that I enjoyed, and I missed tea every day. I prayed and prayed for a miracle: that the temptations and the unwanted erections would subside.

One night, assailed by erotic fantasies, I got up and stood by my bed for several minutes. In a state of agitation I decided to go to church. Creeping along the darkened cloisters I re-membered the story that the ghost of a priest, who had lain unburied in his coffin for many months in the bursar's office, had been seen walking up and down in the night moaning softly to himself like melancholy wind. I was also terrified of being caught. Yet I felt exhilarated on my release from the narrow bed, the cockpit of unbidden urges.

I knelt shivering in the Lady chapel, praying over and over again: 'Our Blessed Lady, please help me.' Again and again I prayed the special prayer Father Owen had recommended, the *Memorare*.

I must have been kneeling for an hour when I heard the door of the church opening and banging, then the sound of footsteps coming up the central aisle. I was petrified, thinking of the ghost of the unburied priest. The confident footsteps continued right up to the sanctuary, which was fully in view to my left. A shadowy figure, too small to be a priest, went down on its knees, then prostrated itself before the Blessed Sacrament face down on the parquet floor, as the young priest-to-be had done at his ordination. After a while the figure, straightening up, began to speak in clear tones: 'Jesus, Lord! . . . Jesus, Lord! . . . Jesus, Lord! . . .' It was the unmistakable voice of Paul Moreland.

After a while I crept away down the side aisle and left the church. As I went along the clock cloister I could still hear that voice, dim now, calling out: 'Jesus, Lord! . . . Jesus, Lord! . . .'

68

ON THE DAY the annual Holy Week retreat began, I again took from the library Archbishop Goodier's book on the passion and death of Jesus. I wanted to relive the way of the Cross step by step with the liturgy and to identify wholly with his suffering. I believed that I was beginning to bring the 'irregular motions of the flesh' under control by sheer grim and persistent determination. I was still embattled, and there had been lapses and raging scruples. But what successes I had gained, had been achieved, I felt, at the cost of remorseless self-pummelling: hard work. At times I felt like the lurid picture of Saint Sebastian prominently displayed in the clock cloister: the naked boy covered in vicious arrows. Was a heavy point being made by Father Doran in having that picture thrust into our imaginations before night prayers and bed?

The retreat father, who emerged on to the sanctuary after Tennebrae on Spy Wednesday evening was a member of the Catholic Missionary Society who announced himself as Father Buxton. He was slight in build and middle-aged; his grey hair contrasted with a fresh outdoor face. He spoke to us gently that evening of the love of God.

On Maundy Thursday morning I went to see him in the archbishop's room. He greeted me in silence, gesturing that I should sit down. What struck me first was a quality of simplicity, as if he had stripped from his life everything that was inessential. He sat with his head a little bowed as if he was content just to sit there without speaking for as long as it took. I felt as if the love of God was shining through him. Then, suddenly, it was like the sun itself, rising after a dark, turbulent night. I had a sense of Jesus himself – not an imaginary picture, or a sentimental statue, but the very person of Jesus present in the room.

'What's troubling you?' he asked.

I began to cry. Then it all came out. The misery of my impurities and the struggles with my body. 'The worst of it,' I said, 'is that I know that I am not worthy to be a priest. If I stay here God can't bestow his grace upon the college.'

When I had stopped crying, Father Buxton talked for a while. What he said rescued me instantly from turmoil. At the same time, I was aware of an atmosphere like a pure fragrance pervading the room.

Jesus loved me very much, he said. Everything I was experiencing was normal in many boys, and our mode of life in the seminary exaggerated everything. Jesus did not expect the impossible. He told me to stop going to confession so often and to make an act of contrition if I failed, and to confess just once a week to one confessor who knew me well. I was not to stay away from Holy Communion, as this would give me strength. The important thing, always, was not to do harm to others and to trust in the love of Jesus Christ. As for my doubts about the priesthood, there were many years to go before I reached that goal, and many other trials lay in store. I would change with the years, and with maturity. God would not punish the entire community, he went on, because of the temptations bravely resisted by one boy.

Now he asked me to kneel by the side of his armchair and he blessed me, placing his hands on my head. I had an impression of strength and warmth flooding through my body.

As I walked in spring sunshine, up and down the lime grove by the side of the church, I felt that I had never experienced such inward peace in the whole of my life. I felt that I had been touched by Jesus himself.

69

BACK AT HOME for the Easter break I found that my father had returned from Saint Clement's and was working again, more or less. It was decided that I would help him for several hours each day. He was still frail-looking and his hands were trembling. It was obvious that the sports field and its facilities had been allowed to slip. The cricket tables were suffering from a form of mildew; moles had been burrowing and were devastating large areas of turf; there were plantains and moss where smooth swards of grass should have been. His equipment had been neglected, and he was taking longer each day to get his tractor working.

In the living room, Rosemary Clooney's 'Mambo Italiano' was belting out from the record player till late at night. My brother Michael, in his second year at Jesuit college, looked stricken. In addition to his long stints of homework, and the long journey to school, he had been suffering the over-strict disciplines of the Jesuits. He had tales of grim injustice involving savage beatings on the hand with the tolley, a piece of whalebone covered in rubber. Jimmy was still glued to the television, unable to take his eyes off the lurid greenish screen even during the long intervals between programmes when the BBC showed a windmill or daffodils swaying in the breeze. Mum, who was working harder than ever, spent her precious free time preparing for formation dance exhibitions, recklessly sewing ever more dense layers of sequins on her dresses, the outer skirts of which stood at right angles to her hips. She had the look of a femme fatale Cinderella.

I called on Miss Racine several times in the evening when I was out on a run. She never answered the door. But I saw her one day sitting on a public bench by the side of Eastern Avenue watching the traffic go by. Her clothes were filthy, and she barely recognised me. I asked her if I could do anything for her, but she just shook her head and said that she was waiting for someone.

Lonely for conversation I decided to visit Father Cooney in his presbytery, with the pretext that I needed a book on the theology of grace. I was hoping to be invited in for a cup of tea and some innocent clerical chat. His sister, who had cheeks like wizened apples, was acting as his housekeeper. She answered the door and in a brogue, Mum would say, 'you could tar the road with', cried out: 'Wait on da treshold now, willya.'

Eventually he arrived. When I explained my errand his eyes froze hare-like with alarm. He seemed to be gazing with that listing, now snow-white head, somewhere to the right of my ear as if witnessing a traffic accident on the high road. 'Tee-ology of grace is it! Our dear Lord help us and save us! ... Wisswiss ... Out in the fresh air witcha!' The door slammed heavily behind me.

70

THERE WERE THREE sets of cricket practice nets on the Peel ground, and I decided to practise by myself. One evening, after watching me bowling, Terry gave me a lesson on how to hold the ball, how to bring my arm over my shoulder, and how to aim surely. He told me that my eye problem would mean that I would always find it difficult to succeed as a batsman, but there was no reason why I shouldn't become a reasonable bowler. He said that most bowlers only focus with one eye anyway, and I wondered if he was pulling my leg. I began to practise, hour after hour, putting as much concentrated effort into it as I had into my running.

One evening, Dad came limping along and showed me how to bowl a googly, a slow ball that spun in such a way that it would shoot suddenly in a new direction on bouncing. He stayed for an hour or so and suddenly he appeared younger and less anguished than I had seen him for a long time.

One morning I told Dad that I wanted to take the day off. I pumped up the tyres on my sister's bike, and with nothing more than a bottle of water in the saddlebag, and my copy of *The Imitation of Christ* given to me four years earlier by Father Malachy Lynch, I set off to find Aylesford priory by road.

I had somehow thought that I would reach my destination by lunchtime. I did not arrive at Aylesford village until early evening, exhausted and hungry after a journey on busy main roads lasting eight hours. I had no money in my pocket, and on several occasions after I had emptied my bottle I had knocked on the doors of strangers to beg a cup of water. I could barely stand. The guest master, an Irish brother with a cheerful grin, emerged from the monastery as I wheeled the bike into the quadrangle known as Pilgrims' Court. He arranged a bath and something for me to eat before finding a bed for me in a pilgrim's guest room.

That night I rose from the bed, sleepwalking, and fell on the floor; my legs refused to stop cycling. Several times I screamed out in my sleep. Eventually the guest master appeared in pyjamas and fetched a mug of hot milk, sitting with me until I calmed down and fell asleep.

When I awoke, I went to pray at the shrine of Saint Simon Stock. Afterwards I joined a band of pilgrims in the ancient galleried dining hall for breakfast. They were gossiping among themselves about different pilgrimages they had enjoyed in places like Walsingham and Lourdes. They came from Stratford in east London and they were intrigued that I had cycled all the way on my sister's bicycle without eating. Then Father Malachy Lynch appeared, tall, red in the face, with his great swathe of silver hair combed across the top of his head, and the room fell silent. He moved among the pilgrims, greeting them one by one, touching a head here, a shoulder there, his face lighting up occasionally when he seemed to recognise someone. At last he came to me and stopped for a few moments. I showed him my copy of *The Imitation of Christ*. He smiled benignly and blessed the book with a flowing gesture of his hand. I was not sure whether he remembered me, but it did not seem to matter. I felt that I was in the presence of holiness, although it was a different kind of holiness from the simplicity of Father Buxton, the retreat father at Cotton, or the grim austerity of Father Cooney. Father Malachy's holiness was romantic, theatrical, suggestive of signs and wonders.

At midday Father Malachy talked to the pilgrims about Our

Lady and the scapular. He rambled, but he held us entranced. I remembered Miss Racine's devotion to the scapular, and I was saddened to think of her sitting by the side of the highway at Redbridge. I had long ago lost the scapular she gave me. After the talk I went up to Father Malachy and asked him how I could obtain a scapular. He took me over to the guest master's office and produced a substantial scapular from a drawer. He blessed the object before placing the ribbons over my head and tucking the squares into my shirt back and front. 'And now,' he said, 'you are a true Carmelite.' Then he asked me to kneel while he recited over me Saint Patrick's blessing, a prayer about protection from evil, behind, in front, all around.

The guest master arranged for me to return to London on the bus with the visiting pilgrims, the bike strapped on to the luggage rack on the top. I felt happy sitting on the bus with the pilgrims, who were laughing and sharing sandwiches.

When I arrived back home later that evening, having cycled from Stratford, Mum was angry that I had gone off without telling her of my whereabouts. 'I hope you're not turning out like your father!' she said. That night in bed I fingered the scapular about my neck and felt safe and secure from every kind of evil.

PART THREE

THE HALFWAY HOUSE

71

RETURNING TO COTTON was like dawn after a long dark night. I sensed that this was going to be a new beginning. I was going to pray hard and work hard, as never before. Father Owen had promised that he would give me a new voice test for the choir. I longed to be back among the privileged group singing our sacred music in the sanctuary. After depositing my case in the dorm, I hurried to the church to go on my knees before the Blessed Sacrament. The sanctuary lamp was shining clear and steady.

On the second day of term Father Gavin announced that he was conducting trials after lunch in the cricket nets on the field above Top Bounds. He was selecting for two reserve places in the college team, and I was confident that I could make an impression with my bowling alone. About twenty boys turned up in cricket boots. I was among those told to pad up to bat, which disappointed me as I knew that I would not perform well. I faced twenty or so balls, most of which I missed, before Father Gavin told me to take my pads off and join the bowlers.

There were six of us taking turns to bowl. My first two balls were grotesque wides and several boys groaned derisively. For my third, I took a long run-up. This knocked out the middle stump with such force that the wicket-keeper hollered with alarm. My confidence was soaring: I could do no wrong. I was my brother Terry. Ball after ball I sent the stumps flying; the batsmen were leaping back at the ferocious speed. Now Father Gavin went to the crease to confront me. The first two balls he smacked skywards, and everybody cheered. The next ball I bowled a googly. As his leg stump was nicked, and the wicket-keeper yelled: 'Howzatt!' Father Gavin stood stunned for a moment, then his face was suffused with delight. 'Good Lord, Fru, where did you learn to bowl like that!'

In church that night I could barely concentrate on my prayers. I was thinking about my success in the practice nets. Later, after going to bed, I felt discomfort across my chest and shooting pains down my left arm; which was strange, for I bowled with my right arm.

The next morning, I looked up at the dormer window to see the sky cloudless, the trees tranquil, promising a fair day. If the weather held we would have cricket practice, and perhaps a swim. I leapt out of bed and got dressed, but as I began to walk down the dorm on my way to the wash places I felt my heart pounding in my chest and an excruciating pain in my left arm. I sat down on the floor, where I was. James was next to me, speaking soothingly. Several boys paused to look at me with concerned curiosity. A member of the big sixth came along and said I had better lay on my bed and wait for Matron. He told the dawdlers to get on down to the wash places.

I lay in the silent dormitory wondering what could be the matter. Eventually the pain went away. Then Mère Saint Luc, our stout little nun matron, bustled in. As I tried to explain the pain, she was looking directly in my face as if to discover signs of my ailment somewhere around my eyes and forehead. Eventually she asked me to stand up. 'Good, good, now let's just walk a little way,' she said in her French Belgian accent. 'Let's see if we can walk you as far as the infirmary.' I had walked about ten paces when I felt as if I had been slammed in the chest with a sledgehammer. I went down on the floor, my lungs heaving with agony. The nun turned me over on my side and made me raise my knees a little: she held my hand in silence, and I was aware of her looking at me with strange anxiety. Next Father McCartie appeared. I heard him saying:

'What's happened?' His voice sounded brittle. Then I heard Matron whispering: 'This boy is having a heart attack! Call the doctor, Father.'

The pain came in a terrible rhythm as if an engine was sending a pile driver through my chest. Matron put a pillow under my head and knelt beside me soothing my hair. I felt a sudden wave of terror and self-pity.

Matron said softly: 'Don't worry, *mon cher*, we are all in God's hands!' Part of my mind told me that I was dying, and that this event had been lying in wait for me every moment of my existence. I saw a fleeting image of myself being carried in my coffin past the old hall to the little cemetery at the head of the valley. I could see, where I lay, the statue to Saint Joseph in memory of the long-dead Cottonian boy.

Dr Hall, the school doctor, arrived, a dapper man whose dark hair was smoothly plastered down on his scalp. He was wearing a tweed suit and a mustard-coloured waistcoat. His hands smelt of antiseptic lotion. He gave me an injection, and the pain began to ease. He helped me to sit up a little and took off my shirt. He expressed mild surprise at my scapular. 'And what is the meaning of this?' he asked as he took it off. He was not a Catholic. The nun explained that it was an item of devotion. I was not happy that the scapular had been taken off, remembering the special indulgence accorded those who died wearing it.

He questioned me in a quiet authoritative voice and spent a lot of time taking my pulse and listening to my back and my chest with his stethoscope. Eventually he said that he didn't think that I had had a severe heart attack; but he wanted me in hospital straight away. As he went off to make some phone calls, Father McCartie appeared with three hefty members of the sixth form. They carried me downstairs and out through the front door of the old hall to where the doctor's car was parked. They placed me in a lying position on the back seat.

The doctor drove and Matron sat next to him. As we passed

through the country lanes, Matron did not take her eyes off me once; but she chatted a little with the doctor, telling him about her war service as a nurse. After driving for an hour or so I was conscious that we had left the countryside and entered a town. From where I lay looking up at the car windows I could see terraces of dark red-brick houses rising up the sides of the hills. Then there were clusters of strangely shaped chimneys, like fat black bottles, belching smoke. The doctor explained that the town was called Stoke-on-Trent, and it was also known as the Potteries, where china like Wedgwood was made to be sold all over the world. We were destined for the hospital known as the Staffordshire Royal Infirmary.

At the hospital I was placed in a wheelchair and propelled very slowly down a corridor to a room with various machines. A bespectacled man in a white coat came in. He introduced himself as Dr Gardiner and explained that he was a cardiologist, a heart specialist. He placed a number of wires with suction pads at various points over my chest and proceeded to work a machine placed on a trolley. As the contraption whirred and crackled, a paper printout emerged. It seemed strange to see my heart registered on paper as a series of peaks and troughs. Showing Dr Hall the results, Dr Gardiner said that he had never seen anything quite like it before. 'This boy seems to have angina,' he said, 'but he is only fifteen or sixteen years of age.'

Before she and Dr Hall left, Mère Saint Luc asked if I wanted anything. I said impulsively: 'Please bring me the life of Saint Thérèse from the library.'

Dr Gardiner said that until I was told otherwise I should have to lie flat and not raise my arms above my head. I asked him whether I could have caused my illness by bowling too vigorously. 'Oh no,' he said. 'I don't think that we can blame this on cricket.'

I was taken in a lift to a ward on the top storey of the hospital with views out over a residential district – rows and rows of red-brick houses with smoking chimneys. There was a strong smell of antiseptic.

The ward sister came to see me. She was a short woman with an ample figure, wearing a starched frilly cap and a belted blue dress. She had a flat, shiny face, with placid eyes, and she sounded a little dreamy in her voice and manner. She pulled a screen around the bed and told me to take off all my clothes and put on a nightgown which opened at the back. As I did all this in full view of the woman I felt myself blushing with shame. She tied up the strings at the back of the gown and I felt her cold fingers on my back. After I had got between the sheets she sat for a while on the bed with my clothes, as if she had my life and my privacy just casually placed across her starched apron. I had a strong sense of her femininity; she was wearing nail varnish, and had an aura of faintly sweet scent.

When I asked her what was wrong with me, she said with a crooked little smile that I was a 'mystery boy with a heart disease only suffered by old men'. This frightened me; I wondered whether my hair would go grey and fall out prematurely. As she walked off with my clothes, I felt as though she was taking my freedom and modesty down the ward with her.

I was the youngest person in the ward and found myself in a bay facing a man in his late fifties, called Mr Raymont. He told me that he was waiting for an operation on a 'delicate part' of his anatomy, but that when he was under the anaesthetic they would also take away an unsightly little polyp. He pointed to a red blob on the side of his nose. 'I'm much more interested in losing this horrible thing,' he said with a cheerless laugh. He wanted to engage me in conversation, but I felt too sad and tired.

The sister had told me that a nurse would come and give me a 'blanket bath' and I would have to use a bottle and a bedpan. I had earphones to listen to the radio, but I had nothing to read. I lay for along time rapt in my thoughts, watching the comings and goings on the ward, and looking out at the view over the rooftops. If I was going to die, I thought, it would be a lonely death.

There was a ward maid called Hilda. She grumbled to herself while she cleaned around with a feather duster. I couldn't possibly be dying, I thought, while a woman grumbled and cleaned under my bed with a ludicrous-looking set of feathers on a bamboo cane.

As it was getting dark Dr Gardiner appeared on the ward with two other younger doctors. Sister was in attendance. He told me that I was very ill, and that I must take great care not to put a strain on my heart otherwise there would be a recurrence of the attack I had experienced at school. He was not sure of the diagnosis, he said, but there were various possibilities. My symptoms were identical with those of angina pectoris caused by lack of blood supply to the heart muscle, but it was also possible that I was suffering from a disease known as pericarditis. He explained that the heart floats in a sac known as the pericardium and that sometimes the membrane becomes infected and inflamed, creating pain, palpitation and the build-up of fluid around the heart. He was hoping that it was pericarditis, but he was not taking any chances. He suggested that I now sit up a little, propped up by my pillows, rather than completely flat. On no account should I get out of bed until I had been given permission to do so, nor should I raise my hands above my head or strain myself.

'Am I likely to die?' I asked him.

He smiled. 'No,' he said, 'we won't let that happen.'

From that moment I put all thoughts of death out of my mind.

72

THE FIRST DAY passed in a painless routine of meals and blood tests. I had no recurrence of the pain and tightness in my chest, except for several isolated occasions when I strained, against advice, to reach things on my bedside locker. One afternoon, early in my hospital stay, I was tempted to stroke my penis. But I felt the palpitation coming on, and stopped. A male nurse named Eamon gave me a blanket bath later that day. When the flannel reached my private parts he said: 'Right young fellah, you do that bit for yourself, I think.'

With nothing to read, I listened to the Light programme on the radio. Tony Bennett's song 'Stranger in Paradise' was being played over and over. I felt especially isolated at visiting times as there was no one to visit me and the nurses seemed to vanish too. I thought to myself: this is what it must feel like to be a leper.

On the third day Father McCartie arrived bearing the autobiography of Saint Thérèse. He sat on a chair at the end of the bed. His face was expressionless. He talked about the weather at Cotton and how Father Piercy had got the swimming pool in operation, but he soon ran out of conversation. Then he looked at his watch and said that he had to get back. When he asked me if I needed anything, I said that I would like a rosary. He fished into his pocket and brought out a substantial black and silver one. 'You can have this,' he said. 'Keep it.' Before he gave it to me, he blessed it. I thought to myself that he was not so bad after all. It occurred to me that he hated being at Cotton and longed to have a parish.

The next day Father Doran appeared in the ward outside visiting hours. He set up two small candles and a crucifix and said prayers in Latin before giving me Holy Communion. We both sat in silence as I made my thanksgiving. Then he said that the local Catholic hospital chaplain would bring me Communion regularly now. He told me that he had written to my mother and that she would come to see me, but there was a problem with funds. 'Your bishop,' said Father Doran with an edge of severity, 'will arrange for a postal order to be sent to her to cover her expenses.' I felt ashamed. I hated to think that I was being a cost to the diocese on account of my illness.

He fiddled with his hands a great deal, as if he was longing to smoke a cigarette. He was not looking at me, but gazing out of the window. At last he got up to go and shook my hand. 'Now get yourself better and back to Cotton as soon as you can,' he said.

73

AT THE BEGINNING of the second week, there was a new staff nurse on night duty. She was appealing without being pretty or beautiful; she had a neat figure and auburn hair done up in a bun under her little nurse's cap. She was very pale and did not wear make-up. She went around the ward speaking to each of the patients in turn before going about her normal ward business. When she came to me, she spotted my copy of Saint Thérèse of Lisieux on the locker. She picked it up with a faint smile about her lips.

'Oh, are you a Catholic?'

'Yes.'

'I'm a Catholic, too. Where do you go to school?'

'I'm at Cotton College.'

'Oh, you're a seminarian.'

'Yes.'

She seemed embarrassed and yet pleased at the same time. When she brought me my pills, she leant against the bed a little. 'How are you feeling, John?' Most of the staff called me 'laddie' or 'young man' or 'son'. This young woman, who seemed to be in her late twenties or even older, spoke to me directly as an equal. She told me that her name was Philomena, that she lived in Burslem, and that she would be working nights for several weeks.

I had not been sleeping well at night as I often dozed during the day. At eleven o'clock, after most of the patients had fallen asleep and the ward was in darkness, I was saying the Rosary. The beads lay outside the bedclothes. Philomena came by and stood for a while, as if trying to work out whether I was asleep in the semi-darkness. I gave a small wave with my free hand and she came over.

'Still awake, John?'

'Yes.'

'Saying your Rosary?'

'Yes.'

'Can't sleep?'

'No.'

'How would you like a hot milk drink?'

'That would be nice.'

She came back several minutes later with a mug of cocoa and two biscuits.

She sat on the bed, smoothing out her apron. She seemed a little nervous. As I sipped the cocoa she asked me a lot of questions. Our conversation was conducted in whispers. When did I first have a desire to become a priest? What did my mother think? What did my father think? What about my siblings? I gave her carefully edited answers, designed to enhance an idealised picture of myself and my family. That's what I thought she wanted; and I wanted her to like me and to stay talking with me.

She asked about my prayer life, and my favourite saints. She was curious about Cotton and the routine of the day, and the discipline, and how I liked it. As I answered all these things, I was conscious of her gazing at me in the semi-darkness, her body and her face very taut and very close.

Eventually she looked at her watch and said that the night superintendent would be making her rounds. I must try to go to sleep and she would come and see me in the morning.

Several times in the night, Nurse Philomena came by the bed and stood looking at me. I watched her through half-shut eyes, pretending to sleep because I did not want her to be concerned about me.

One day Father Armishaw turned up. He had come to the hospital on his motorbike and was wearing his dashing leather flying jacket. He pretended to be gruff, almost unsympathetic, as if I were a malingerer. 'So what's all this, Cornwell? Decided to take a little holiday, eh?' But I could tell that he was really concerned. He had brought me a book: Robert Louis Stevenson's *Travels with a Donkey*. Instead of sitting on a chair some distance away, he sat on the bed quite close to me. He asked about my condition, how I felt, what sorts of drugs I was taking, and whether I slept at night. He told me that he had spent time in hospital when he was an undergraduate at Cambridge. He had suffered, he told me, from a perforated ulcer. He gave a strange guffaw as he explained in detail what happened when the ulcer burst. 'I had to have an operation,' he said, 'and they give you a drug that makes you feel completely at ease before you take the anaesthetic and go under the knife. When we came to the lift to go to the operating theatre, I remember thinking . . . I couldn't care less if they threw me down the lift shaft. Now isn't that strange! The power of drugs over the mind.' When Hilda came around with the tea, he said that he would like nothing better than to try her cake, but he had to get back to duty. She looked at him awestruck, as if he was a film star.

He stood at the door of the ward and waved before he left. A moment later he appeared again, and waved once more. Then he did it again. It was a good joke, and I laughed. He had a broad grin on his face. He gave me a big thumbs-up sign and really went.

My talks with Nurse Philomena had become a regular fixture: gentle, clandestine, whispered. Night after night, she came to my bedside. Eventually, she waited until the night superintendent had done her first round so that we had longer to talk. Our conversations would last for as long as two hours, and there would be cocoa, and more cocoa, and biscuits, and more biscuits.

I rarely saw her face clearly as we always talked in the half-light. She spoke rapidly and self-consciously. She shut her eyes frequently for a few moments as she spoke. He expression, as far as I could tell in the twilight, was usually bland; she did not smile much or laugh much. She did not use her hands when she spoke. They usually rested on her lap. She spoke in an earnest monotone.

One night she brought in a replica of an icon of Our Lady of Perpetual Succour, which she placed on my bedside locker. On another evening she brought in the Miraculous Medal on a very fine silver chain. She asked me to wear it around my neck.

After she had satisfied herself with questions about every detail of my life and my vocation, she began to talk rather than question. She had a lot of stories about the power of prayer, patients brought back from the brink of death, patients relieved of incurable diseases, and brought out of comas. Then there were tales of saints and martyrs. She told me about a Franciscan friar in the South of Italy called Padre Pio who could tell penitents' sins in confession before they had admitted to them. His advice to all Christians, she said, was: 'Pray! Hope! And don't worry!'

Every time she came to sit on my bed she started by saying that she had been praying for me. One day, after looking at me for a long time in silence, she said: 'You are going to make a wonderful priest. I can tell.'

74

TWO WEEKS INTO my hospital stay, I had been sleeping after lunch and woke up to find Mum standing by the bed. She was dressed in a floral frock and had a peculiar flat hat pinned into her stiffly permed hair. She was wearing a lot of make-up and looked quite glamorous. She bent over and kissed me, her eyes smiling, and said: 'Aren't you the poor little soldier!' I was overjoyed to see her, and I wept a little. She dried my eyes tenderly with a handkerchief that smelt of lavender water.

She sat on the bed talking, stroking me with one large, firm hand. Every so often she would plunge into her shopping bag to bring out another item. Apples, biscuits, comic books, a bottle of Lucozade. Each time she delved into the bag, she would say: 'Oh yes, and I've brought you this . . .' as if to stretch out the gift ritual. She talked about the adventure of her journey from Euston to Stoke-on-Trent, and the huge cost; then there was the latest saga of her job at Wanstead hospital; then she went through every member of the family one by one. When Hilda appeared with the trolley she offered Mum a cup of tea and a piece of cake, for which she was effusively thankful. She told Hilda that she worked in a hospital too, on nights.

Eventually she said she had to catch the train back to London, but she must see the consultant before leaving the hospital. She gave me a strong hug, and she was gone.

That evening Dr Gardiner appeared and said that I could get up and try to walk. At first my legs gave way under me, but I soon found my feet and began to stroll slowly up and down the ward in a hospital dressing gown under the watchful eye of the placid-faced sister. There was no recurrence of my chest pains.

That night Philomena was off duty and I began to read

Travels with a Donkey. It seemed like a gate into an enchanted world, and yet the account of the author's arrival at Our Lady of the Snows seemed familiar too: I could imagine every incident with an intensely tangible and visible reality. I became so gripped that I read by my night light until I fell asleep. I awoke briefly as a strange nurse took the book softly from my hands and turned out the light.

75

THE NEXT DAY I was allowed to sit out in the early summer sunshine on a balcony at the end of the ward. A patient named Geoff, an ex-soldier suffering from kidney disease, was there smoking a cigarette. When one of the nurses, a short dark-haired trainee, came on to the balcony to take our temperatures, he addressed her to her face as 'Gorgeous Gussie'. After she left, he said: 'Has Gorgeous Gussie ever given you a blanket bath? I made 'er blush. My prick stood up like a flagpole on a parade-ground.' And he gave a wicked laugh. My heart missed a beat when he said this. Then another nurse appeared, a staff nurse I had always thought to be strict and prim in manner. 'Oh,' said Geoff, 'here's Sweetie Pie.' To my surprise she smiled and blushed, then ruffled his hair and told him not to be cheeky. After so much isolation, I was reminded by his banter with 'Sweetie Pie' that I had watched the nurses coming and going with a quiet subterranean interest of my own. I felt a pang of jealousy when the staff nurse ruffled Geoff's hair.

That afternoon I was taken down to Dr Gardiner's clinic where I was put through a battery of tests. When I came back to the ward the man opposite was lying waxen-faced and asleep; he had undergone his operation and his mouth was wide open so that I could see all the metal fillings in his back teeth. There was a small piece of plaster on his nose where his polyp had been.

I wanted to talk to somebody so I went back down to the balcony where Geoff was reading a magazine and smoking as usual. He began to speak about women again. He asked if I had ever had a girlfriend. I would never have girlfriends, I told him, because I was going to be a Catholic priest and I would never get married. He gawped at me in an exaggerated fashion. 'Jesus H. Christ!' he swore. 'D'you mean to say you're never going to have a fuck? Ever?'

I sat frozen, appalled, unsure what to do or what to say.

He said: 'Listen, son, you obviously don't know what you're going to be missing. There's nothing better in the whole of this wide world than a good fuck. It's the whole point. That's why we're put on this earth. You tell me what's better! Go on, tell me what's better!'

At that moment an old dodderer, as Geoffrey called the elderly patients, appeared on the balcony, and there was a change of subject.

76

THAT EVENING NURSE Philomena came back on duty. The evenings were getting lighter and I had a better look at her when she made her ward round. I noticed for the first time that she had nice legs, not particularly shapely, but slender; and I liked the way she walked, swinging her hips slightly as she moved with neat steps along the ward in her low-heeled shoes, looking from side to side. She gave me a private smile when she passed, as if to say we would be talking later. I felt the stirring, perhaps for the first time, of more than seminary-boy interest in Philomena. Yet I could not envisage anything other than our just sitting close to each other in the depths of the night.

I lay in a reverie as the ward wound down and it got dark. I could see Philomena's auburn head bent to her tasks at the nurses' station. Her hair in the light, I noticed for the first time, was like burnished copper. At last the night superintendent came through and I pretended to be asleep. She stood for a while whispering with Philomena. Then she went, and I heard Philomena going into the kitchen.

At last she came, carrying cocoa and biscuits as usual. She sat on the bed and smoothed out her starched apron. She was looking at me intently.

'Hello, John,' she said. 'I prayed for you again today.'

What got into me? What strange adolescent madness led me to say it? With a mouth full of biscuit, I said to her in a winsome voice: 'Hello, Sweetie Pie!'

There were several moments of silence, long enough for me to realise that I had made a drastic miscalculation. She stood up. She was staring at me as if in shock.

She said, quite loudly: 'How dare you!' She took a sharp intake of breath, like a little sob.

'You don't ever speak to me like that! You little hypocrite! How dare you!' She snatched the mug of cocoa from my hands, spilling some of it as she did so, and walked rapidly away up the ward towards the kitchen.

My head was raging with shame. I lay there, my heart pounding, although not with pericarditis now. I wondered whether I should get out of bed and go in search of her. I had to apologise, to make it all right again. But I was now afraid of her righteous anger, and her authority. She was the woman in charge of the ward.

As the night progressed I would fall asleep for a while, then wake up again. I was awake when the skyline over the houses became a wedge of sandy light at dawn. Still she had not come and I was distraught in my disgrace.

I was asleep when she came to take my temperature and pulse. She woke me up, but did not speak as she went through the routine. After she took the thermometer out of my mouth, with tears in my eyes, my voice breaking, I said: 'Philomena, please listen. It was a just a joke. Please . . . ?'

Shaking the thermometer vigorously, her face hard, she said: 'I don't want your apologies. I am just so disappointed in you. God help us if you ever become a priest. That's all I can say.' She walked away, her neck stiff. Then I noticed that the icon of Our Lady of Perpetual Succour had disappeared from the bedside locker.

Later that morning, Dr Gardiner came to tell me that all my tests were good. I was better and I could go home to London. He confirmed that my illness had almost certainly been a bout of transient pericarditis.

I expressed surprise at being sent home as there were more than two months of the summer term left. He told me that my mother had been to see him on her recent visit and that she was insistent that I should not return to Cotton until the autumn; that she would look after me at home. As Dr Gardiner put it: 'She wants to consolidate your convalescence.'

The news filled me with alarm. I tried to expostulate; but Dr Gardiner told me that it was out of his hands. It had been discussed with Father Doran and everything had been arranged. I was to be driven to the London hospital in Whitechapel, the closest teaching hospital to home, where I would be seen by a local consultant who would check me over before discharging me.

My last night in Stoke-on-Trent, Philomena came to take my temperature and pulse but she refused to speak to me. I felt aggrieved; and yet, I also felt guilty at having transformed so easily from the pious seminarian she had believed me to be into a cocky little flirt. Which was I?

Now one thing was certain: my mother still had a significant degree of power over me. Whatever Father Doran, in the name of the bishop, had to say about the conduct of my vocation, Mum could legitimately step in and take control.

Early next morning I made my farewells to everyone on the ward, including Geoff who said with a wink: 'You tell me what's better, eh!' Then the ward sister, cool and very collected, accompanied me down to a waiting ambulance. She shook my hand in a formal way and I wondered if Philomena had told her of my disgrace. I felt a spasm of resentment, and fear, at the controlling power of women. Then I got into an old-fashioned Daimler ambulance and was driven at a sedate speed down the A5 towards London.

77

IN THE LATE afternoon the ambulance deposited me at the London Hospital reception and I was taken in a wheelchair to the cardiology unit where Mum was waiting. She hugged me and said that I would have some tests which were just a formality. After the examination we were led by a nurse down a corridor and into a lecture theatre where young men and women were seated on tiered benches. They were taking notes while being addressed by a tall man with a bald head and gold-rimmed half-moon glasses. He looked very grand in a flamboyant yellow-and-blue polka-dotted bow tie and a double-breasted white doctor's coat (I had never seen double-breasted in Stoke). He now sat down at a desk, indicating that my wheelchair should be brought closer to him. With a vague gesture of the hand he waved Mum into the front row of the theatre benches. The nurse handed the man a sheaf of files and he flicked through them humming a little as he did so.

'Here we have a boy of fifteen or sixteen' he said, 'who was taken ill two or three weeks ago up in Staffordshire. I am going to ask him to relate to you his symptoms. Please raise your hands if you wish to ask him a question when he has finished.'

Turning to me, he introduced himself as 'Lord Evans' and said that he was the Professor of Cardiology. 'Speak loudly.' I welcomed the opportunity to act a part and I projected my voice up to the gallery. I said: 'I was playing a lot of cricket on one day; the next I got pain in my left arm, and palpitations. I collapsed on the dormitory floor and I was taken to the hospital . . . the cardiologist diagnosed . . .'

The consultant cut me off. 'No, my boy, we don't want to hear from *you* about diagnoses . . .'

'Observe,' he said to the audience, 'that the lad speaks of palpitations, a nice word which he has no doubt picked up in the course of his stay in hospital. Palpitation, of course, is a collective noun which does not express a plural. I want to see no mention of palpitations in your examination papers.'

A student asked me whether I thought that I had strained myself playing cricket, and I said that I had thought there might be a link, but then when I was diagnosed with—. Before I could get another word out the professor cut me short.

Explaining the whole thing to the students, namely, pericarditis, he ended by saying that my condition had cleared up and there was no reason why it should recur. Then he said: 'Well, you can abandon that wheelchair Master Cornwell, and get back to your cricket.' But, as I realised, there was no getting back to my cricket.

Mum led me out to the Whitechapel Road, to take a bus back towards Ilford. It seemed strange to be in a street, deprived of ambulances and wheelchairs and the protection of hospitals and nurses. On the bus, sitting at the front of the top deck, Mum outlined how she saw things developing over the next few months until I would return to Cotton in late September.

'I want you at home where I can keep an eye on you,' she said.

'But I want to go back to Cotton,' I said, my anxiety mounting. 'I'm going to miss a lot of school work otherwise.'

'Well, your health comes first.'

'But the doctor said that I was all right. There's nothing wrong with me.'

'You've been very ill, and I'm going to make sure that I keep an eye on you. And that's that. What if it comes back? So don't think you can argue with me ... I'm your mother!' She was raising her voice, and I could see from the mottled neck that her temper was rising too.

'But what am I going to do for the next four months?'

'You're going to go out to work. I can't have you sitting around at home.'

'What will I do?'

'I've got you an interview. There's an ideal job at Bearmans department store in Leytonstone; just walking about the store.'

I felt cruelly ill-used; utterly cast down with injustice and grief. But I was powerless to resist Mum's will.

78

I HAD RETURNED home on a Wednesday; on the Friday I had my interview with the personnel manager of Bearmans. He asked me to fill out a form and told me immediately that I was accepted. My pay was to be two pounds eight shillings a week. Mr Grey showed me about the store and took me out to the dispatch department where I was to work. It was an area at the back of the store where the goods arrived by lorry from various suppliers. There were four men working there; the senior man was Sam, a fellow in his mid- to late-sixties with enormous shoulders and biceps. He seemed friendly enough, but once or twice he looked me up and down as if

I was about to face a firing squad. He shook my hand and painfully squeezed the life out of it. I was told that my hours started at 7.30 a.m. and finished at 5.30 p.m., six days a week. I was to start on the following Monday.

I realised with foreboding that the early start meant I would not be able to attend Mass in the morning. I would not be able to receive daily Communion, which had become a routine for me since the age of eleven. I wondered whether Father Cooney would be able to intervene on my behalf.

On Saturday morning I served Father Cooney's early morning Mass at Saint Augustine's in his vast unadorned new church (occasion now of fresh anxieties about the interest on the loan). There were two other servers on the altar, boys aged about ten or eleven. The old sanctury bell had been replaced with an ugly gong. I noticed that when Father Cooney came to the part of the Mass known as the *Domine non sum dignus*, acknowledging that we are not worthy to enter under the Lord's roof, he reverently recited: '*Et sab-anitur anima mea*.' As most third-year minor seminarians would have known, the correct Latin was: '*Et san-abitur anima mea*.' 'And my soul shall be cleansed.' He seemed to have become slow and uncertain.

I stayed behind to talk with him in the spacious new sacristy. As he took off his vestments and folded them he listened to the account of my illness, nodding, and occasionally muttering his 'Wisswiss . . .' Then I told him about the job and how I would not be able to go to Mass in the morning. When I had finished he fixed me sternly with his slate-grey eyes. 'Sure this is a test of your vocation,' he said firmly, although breathing as if with difficulty. 'Thank God for the privilege you've had of daily Communion, and think of all those who have to do without . . . Now each morning on your way to work say a special prayer. Desire the sacrament and you won't be without the fruit of it . . . And think of the words of the Mass . . . Lord I am not worthy . . . Wisswiss . . . Very good! . . . Run along now!'

79

THE JOB OF the dispatch workers was to take goods from the incoming lorries and deliver them to the departments. At the same time, we delivered goods from the departments back to the bay for distribution to customers by Bearmans own lorries. There was an inward flow of goods all day: sofas, carpets, bedding, kitchenware, lampshades, lingerie, hosiery. When the items were light they were frequently awkward to carry; often they were both heavy and awkward. Some items had a will of their own, especially mattresses, and we had to struggle and strain ourselves getting them on and off the lorries. They were transported around the shop on deep open-sided trolleys which we heaved to their destinations, travelling between floors in slow-moving lifts.

Sam's first assistant, Eric, was elderly, probably well into his seventies. He had a coarse little white moustache and ill-fitting false teeth. He was deputed to do the paperwork. Being short-sighted, he found it difficult to read what was written on the order sheets. He was supposed to put stickers on the goods indicating their destination in the shop, and invariably got it wrong. Sam was patient with him when this happened.

Two others, Bill and Reg, were in late middle-age. Bill, a cockney born and bred, had a huge girth and walked with splayed feet carrying all before him with self-satisfied dignity. He had a slack jaw and a bottom row of tarnished teeth. Reg was a former merchant seaman from Glasgow. He was squat and leathery with steel-grey hair. He had a belligerent way of flinching one shoulder. He and Bill worked with a kind of brutish, muscular relish. All four men were foul-mouthed, and attempted to outdo each other when they had to struggle with an awkward item. 'Wassiss fuckin' thing then?' They often broke fragile objects and Eric had to write down that the goods had arrived broken. Looking up at Sam conspiratorially, he would pronounce: 'Thass fuckin' broke on arrival, mate, innit!'

'Fuckin' oath it wass!' Sam would agree, usually shortening it to 'C'n'oath, mate!'

Sam was proud of working at Bearmans: 'This 'ere shop,' he used to say, 'is the fuckin' 'Arrods of the East End.' He made it clear that he was my boss and that I would respond to his every command. He was a lot older than he looked. He told me that he was too old to fight in the Second World War, but he had fought in the First War.

He worked steadily all day long. 'Fuckin' pace yourself, mate,' he used to say. 'Then you'll get through the fuckin' day.' He called me 'the lad', or 'young Jack'.

Sam was scrupulously fair when it came to sending us off to the employees' canteen for tea breaks and for lunch. Mum had anticipated that I would need pocket money for these breaks, for which she provided one shilling and sixpence a day which she handed to me before I set out. The cooked lunch was always the same: meat pie, gravy and chips. I usually found myself taking my break with Bill, who smoked between mouthfuls of meat pie. He had little conversation beyond a periodic: 'Fuckit! . . . Thass what I say, mate. Fuckit!'

The First War had made a deep impression on Sam. One day, as we had a tea break together, I told him after his persistent questioning that I was studying to be a priest. He seemed intrigued and annoyed at the same time.

'Believe in a God then, do you, young Jack?'

'Yes.'

'There can't be no such fuckin' thing as a God, Jack.'

'How can you be sure?'

'Durin' the Great War, Jack, I saw stacks of bodies piled up be'ind the trenches. Great stacks of them: cuntin' great pyramids of 'em. And when you seen fuckin' great stacks of corpses like that, Jack, you *know*. You *know* there ain't no such fuckin' thing as a bleedin' God.'

80

I WOULD COME home via Our Lady of Lourdes at Wanstead and say the Rosary each day. There was a special prayer I said in reparation for profanities against Almighty God. When I got home I used to lie on my bed resting. I would read the book Father Armishaw had given me, *Travels with a Donkey*, which transported me to the southern landscapes and forests of France. I loved reading about the monastery of Our Lady of the Snows.

The television was always blaring downstairs and Mum was usually crashing pots and pans or putting chairs up on the table to sweep and mop in a flurry of impatient semi-cleaning before departing for her night shift at the hospital.

For the first time I nourished sympathy for my younger brother Michael, a highly intelligent boy who was struggling to do a dozen subjects at his grammar school. He would bring back homework along with his Jesuit-flayed hands. His fingers were so bruised at times that he could scarcely move them. 'Hope you're not aiming to be a brain surgeon, Mick!' I said to him one evening as he sat with his swollen, purple hands in a basin of cold water. He shook his head wryly, old before his time. Like everybody in the house, except our blissfully contented television-glued youngest, Jim, Michael seemed to be biding his time.

I also had my copy of the autobiography of Saint Thérèse, which I was reading for a short period each day. I felt that her writing kept me in touch with the world from which I had been so unfairly excluded. I was living in a limbo where the sustenance of my soul and my mind had been suspended. Sometimes, though, it felt as if I was in a desert which brought me closer to God in an unforeseen way. I sensed a grim, monk-like austerity about my way of life now. I was acquainted with the word 'asceticism', and understood its meaning. And there was a curious parallel with Thérèse. Even though Thérèse was living in a convent, she was sometimes close to despair. She wrote that her doubts rose like a great dark mountain blotting out belief in God and hope of heaven. It seemed to connect with Grandma Egan's final hours of near despair on her deathbed, when Mum had brought her a rose from the garden.

'Think of the little flower of Jesus, Mum.'

'Don't be stupid!'

There were times at Bearmans when my soul felt as flayed as Michael's hands. The worst was Reg, with his flinching shoulder. The entrance to the lorry bay looked out on to a side road off Leytonstone Road. Every so often a woman would pass along the pavement and Eric would wolf-whistle. He didn't care if she was hobbling with a stick or pushing a pram, so long as she was wearing a skirt. Then he would turn to whoever was listening, invariably me, and voice his fantasies. One of his repeated observations was: 'Looka tha' fuckin' cunt, laddie. Ard lake ta ger' ma cork arp tha'.' After a demonic nasal laugh, he would start badgering me. 'Wouldncha, eh? Wouldncha lake ta ger' ya cork arp tha', laddie!'

Then Sam would intervene to say: 'Nah, Reg, young Jack's goin' ter wear 'is collar and 'is trouzis back to front, ain'tcha, Jack!' And they would laugh together, their eyes aglint at my discomfort.

I derived no consolation from getting paid. We had to clock on in the morning and clock off at night. Any deviation from timekeeping, by minutes, meant that we lost an hour's pay. I was often five or ten minutes late because I had to wait my turn to get into the bathroom in the mornings. My sister was taking longer and longer to achieve whatever she was up to in there, so my wage packet was regularly docked. I was paid in cash every Friday by Sam who would hand me the brown envelope which he brought from the general manager's office. Mum insisted that the pay packet was delivered into her hand unopened. When I gave her my first week's wages she put it behind a vase on the mantelpiece. I stood there, hoping at least for a 'thank you'. I was proud to have earned my first serious wage. She looked at me for a moment. Then she said: 'Well ... what are *you* waiting for? A round of applause?'

'You even get a thank you when the bus conductor takes your fare,' I said pompously.

'Well, I'm not a bus conductor, am I, you cheeky brat!'

81

ODD THINGS HAD been happening with Dad. Not long after I arrived home it was announced that he was going to take a holiday in Portsmouth with a married couple called the Pierces who were friends of the family. Mr Pierce was a tall saturnine man who originally came from Dorset. He had a strong West Country accent and smoked a pipe. He had a dumpy cockney wife with glasses who laughed uproariously every time her husband said anything mildly amusing.

Mum was happy for Dad to go off on this 'convalescent' break before the height of the cricket season. On the morning of his departure he appeared in the living room wearing a new blazer with a Plessey sports club badge sewn on the pocket patch. I saw my mother carefully hand over to him two pound notes which he put in his top pocket. She said: 'By the way, you know you're not entitled to wear that badge. I hope you don't run into anybody who *is* entitled to wear it.'

He just blinked.

He was away for two weeks. I was at home on the evening of his return. The Pierces brought him to the house in their car. Dad had a pipe stuck between his teeth and he was wearing sunglasses and a boater which he did not take off. He sat down in the midst of the family, puffing at the pipe, which had no tobacco in it, and embarked on an eloquent description of the delights of Portsmouth and neighbouring Southsea, with anecdotes and funny asides about the characters he had met – mostly in pubs. It was all delivered in a broad West Country accent. Every time Dad said anything funny, Mrs Pierce would screech with laughter, but Mum's face did not smile once: her jaw and mouth seemed to be set in concrete.

82

SIX OR SEVEN weeks into my time in the dispatch department, I found myself thinking about a young shop assistant who worked in the lampshade department. The silken pastel shades were like banks of brilliant blooms. Among them stood Iris, a pretty, petite, well-groomed brunette with large dark blue eyes. She was older than me, I guessed, but I felt that we were equals, and I liked her apparent shyness. She had a pretty, bashful way of looking down whenever she was spoken to.

The principal shop assistant on lampshades was Sheila, a raw-boned girl with gypsy looks who had been at my primary school four years ahead of me. She knew my family, and vaguely knew me. When I approached the section with my trolley Sheila would nudge Iris and whisper to her. Iris would steal a look at me, followed by an appealing inward-looking smile.

It seemed no more than an innocent workplace flirtation, until the day Sheila found me sitting alone in the canteen.

'Oy! You like Iris, don't you?' she said.

'She's all right.'

'Come on . . . Yes, you do. I've seen you looking at her. She's more than all right, isn't she. And she doesn't have a boyfriend. And . . . guess what: she really likes you.'

The idea that pretty Iris was interested in me made her suddenly fascinating. It had never occurred to me that I would ever speak to her.

'Do you want to take her out?'

I just stared, a delicious feeling of anticipation stirring inside me. I could not say a word. Sheila giggled. She placed a hand on my arm. 'She's really sweet . . . You should take her out.'

As the days passed, an acute sense of that unmistakable and exquisite thrill of infatuation began to blossom. I was thinking about Iris all the time. Visiting the lampshade section was pleasurable torture. I began to invent reasons for passing by. It was a short cut on the way to blankets, bath towels, curtain materials and several other sections if I really came to think about it. There she stood, demure, ever-so-pretty Iris, a delightful ornament among the glowing lamps, looking more and more lovely every day. And there was Sheila, casting knowing looks, whispering and giggling. Whenever I found myself humming the song of that summer, Slim Whitman's 'Rose Marie', she was my Rose Marie. I was always thinking of her.

Kneeling before the statue of the Virgin at Our Lady of Lourdes in Wanstead after work each evening, I was bound to ask myself whether it would be a sin to take Iris out. There was surely no guilt in accompanying a girl to the cinema. But there had been fleeting fantasies of placing my lips on her lovely, innocent, pouting mouth. In the meantime I was saving my daily lunch allowance so that I could afford a trip to the cinema.

It was Sheila who fixed it. She came up to me in the canteen and whispered in my ear: 'Granada, Walthamstow, Saturday night, seven o'clock. All right?'

I stared at her.

'All right? Come on! And you'd better be there on time, 'cos you can't keep a girl waiting!' We were staring at each other, Sheila's eyes wide with anticipation.

Then I said it: 'All right.' With those two little words began a juggernaut of anxiety. What would we say to each other? Would I walk her home? Would we kiss? Was this the beginning of the end of my vocation?

On the Saturday of the assignation I cycled home, took a bath and made myself ready to set off for Walthamstow, a rough district of north-east London. I was under no illusions as to the step that I was taking. Saturday evenings were usually spent going to confession. Instead I was outside the Granada by half-past six, standing in a light rain, four shillings in my pocket.

I waited until nine o'clock. Iris did not turn up. The main film, *The Night of the Hunter*, had already started when I decided to go in. Robert Mitchum played the widow-slaying preacher man. His character, it seemed to me, was appropriate for a hypocrite seminarian making dates with pretty girls. The contradiction expressed on his fists, LOVE tattooed on the knuckles of one hand and HATE on the other, summed up my own attempt to have my cake and eat it. I was fascinated by the guilt-ridden widow, played by Shelley Winters, who declared: 'My whole body's just aquiv'rin, with cleanness.' I even found myself identifying with her when she prayed imploringly to the Lord: 'Help me to get clean!'

How disturbing it was, hearing over and over again the hymn that was the film's sinister refrain, as if the sacred words were mocking my duplicity:

> Leaning, leaning!
> Safe and secure from all alarms.
> Leaning, leaning!
> Leaning on the everlasting arms.

I cycled back to the Peel in the rain and arrived soaked. I felt a fool, a victim, and I was full of remorse. But I was also relieved. In a month's time I would be going back to Cotton. I had eaten shame and humiliation over a silly girl, and I had learnt my lesson. I wanted to be going back to Cotton more than anything in the world.

On Monday morning, when I passed the lampshade section, Iris and Sheila were shaking with mirth.

Sheila called out: 'Hey, you!'

I paused with my trolley; head down.

'You kept Iris waiting outside the Rialto in Leytonstone all Saturday evening. That wasn't very nice, was it!'

I looked up. 'But you said the Granada in Walthamstow.'

'No, you stupid boy, you obviously don't know your Granada from your Rialto.' Then she turned to Iris and said, just loud enough for me to hear: 'Or 'is arse from 'is elbow.' Then they both erupted with laughter. Now I saw that Iris was no coy maiden: she was, as my brother Terry put it to me later, 'a sly little bitch'. I had been well and truly had.

As I looked around the store I could see several other assistants laughing at me. From that moment I knew that life at Bearmans was going to prove difficult for the next month. I was to be rescued sooner than I could have guessed.

83

MY SISTER MAUREEN was mature for her age and a thoughtful commentator on family affairs and relationships. Sitting in the kitchen by ourselves one Sunday evening after I had returned from serving Benediction, she was talking about Mum and Dad. I must have been listening with only half an ear, since it did not occur to me that she was alluding to the possible break-up of their marriage.

Then she asked me about my job. When I told Maureen

about the foul-mouthed talk of the men in my hearing, she was appalled. She clutched her head with both hands, mussing up her beautifully groomed hair.

'They talk like this in front of you all day? And you a seminarian?' Not for nothing had my demure and devout sister attended the Ursuline convent in Ilford for five years.

Then she mentioned the matter to Mum, who saw herself, when the fit took her, as the embodiment of Catholic female rectitude, especially in the matter of dirty talk. Memories of that lump of carbolic soap were still fresh on my tongue. Mum, her voice low and trembling with menace, questioned me closely. Finally, she wanted to know: 'Do they use the "f" word?' I told her that they not only used the 'f' word, but the 'b' word and the 'c' word too; and they used them almost every other word in every sentence they spoke. Whereupon she let forth a tidal wave of wrath punctuated by the insistent question: 'Why didn't you tell me this before?'

Much as Mum was capable of vulgarity I had never heard her utter what we would term a 'swear-word' with sexual connotations. She was genuinely upset. And clearly she was at last suffering an element of inchoate remorse at having exposed her seminary boy to this abomination. What alarmed me, though, was her express determination that she would go into Bearmans the very next day – 'you see if I don't' – to speak to the general manager and have it stopped.

She was as good as her word. Two hours after I had clocked on, Mum apparently arrived outside the general manager's office door and, according to her subsequent version of events, set before him the verbal misdemeanours of my work mates. Sam was sent for. 'Your son, madam,' Sam said, 'has a vivid imagination. We wouldn't use bad language. Never.'

'And *my* son, I'll have you know, would be incapable of a lie!'

After which Mum appeared like an avenging angel in the dispatch bay just as I was about to load an armchair on to the trolley. 'John,' she said in her most stentorian voice, large hands on hips, 'put that thing down! You're not staying here a moment longer.' Eric, Reg, Bill and Sam stood shoulder to shoulder facing her. 'And as for you lot,' she said in a tone of withering disgust, 'you're not real men, you're a disgrace to decent manhood.'

Reg flinched his shoulder, opened his mouth; and thought better of it.

84

MUM, WHO HAD never had a day's unemployment from the age of fourteen, was not slow in finding me a new job. She returned from her night shift announcing that I would work for two weeks in the pathology lab at the hospital, and then a further two weeks mopping the hospital corridors. I was to cover for workers who were taking their holidays. The pay would be less than at Bearmans, but the hours were the same. It would be six days a week, but with a half-day on Saturdays.

I started on the following Monday. The pathology department was situated in the basement of the hospital, a gloomy Victorian edifice. My task was to wash Petri dishes and test-tubes containing every kind of secretion, excretion and excision from the anatomies of the patients in the wards above. The dishes and tubes were made of glass and were not disposable. They had to be rinsed and scrubbed individually by hand, before being placed inside an oven and sterilised. The worst of it was the first rinsing in the deep butler's sink. As I continually took splashes of ordure in the face I reflected that even Saint Thérèse had not been obliged to endure such nastiness.

The wash-up room was separate from the laboratories where the technicians sat in their white coats doing biopsies and assays, staring into microscopes and writing up notes. Sometimes they would grumble about the doctors upstairs when there was a rush on. For no good reason, other than not being a member of their caste of biochemical boffins, they treated me like one of my specimens. The head of the lab bawled me out one day for heating a quantity of cotton-wool swabs at the wrong temperature so that they went brown. In front of his colleagues he called me 'cloth ears' and a 'stupid berk', highly insulting epithets to English ears in those days. My arms and fists, hardened by weeks in the dispatch department, twitched. But I kept the peace and went home smelling and feeling like something nasty in that sink.

The next job, sweeping and mopping the corridors and public areas of the hospital, came as a relief. Anywhere on God's earth seemed preferable to the path-lab wash room. I found that the best way to get through the day was, as Sam had recommended, to pace myself. I got into a rhythm and hummed to myself as I worked. Sometimes I prayed, saying the Rosary rhythmically in my head as I slapped the mop down, then squeezed it out. Plunge. 'Hail Mary . . . full of grace . . .' Slap slop. 'The Lord is with thee . . .' Squeeze squeeze. The corridors seemed to stretch to infinity, and there was no human contact, except when I got in somebody's way. A cleaner should have sufficient good sense and manners not to impede the progress of important personages.

I thought I was working as hard as I possibly could. At the day's end I was utterly exhausted and aching all over. But my efforts evidently fell short of the full-timer for whom I was covering. One day I was pausing outside a storeroom when I heard two ward maids gossiping within. One of them said: ''Ave you seen that lazy little bugger they've got mopping the corridors? That's Kath Cornwell's son. I'd like to chuck that bucket of water all over 'im: that'd get the idle little sod going.' So much for worker solidarity!

The remark annoyed me; but not so much as when I was

criticised by the matron herself, a hugely self-important lady with a mountainous bosom and very thin ankles who sailed sedately along the corridors sweeping me aside in her wake. Every so often, however, she would stop to examine the terrazzo flooring in order to ensure that it was, as she insisted, 'deep-down clean', and not just 'spit-and-lick dirty'. Sometimes she would say, very rapidly: 'Change the water, change the water, change the water,' because she thought that I was washing the corridors with dirty water, and she obviously believed that three imperatives worked better than one.

Our altercation occurred two days before I was due to leave. She came bearing down on me with an empty cigarette pack which she said she had found in the operating-theatre corridor, always the first to be cleaned each morning. She waved it in front of my nose between her thumb and forefinger as if it were a rat swinging by its tail. 'Boy, boy, boy!' she cried. 'What's this, what's this, what's this?' I could see that it was a cigarette pack so there was no point in saying anything, but my silence evidently provoked her wrath.

'What have you to say for yourself?' she demanded.

'I did sweep and mop that corridor, Matron,' I said.

'How could you have done? Here's the evidence!'

In a voice that was not a bad approximation of Father Armishaw's educated Black Country drawl, and with a raised forefinger for emphasis, I riposted: 'Matron, has it not occurred to you that some individual might have dropped that cigarette packet after I cleaned the corridor? I did that stretch at half past seven this morning and it is now half past eleven. By my calculation, give or take a few minutes, that allows for four whole hours in which somebody might have perpetrated the dastardly crime.'

Her thunderous 'How dare you!' reverberated down the corridors. Then: 'You will go back to the theatre corridor and clean it again. You will clean it so that I can see my face in it.' With which she seemed to gather her skirts before heading off,

Mum and I out for a stroll in 1956.

calling out to the various people who were popping their heads around doors: 'Never have I been spoken to like that in all my life! In all my life! In all my life! . . . In all my life!'

I did as I was told, since I knew that I had still to collect my last pay packet at the end of the week. Also I had my mother to face, which I did the following morning when she came back off night duty, having heard the saga from Matron's point of view.

Mum was already in an extremely volatile mood, as the domestic situation had been brewing and bubbling, and there was a sense of things coming to a head. Sam and his cohort at Bearmans were one thing, getting into quarrels with the matron of Wanstead hospital was another. Mum came very close to striking me as in days of yore. I saw all the warning signs: the mottling around the upper chest and neck, the itchy fingers, the flexing forearms, the restless prizefighter's foot shuffle; but somehow she thought better of it. Four months of being a sofa carrier, a sink operator, and floor swabber, and I was as hard as a concrete lamp-post. In any case, as that week came to a close, unknown to me then, Mum had much fatter flounders to baste.

85

AFTER TAKING LEAVE of Wanstead hospital for the last time, I cycled home to find the back door bolted. My sister Maureen looked through the diamond-shaped window to check who was knocking before admitting me and bolting the door again. She had been crying, and so had my younger brothers. Terry was playing cricket somewhere. My mother was in the club-house canteen.

According to Maureen, Dad had left home. I was shocked and mystified. 'Is the door bolted against Dad?' I could get no straight answer. But I began to see things from a perspective appropriate for a seminary boy. The sibling tears were tears of abandonment. Dad had left us and this was an economic as well as an emotional abandonment; I was sensitive to moral considerations too. I saw it as my duty to bring him back.

The sports-ground activities were continuing as usual. A late-season cricket match was in progress; there were couples playing on the tennis courts, laughing and calling out to each other. I went to see Mum in the canteen. I handed over my last pay packet, and she thrust it into her apron pocket. She was pouring tea into cups from an enormous brown enamel teapot.

I said: 'What's happened to Dad?'

'He's gone.'

'Where?'

'I've no idea, and I couldn't care less.'

Her face looked closed up; I took it to be the bitter reaction of a deserted wife and mother.

I left the club room and stood outside, watching the cricket for a while. Where could he be? Then it occurred to me that he had only one place to go: Grandma's. So I set off for Woodford and her basement flat.

When I arrived, there was Dad, sitting in my late Granddad's armchair, listening to a football match on the radio, and there was Grandma, sitting on the other side of the fireplace. Stroking her arms, she said to me: 'I always keep an extra bed, Jack, case any o' me sons come 'ome.'

We talked. Dad's version of the morning was different. When he had tried to get into the house for his mid-morning break, he said, he had found himself locked out. As he stood in the yard his clothes were thrown down at him from an upstairs window.

I said: 'Do you want to come home?'

'They don't want me there.'

'But it's your home. We love you, Dad.'

'No, son. They don't want me.'

After a little more of this, I said: 'Why don't we let things quieten down. Come home on Monday and everything will be normal. You'll see how much we love you, Dad.' He seemed happy with the proposition. He said that he would come home on Monday.

As I cycled back to the Peel, it did not occur to me that Mum and Dad were each promoting versions of the marriage break-up that suited them. I was feeling pleased with myself. When I got home, Mum was in the house. Once again the door had to be unbolted.

I said: 'It's all right, Mum. I've found him. He's at Grandma's and he's coming back on Monday.'

Her reaction was explosive. Who did I think I was! Who said that I could go telling him that he could come back! He walked out, so he can stay out! Mum thought this equation squared the riddle. But I could not, would not, understand. And the more I tried to get to the bottom of it, the more angry she became. It ended with a swift and unexpected act of violence.

I was due to return to Cotton on the following Tuesday. I departed from Saint Pancras with five deep scratch wounds down the side of my face which I would carry to the other side of Saint Wilfred's Day.

86

ONCE AGAIN I was riding the train alongside the fast flowing River Churnet. Once again the bus was climbing those hairpin bends above Oakamoor, rising through our beautiful valley in the fading autumn light. It felt strange to be back at Cotton. I had changed: I had started to shave; I was suffering from a bout of adolescent acne, five deep scratches; and, as Peter Gladden told me on the bus, 'a smidgen of the old cockney'. I was returning wiser and tougher, I suspected, than most of my peers, and I had lost a large measure of seminary-boy inno-cence. I had also lost a father. Dad had returned to the house briefly the day before I departed. I did not see him because I was serving Mass at Saint Augustine's. He had stayed long enough to collect the rest of his things before departing: as far as Mum and Dad were both concerned, forever.

I arrived to find myself in an odd predicament. The idea had taken hold that my health required careful monitoring for a term or two. Instead of going into a dormitory I was placed, temporarily at least, in the infirmary opposite Mère Saint Luc's dispensary. I would have my own wash basin and there was a toilet and bathroom close by. Since there were no sick boys that early in the term I had the entire place to myself.

Matron explained that Dr Hall insisted that I should be one hundred per cent fit before returning to the rigorous Cotton routine. I was to be excused games, ditch digging and arduous walks. I would be dosed with cod liver oil and malt, and brought a mug of cocoa when I retired each night. I laughed inwardly when Mère Saint Luc said that she hoped I had enjoyed 'a restful convalescence'. Then she noticed the scratches. When I told her that the cat had scratched me, she looked me in the eye wonderingly.

'What a very strange cat, to have claws just like human fingernails.' She dabbed the wounds with iodine, saying, '*Mon cher*, I think *le chat* Cornvell needs to be placed in the sack with a rock and drowned in the river.' She regarded me with such protective affection, it made me feel a little tearful. She had never got over the sight of me collapsed on the dormitory floor.

Cotton and its routines stretched ahead, secure and dependable. Kneeling in night prayers, conscious of the bruising experience of the previous months, I felt that I was trespassing within the seminary sanctum. I could not stop thinking about home and what was to become of the family. Our house went with my father's job. It seemed obvious that Dad would leave his job as grounds keeper. Soon we would be homeless. I wondered whether it would end with my being taken away from Cotton to help support my younger brothers who were still at school.

It was the troubled relief of being back in our valley retreat, and the anxious conviction that it could be taken away, that compelled me to do what I did next. That evening I yearned for fatherly affection.

After night prayers I went up the staircase to Father Armishaw's room. I knocked. A few moments later the door was opened wide with a sudden sweep. There he was: wearing black trousers and a collarless white shirt; he had no shoes on his feet. I was ready for him to tell me to bugger off and come back in the morning, but after a few moments' delay, he asked me in. We sat facing each other. His breviary lay open on the desk. He lit a cigarette. Without invitation I began to talk; to gabble. I told him about my father leaving home. I told him the story of my return to the house after leaving the hospital. I explained that our house went with his job; that I had come back to Cotton not knowing whether I would be able to stay.

When I had finished, he looked at my face searchingly. 'Did you get those scratches at home?'

I nodded. I felt on the edge of tears, but intuition told me to resist weeping with all my might.

'Look, you shouldn't be here,' he said gently. 'You should be in bed . . . But since you're here, I just want to say this . . .'

The quiet reprimand, followed by the sudden change of tone, upset me for a moment, then relieved me.

'You're feeling lost, Cornwell,' he began, ' because your father has left you; but I think you're also feeling responsible for him leaving. There comes a time when you have to stop being a boy, and begin to think of yourself as an adult. You're going to have to do without a father. You can't solve the problems of your parents' marriage. You're not responsible. What you have to do now is be your own person, independent. Stand on your own two feet, Cornwell.'

Then he talked for a while about a friend who had been in a similar circumstance. This friend's father, he went on, was gassed during the Great War and never recovered. The father died when his friend was twelve years of age. Something told me that he was speaking not about a friend, but about himself.

Then he said: 'You're not called to the priesthood by your mother. You're called by the Church. It's a good sign that she's allowed you to return. But if she takes you away you'll be free again the moment you reach the age of seventeen. I'm sure your bishop will support you.'

Now, peremptorily, he told me to go to bed. Pausing by the door, and before opening it, he said: 'Come back if you ever feel the need.' I knew that he was prepared, within limits, to allow me to go on reaching out to him. There was something between us.

As I passed into the corridor, I said: 'Thank you, Father.' He did not correct me.

87

As I joined Derek, James and Peter for our morning constitutional on Top Bounds my heart was singing, although my happiness was not without anxiety. I knew that the problems at home were not about to disappear; that they could get worse. But I felt a secret pride in having established a special friendship with the one priest at Cotton who had beguiled me from my first days.

They were talking cheerfully, but I did not hear what they were saying. Then Derek said: 'Armishaw is taking us for English this term.'

My relief from games and manual labour, and my temporary residence in the infirmary, which I had made my own domain (there was a table to work on, with a chair, as well as an armchair), was an ideal circumstance to make up for my lost term. I planned to work all through the afternoons when the rest of the college was outside, and there would be nobody to stop me reading late into the night. I was determined to excel in every subject, but especially in English.

The first set book was Chaucer's *Prologue* to the *Canterbury Tales*. I aimed to learn it by heart, to bask in Father Armishaw's approval, but from his very first lesson I was disabused of making progress just by slog and memory work.

He arrived with his American edition of *Chaucer's Works*, a beautifully bound volume that lay completely flat at whichever page he opened it. Ensconced on the stool of his high teacher's desk he went straight to work. He had a unique way of reading, with an occasional inward smile or an upward look at the class, or towards the tall windows.

He began teaching us how to pronounce Chaucerian English, commenting on the elements of French derivation and showing us how to detect pronunciation from rhyming schemes and meter. He wanted us to relish the music of the sounds and rhythms before we began translating unfamiliar words and getting the drift of the characterisations.

The next lesson he began a line-by-line explication. He approached the text with subtlety: listening, scenting, doubling back to pick up subtle clues. He was inviting us to be open; to respond to the range of Chaucer's mood and wit, the striking connections of his metaphors and similes; the vivid evocation of an entire sensory world.

Entering the daily rhythm of the liturgy once more (I was back in the choir as a tenor now), I had resumed the daily religious routines of meditation, twice-daily examination of conscience. I was taking stock once again of my soul. With my illness, the plague of impure thoughts and 'irregular motions of the flesh' had subsided like the passing of a bad dream. Not since that day in hospital, when bored, trapped and anxious in bed, had I been tempted to an 'impure act by myself'. During the months of hard labour since the end of my illness I had usually been too tired to act upon 'irregular motions of the flesh'. If anything, the filthy talk at Bearmans and the silly behaviour of Sheila and Iris, had only served as a discouragement to the sins of the flesh.

I seemed to have settled into a state of more or less becalmed chastity; and was gaining confidence in my ability to control my thoughts and resist temptation. The confidence arose in part from a new conviction of what a Catholic was capable of, given God's grace: a strength of iron purpose even to the point of death. The sentiments expressed in the popular English hymn 'Faith of Our Fathers', composed at Cotton a hundred years earlier by Father William Faber, had begun to work on me. The hymn celebrated the English Catholic martyrs who had been executed during the time of persecution in the reigns of Henry VIII, Edward VI and Elizabeth I:

> Faith of our Fathers! living still
> In spite of dungeon, fire and sword
> O how our hearts beat high with joy
> Whene'er we hear that glorious word.
>
> Faith of our Fathers! Holy Faith!
> We will be true to Thee till death.

One afternoon I was visiting the library, the entire school being up on the playing fields, when a lay prof we called 'Whisky Roberts' appeared. Mr Frank Roberts, a stout man with red hair and a stentorian voice, was the college archivist. 'Ah, a boy with time on his hands,' he said. He invited me into the archive room to the right of the library exit. An acrid stench arose from the stacks of documents, records and ledgers dating back to the foundation of the college in 1763 by Bishop Richard Challoner. Whisky was a serious historian of the Reformation and 'Re-cusancy' – the refusal of Catholics to deny their faith – when Masses were celebrated behind false walls in the dead of night, and priests hid in 'priest holes' during the day. He was delighted to have the opportunity to talk about the early days of the college and the long years of persecution that preceded it: the courage, the betrayals, the torture, the executions.

As he spoke I had an impression of ancient blood and burning flesh emanating from the piles of documents. The leather-bound volumes containing the lives of martyrs and recusants seemed to glower down from the shelves, baleful-eyed, watchful, eager to impart their *esprit de corps* on the living generation of Cottonians. Mr Roberts was enthused with his subject, and would have gone on all afternoon.

At length I said to him, partly out of mischief, and partly for the sake of something to say: 'But didn't we Catholics do a lot of burning ourselves, sir? What about the Protestant martyrs who were burnt at the stake?'

He winced with evident irritation. 'Oh, burning at the stake is nothing,' he muttered. 'It only takes a few minutes.'

88

THE ENCOUNTER IN the archive room stimulated a renewed interest in Father Grady's history class on the Reformation. That term I had learnt details of the martyrdom of Catholics under Henry VIII. Father Grady dwelt on the deaths of the monks of the London Charterhouse in the sixteenth century, simple enclosed monks who had taken vows of silence and who refused to utter an oath that would have sanctioned the king's illicit marriage to his mistress Anne Boleyn. The deaths of these monks, some by hanging and disembowelling, others by being starved to death in prison, affected me deeply. I asked Father Grady where I could learn more. He recommended the two-volume work by Dom Bede Camm, *Lives of the English Martyrs*, which was in the college library. I carried them off to the infirmary and read both volumes within several days.

I read how a Carthusian martyr was hung at Tyburn gallows in such a way that he was still alive when he was cut down; the executioner disembowelled him so swiftly that the monk saw his own entrails and testicles ('organs of generation') in the executioner's hands before he expired. When I mentioned this to Mr Roberts later, he snorted: 'That's nothing; there was an executioner who would fish out a priest's heart like a plum from a porridge bowl and rub it in the victim's face while he was still alive!'

I also took from the library a history of the Catholic Church by Father Philip Hughes. In the reign of Queen Elizabeth I, I learnt, celebrating or hearing Mass could entail execution. I was not alone among the boys at Cotton awakening, yet again, to a tradition that called us to loyalty to our Faith even to the extent of the supreme sacrifice. As the hymn, 'Faith of Our Fathers', went:

> How sweet would be their children's fate
> If they like them could die for Thee.

I began to meditate on whether I would have the courage to go to the gallows for my Faith. Striving to imagine myself in that situation, faced with the choice of apostasy or death, I knew one thing was sure: when it came to resisting sexual temptation I could look for inspiration to the English martyrs who gladly went to their deaths rather than betray the Lord. I saw a direct link between the *esprit de corps* of the English martyr priests and Cotton's early teaching priests, who had taught Catholic youths in secrecy, and the current generation of Cottonian priests with their selfless unostentatious austerity.

But then, a different kind of priestly role model entered my life.

89

ONE AFTERNOON THE door of the infirmary opened and a strange priest entered, to find me sitting in the armchair, my head in a book. He was of medium height and had a rounded face with swarthy Latin features. He was aged about fifty and he introduced himself as Father Lesley McCallum. His hair appeared to be dyed and artificially waved, his eyebrows plucked. He was smoking a cigarette in a cigarette holder.

'What have we here?' he said. 'What ails you, my dear?'

As I attempted to explain my circumstances, his face went through a series of histrionic reactions: anxiety, horror, sympathy and, finally, huge relief at the happy current conclusion of my bout of pericarditis.

He told me that he was the new assistant bursar, Father Browne being away on sick leave. He spoke with a creamy, self-mocking voice. He used his eyes, with sidelong looks, for emphasis and effect. From his voice and demeanour it was obvious that although he was a priest, he was not a priest in the tough, no-nonsense Cotton tradition. He was wearing a caped cloak like Father Doran's, and every so often he turned his shoulders to allow its folds to flourish.

Having ascertained my name and predicament, he enlarged on his own situation. He was, he told me, a 'late vocation'. He had been born and brought up in the British community of Buenos Aires and had gone into journalism, eventually becoming the publisher and editor of a popular lifestyle magazine. 'A strange appointment, you might think, putting me out here in the sticks,' he drawled, 'but these people have no idea about finance; the archbishop is hoping to inject a bit of professionalism into the management of Cotton College at last.' I thought this an inappropriate comment to make to a pupil of the school – 'these people' evidently meaning the Cotton profs – but I was flattered by the way in which he treated me as an equal.

'Oh, what on earth are you reading?' he said, and he started to go through the books on my bedside table, which included the Dom McCann, the Philip Hughes, the collected works of Chaucer, the collected works of Shakespeare, and Hilaire Belloc's *Europe and the Faith*. 'Good grief! I think you could do with something more jolly. Why don't you come next door and choose something from my shelves.'

He walked ahead of me with a rhythmic swagger. In contrast to Father Browne's fug-heavy pipe smoke, there was a fragrance in Father McCallum's sitting room of aftershave lotion and exotic cigarettes. Bottles of whisky and gin, brightly coloured liqueurs and a soda siphon stood on a side table. His bookcase was lined with novels. In time, during my comfortable sojourn in the infirmary next door, I would come to borrow some of them: Somerset Maugham, Joyce Cary, Nevil Shute, Antonia White, Katherine Mansfield, Graham Greene, Evelyn Waugh. That first visit a fat novel entitled *The Cardinal* by Henry Morton Robinson caught my eye.

'I'd like to read that,' I said.

'A bit syrupy,' he said, 'but why not.' He handed it to me. 'Just come in and help yourself any time if the door is open.'

That was how my acquaintance with him began.

Father McCallum, I soon learnt, had arranged for decorators to descend on the boys' common rooms to have them painted in gay colours. Flowers had already appeared at various vantage points in the church. The hard kneelers were being covered in foam rubber to make our devotions more comfortable, and the bells in the church tower, out of order for many years, were pealing once again. Father McCallum seemed to me a good thing.

90

FATHER MCCALLUM'S LOAN to me of the popular novel, *The Cardinal*, opened up a world that both enthralled and disturbed me. I started the book that night after Matron had brought in my cocoa and I read it into the small hours. For all that it was 'syrupy' it was the first twentieth-century adult novel I had read, and I was gripped. Against the background of three post-First World War decades, and a huge cast of characters, the action swung tempestuously between Europe and North America.

The novel, first published in 1951, and a runaway best-seller in Catholic America, tells the story of Father Stephen Fermoyle, an Irish-American priest of the Boston archdiocese through the 1930s and 1940s. Fermoyle's father is a streetcar motorman, struggling to bring up a second-generation migrant family in 1920s Boston. The novel is an amalgam of rags-to-riches American Dream and the rise of a pious working-class Catholic boy to the highest echelons of the Catholic Church. As Father Fermoyle's pastoral career develops he finds himself confronting poverty, racism, anti-Semitism and union conflict in 1930s America. As he ascends the clerical ranks he does not forget his humble origins, nor does he compromise one iota on Catholic moral teaching. He becomes a close aide to the Cardinal Archbishop of Boston, accompanying him to the Vatican and encountering the operation of Church policy in conflict with the Nazis and Mussolini's Fascists.

What struck me most in the early part of the book was Father Fermoyle's pastoral work in poor parishes of Boston, the world of drugstores, factory workshops, baseball and aspiring, materialist American family life. I came to see how a priestly vocation in the poor districts of inner cities could be heroic, romantic even. As I was reading *The Cardinal*, Father Cooney became for the first time transfigured: the challenge of the priesthood existed not in a cloistered retreat, but in bringing God to the everyday world of factories, busy streets, juveniles on vacant lots, families in suburban backwaters, people striving to keep the Faith against the odds.

So, lying in the comfort of the infirmary in our valley retreat, I came to question the lives we were leading at Cotton: the absence of women (save for our enclosed nuns); the neglect of concern, still less action, for the old, the homeless, the poor, the workers; the distance of our rural redoubt not only from the East End of London, but from those crowded terraced streets and smoking chimney stacks that lay just an hour's drive away from Cotton in the Potteries. With an unaccustomed pang of guilt, I was struck for the first time, having worked now for a living wage, by how the free provision of our daily meals trapped us seminarians in material and emotional dependency: a predicament that stretched before me to my ordination nine years away.

91

I LEARNT CHAUCER's *Prologue* by heart. I did it in the hope of pleasing Father Armishaw, and I contrived an opportunity to demonstrate my achievement by asking him one morning as he arrived in class whether he himself knew the poem by heart.

He smiled down at me from his high desk.

'Oh, I see, Cornwell . . . you're trying to tell me that *you* have learnt it by heart . . . All right. Let's hear it.'

So I launched forth, conscious before long that I was being an insufferable show-off. Too late. As I made progress, getting faster and faster, Father Armishaw corrected a mispronunciation here and there, or an incorrect word, or a missed line. By the time I got to the Wife of Bath, he said: 'OK, OK, that's enough. We believe you . . . Now let's get on with some work.' There was a groan of satisfaction and derision from my classmates. Father Armishaw gave me a look as if to say: You've nobody but yourself to blame.

After class James said to me: 'That was ostentatious of you, Fru. Are you trying to suck up to Armishaw? We know that you couldn't learn to decline "*amo, amas, amat*" when you came here, but now you probably know most of the Bible by heart. But it's understanding that matters, not parroting.' I felt crushed.

Father Armishaw, a good-natured smile on his face, stopped

me in the clock cloister later that day. He said: 'I was pleasantly surprised that you'd learnt the whole of the set book by heart, Cornwell; but I didn't relish listening to Chaucer being gabbled like that. Do you get my drift?' I got his drift all right.

James and Derek and Peter were becoming ever more distant as the term progressed; and the fault was entirely mine. With my privileged situation in the infirmary, I stopped taking morning walks on Top Bounds. I even failed to show up at many of the regular meetings of the League of Christ the King; it was no longer a special privilege to be sitting in Father Grady's room on a Sunday evening. I was also finding the conversations of the LOCK set pious and stilted.

I was working hard, I was reading, I was enjoying singing in the choir; I was more or less spiritually content. But I was bored with the boredom of loneliness. Any hope I had entertained of forming a closer relationship with Father Armishaw had receded with the passing of the days and weeks. I had often been tempted to climb those stairs to his door, but I did not want to risk a rejection. I had to be satisfied with encountering him every day in class.

There *was* a new attachment in my life, however, developing so slowly that I hardly noticed. Father McCallum took to dropping in on me at odd times of the day. Sometimes he would appear in cassock and caped cloak, at other times, and on the same day, without there being a noticeable change in the temperature, he would be wearing a brightly coloured silk shirt, which suggested that he had hardly needed his cloak for comfort earlier. He had a collection of silk shirts in primary colours, which resulted in a boy calling him Rainbow Man. The nickname Father Rainbow soon spread.

In the morning Father Rainbow would leave his newspaper behind for me to read, usually the *Daily Telegraph*; then he had an excuse to come by and pick it up later. He would chat about current affairs, such as the doings of Colonel Nasser in Egypt and the tensions with the Soviets. He liked to gossip about Hollywood film stars and actors. He was obsessed by the doings of Marlon Brando and Frank Sinatra, Grace Kelly and Audrey Hepburn. He also liked to gossip about the profs, whom he continued to refer to collectively as 'these people'. I gathered that he had not made any alliances on the staff.

He professed to admire 'Vince', as he called Father Armishaw, more than the others, although he thought him 'a frustrated mystery man'. He said: 'As the Italians say, "something mysterious is bubbling away in that pot."' He described 'Wilf Doran', as he called him, as 'civilised but dry as dust'; Tank Piercy was 'an overgrown schoolboy and a botcher – whoever told him he was a carpenter!' and Tom Gavin was a 'sentimental brute'. He said, in a condescending way, that he liked the new Prefect of Discipline, Father Peter Ryall (Father McCartie had at last been sent out on a parish). He found 'Peter' sweet, but he went on to say that 'like most of them, he has few resources outside his breviary and the sports field. You know he only has one record – Mozart's *Eine Kleine Nacht Musik* – and five books!'

Father McCallum told me that 'Vince' had asked him at lunch whether his black suede shoes with thick crêpe soles might be characterised as 'brothel creepers'. He pulled a face that managed to be wry and smug at the same time. 'I told him: "No, my dear Vincent, they can be properly described as sodomy cloppers!"'

Although vague as to the full meaning of 'sodomy', I was shocked by the word; and I suspected that Father Armishaw and the rest of the staff were similarly taken aback.

One evening he came in after Matron had delivered my cocoa. 'For heavens' sake! What on earth is that muck?' he said. 'Matron's making a milksop of you. Why don't you come into my room and have a proper drink.'

In his room that evening he poured me a glass of Madeira and offered me a cigarette, which I declined although I was tempted. I found the Madeira delicious and accepted his offer of a second glass which he splashed into my glass with generous abandon.

I felt ambivalent about Father McCallum. I thought that he was vain, and I felt there was something dangerous about his cynicism. I liked the feeling of being indulged, especially by a priest who, unlike the rest of the profs, was a 'man of the world'. He loved talking about films; I had seen very few, and the films we were shown at Cotton were limited in scope as well as being purged of kisses, endearments and plunging necklines.

We had a long discussion about *The Night of the Hunter* (of unhappy memory for me), which he thought 'a very good film'. He deplored the films that we were shown on feast days at Cotton because they were mostly what he called 'bland British war heroics', like *Western Approaches* and *The First of the Few*, or 'silly Ealing comedies' such as *Passport to Pimlico* and *The Lavender Hill Mob*. He told me that there were three hundred cinemas in Buenos Aires where you could see films from all over the world, and especially France, Spain and Italy. He talked about the films of Rossellini, Buñuel, Bresson and Vittoria De Sica.

He sometimes played tangos on his radiogram 'to brighten up the Cotton gloom', but I also saw among his records the music of Mahler, Schumann and Wagner. Sometimes as I sat by his fire sipping my large glass of Madeira, he played the BBC Light programme for background music, and he would turn it up when a current hit tune came on, such as Alma Cogan's 'Dreamboat', which he professed to detest. 'Listen to that abomination,' he would say in his precious fashion. Then he would declare: 'Don't you just detest all that nonsense!' He seemed happy to listen to it all the same.

He told me that he had been an officer in the Argentine Navy, and was once nearly shipwrecked. I was fascinated by his stories of storm-lashed voyages on a destroyer, so long as I maintained strong suspension of disbelief.

92

As THE WEEKS passed, and I became increasingly settled in my infirmary domain, with only occasional invasions from the genuinely sick, I began to take my privileges for granted. Matron, I came to realise, wanted me to stay in the infirmary for as long as she could wangle it. She had a great capacity for friendship and little opportunity to express it. Her indulgence towards her favourite convalescent, however, was not without opposition.

Father Doran descended on me one afternoon to find me lying on my bed reading *Brideshead Revisited*, at Father McCallum's recommendation. He took the book from my hands and made a tutting noise as he handed it back. He seemed appalled at the oasis of comfort I had made for myself within Cotton's stern regime. The piles of books (many of them novels with bright covers), the armchair (Matron had found two cushions to make it more comfortable), the fruit bowl, the biscuit tin, the cake stand, the lemonade bottle. Father McCallum had been in earlier, and had left behind a hint of Sobranie cigarette smoke to add to the air of dissipation.

'You haven't been smoking, have you?' Father Doran asked in his heart-stoppingly caustic voice.

I stood up and put the book down. 'No, Father,' I said respectfully. 'Father McCallum just looked in and has left a puff or two behind.'

Father Doran guffawed huskily, evidently seeing more in the remark than I did; but mention of Father McCallum did not seem to improve his mood. 'Are you not taking any exercise whatsoever?' he asked testily. 'I don't think it such a good idea for you to be lying on your bed all afternoon reading novels; you're hardly an invalid. And you might consider smartening this place up.'

Not long after this, on the Feast of the Immaculate Conception, with just three weeks to the end of the term, the infirmary door opened and in came Paul Moreland.

'Ah, Fru, this is where you are. I've been deputed by Father Doran to entice you out on a walk, just the two of us, at your own pace. Do you think you are up to it?'

93

So I WENT on a walk. During that tranquil afternoon of misty sunlight and hard frost I got to know Paul Moreland. There was something out of control about his gestures and expressions, as well as his frequent digressions; although, at times, I could detect playful connections.

His accent was impeccably upper-class, clipped and, I thought at the time, womanish in the style of English film stars like Anna Neagle and Deborah Kerr. Certain showy words cropped up, with the inevitable superlative: 'too elegant', 'too odious', 'too banal', 'too horrifying', and his images were often strained: the work of Swinburne, whom I had not read, was, he insisted, a 'masterpiece of corruption', and the atom bomb proved 'not a shining young angel of new science but an ancient mushroom-shaped hag'. He quoted Plato – repeatedly invoking the allegory of the cave, which he explained to me – but he seldom strayed long from Catholic subjects. That first afternoon he talked about the dogma of the Immaculate Conception, the doctrine of Mary's birth free of original sin, which he thought 'too stunningly beautiful', while discussing the proposition that Mary conceived the Son of God in her soul before the conception in her body. This led to a lecture on the dogma itself and the papacy of Pius IX, citing Lytton Strachey's 'too wicked' *Eminent Victorians*, and lingering over

the predicament of our 'too weepy' Cardinal John Henry
Newman; then a digression on the 'mountain-top mysticism'
of Meister Eckhart and the 'menopausal ravings' of Saint Teresa
of Avila.

That afternoon he told me that his parents (his father was
a retired civil servant) were divorced, and that his mother
was a Catholic convert; that he had grown up an only child
surrounded by books and intellectual conversation, with an
unusually intense and close friendship with a priest in West
London. This priest, he told me, became his guide and mentor.
The priest had introduced him to philosophy, theology, literature and art. 'But I don't see *him* any more,' he said with
pointed emphasis. He divided his holidays between his mother
in West London and his father in the Midlands.

Halfway through the walk we sat together on a railway bank
close to a tunnel in the Churnet valley. 'I love it here,' he said.
'I come here sometimes by myself and consider how easy it
would be to throw oneself before a train the moment it emerges
into the daylight: sex, birth and death!'

I did not then understand what he meant, but I was shocked.
I took it as an item of affectation, like other things he said.

At one point that day I attempted to share with him my
deepest thoughts. 'Moreland, how do you think about God?
How do you think God to be?'

'Oh, Frumentum Bene!' he wailed in a tone of elated super-
ciliousness. 'The question I want answered is what we think
Father McCallum to be.'

I felt hurt by the instant trivialisation of my question, but I
was instantly amused by what he said next. Father McCallum,
he said, was 'too, too camp for words . . . a veritable sanctuary
queen . . . and what a face: he needs a Velásquez to paint that
corrupt smirk.' Then he changed tack: 'And how do we think
about Vince Armishaw?' He told me that on Saturday nights
he sometimes went to his room with two or three other
members of the sixth form. With this he embarked on a parody

of Father Armishaw, imitating his voice with extraordinary accuracy: '. . . I want this clearly understood, Moreland: I've got the best hair in the whole of this college. That's because I shampoo it in egg white and Guinness every day and massage it before I go to bed . . . Now let me tell you something about the finer features of my motor cycle . . . Moreland, how dare you read Milton for pleasure. Come over here. You see this book, this is F. R. Leavis's *Revaluation*, the most important book in my room. Remember that and you can't go wrong . . . So put that bloody *Paradise Lost* away and read something decent, like *Middlemarch*!'

I was not to realise until the following year that when Father Armishaw was at Cambridge he had sat at the feet of F. R. Leavis, the famous judgemental literary critic, and had come to emulate many of Leavis's attitudes.

Eventually Moreland said: 'Oh, Vincent. He's wasted at Cotton . . . He should have stayed in Cambridge.'

Before we reached Little Bounds, he did what he had done the night of the house play: he stood before me, looked into my eyes and tweaked my nose, gently. I just let it happen. 'You're so sweet, Fru,' he said. 'You're an absolute poppet.'

For the rest of the day and the evening I found it difficult to get Moreland out of my mind. I felt, again, those early symptoms of infatuation, and I was trying to resist.

The next morning at breakfast Moreland handed me a sealed envelope. He whispered in my ear: 'Don't open it here. Open it when you are alone.'

I took it to the infirmary.

I could hear an echo of his speaking voice in the note. It went something like this:

'Dearest John,

Walking with you was *too nice* yesterday. I enjoyed my time with you *too much*. Did you realise that? Can you see it? I dare say you can with your discerning eye.

There are some things I can only just think, so much
do I think them. I expect you know that too. Would
you accompany me again? Say that you will. I loved
you asking me How do I think God to be? That was
so sweet. But I wasn't quite in the mood just then to
launch forth on those deep and mysterious waters.
Dearest, I would love to sit beneath a larch tree talking
with you about How I think God to be.
    Much love,
    Paul

The drift of the letter, with its 'dearest' twice over, its 'sweet',
and its 'much love' opened the prospect of a relationship that
I knew, instinctively, was something more than 'special friendship'. Yet I suspected that these endearments, which affected
tender feelings, were exaggerated mannerisms that Paul uttered
without thinking. I found myself yielding to fascination; but I
remained guarded.

94

PAUL INVITED ME for another walk in the last week of term,
the day after we had finished exams. We walked to Alton via
Oakamoor on a freezing day, the woods white with hoar frost
under a pale cloudless sky. He did not talk about God. He
asked me first about my spiritual reading. When I told him
that I had a great fondness for the autobiography of Saint
Thérèse de Lisieux, he joined his hands, looked upwards and
said in a simpering voice: 'Ah, oui, la petite fleurette.' He went
on to say how much he preferred Teresa of Avila. 'Now there's
a tough lady. Did you know, Fru, that the Devil threw her
down the stairs and she broke her arm in three places? They

had to break it again and again to get it straight.' He said that after she died the odour of sanctity was so great that the nuns in her convent passed out. Did I know, he asked, that when they dug her up a year later her habit was rotten, but the corpse was entirely incorrupt? 'But her devotees tore her fresh, pink incorrupt body to pieces in the violent scramble to get themselves relics . . .'

On and on he went. It was a prelude to an extraordinary monologue ranging over the darker side of sainthood and mysticism: a saint who licked the sores of lepers; another who drank a cup of pus to show solidarity with the sick; one that lived solely on the Eucharistic wafer.

At Alton, strictly against the rules, he insisted that we stop at the Bridge Café where he ordered tea and buttered toast, which we ate by an open wood fire. He told me about Saint Catherine of Genoa's vow of chastity while still married, and how she and her husband founded a hospice for the sick and the dying where she worked and prayed for thirty years until her death. He told me of Saint Catherine of Genoa's visions and 'lights in prayer', as he called them; her unusual experience of odours of sweetness, her great fasts, her experience of fiery darts of love, and her unusual acts of self-abnegation. Once she came upon a patient dying of the plague. The patient was wordlessly uttering the name of Jesus with her dying breath. Catherine could not resist kissing the diseased person's lips, since as far as she was concerned she was kissing Jesus himself. She caught the plague, suffering all its horrid torments, although she was not to die of it.

We walked back to Cotton via Farley and the Old Star crossroads, and all the way Moreland's monologue ranged over the problem of distinguishing between mysticism and madness. He was very worked up; and I gathered that this was more than just a topic of passing interest. One memorable thing he said was that Saint Catherine could tell the difference between a consecrated and an unconsecrated host. 'She knew this,' said Paul, 'because the consecrated host sent forth a ray of love that pierced her heart.'

Before we reached Top Bounds he grabbed me by the shoulders and pressed his forehead, cool in the late afternoon, on my forehead. I felt a momentary return of those breathtaking emotions I had experienced with Charles. But this was different; I was fearful of Paul, and I was determined not to put myself in danger again of being expelled.

95

THAT WEEK I received a letter from Mum telling me that the family had moved from the house at the Peel and into a 'halfway-house hostel' in Ilford. The new address was at the top of the page with directions. She assured me that this was just temporary accommodation until the council provided us with a proper house at an affordable rent. It would be a tight squeeze when I came home, she wrote, but she was determined that we would stay together as a family and that we would have a good Christmas. There was no mention of my having to leave Cotton, but the very phrase 'halfway house' filled me with anxiety. I had a vague childhood memory of our insecure wanderings during the war, and I imagined having to spend the Christmas holiday living temporarily, like the bombed-out homeless, in a public assembly hall.

Paul Moreland and I did not take another walk before the end of term but we exchanged addresses. On the night before GH, Moreland came into the infirmary at about midnight. I was reading. He seemed distracted and restless and kept twisting strands of his thick black hair. Eventually he said: 'God bless and love you, Fru. Have a happy and holy Christmas.' Then he bent over and kissed me on the cheek.

He left me in the infirmary, my face burning with excitement and emotion, and I could tell that his footsteps were echoing in the direction of the church rather than back towards the school cloister and the dormitories. Then I remembered the night when I had seen him prostrating himself before the Blessed Sacrament on the darkened sanctuary, praying in that odd repetitive way out loud. There was something frightening about Moreland; he was, I thought, a troubled person.

On the following day I travelled to London with James and Derek. Then I found my own way from Saint Pancras to Ilford mainline station, walking the rest of the way to our temporary home where I arrived after dark.

The 'halfway house' for the homeless was a barrack-like building in which a number of families shared kitchens in common, but had their own rooms situated off corridors on two floors. The Cornwell family, all six of us, had one living room, with two bedrooms. We shared our kitchen, toilet and bathroom with another couple and their baby who dwelt in the room facing our living room across the corridor. Mum and Maureen slept in one room upstairs, and the boys in the other. I was to sleep on a sofa in the living room which Mum had made comfortable. There was a Christmas tree and decorations. A hissing gas fire was attached to a meter which had to be fed frequently with pennies. My two younger brothers were glued to the television set, which was turned up loud to drown out the screams of the baby in the room opposite. The TV had a poor reception which Michael was constantly trying to improve by placing the aerial in different positions.

Mum showed me the communal kitchen. It was basic. One gas stove, one sink, some cupboards and a table. A window looked out over a concrete yard with a washing line. As we stood watching the kettle boil, the woman with the baby came in. Her dyed hair was unkempt, her bare legs were bruised and covered in sores. The baby was convulsed with crying and the woman awkwardly attempted to heat a bottle of milk. Mum intervened and helped. The baby fell silent as the woman put the teat in its mouth.

We made tea for ourselves and went back into the sitting room. I said: 'That woman looks pitiful.'

Then Mum started to cry: tears of rage. 'Scum of the earth!' she said through her teeth. 'We're living with the scum of the earth, and all because of that dirty rat your father!' There was something melodramatically disingenuous about the way she said this; I thought better than to begin an argument on the point.

After a while my sister and elder brother arrived. Maureen was beautifully dressed and bright-eyed; Terry was relaxed and seemingly unconcerned about our new situation. When Mum went out to the kitchen to prepare supper I spoke to Terry about her 'scum of the earth' comment. He said: 'Don't worry about it. We could have stayed at the Peel longer, but Mum got us into this place because it's the quickest route to a council house.'

It struck me, and not for the first time, that Mum could keep several versions of her life, and several paths of emotion, in train at the same time. Later that evening Uncle Mike, Mum's youngest brother, turned up to stay the night before driving back to Somerset the next day. Even in our homelessness Mum would find room for anybody in need: shades of the old Silvertown hospitality. He was to sleep on the floor in the sitting room with me. We sat around the gas fire talking until late. At one point he said: 'You know, Kath, I went over to Ireland not so long ago and visited Tralee. Our Egan forebears knew what they were doing when they got out of that dump and came to England.' I saw my mother's face cloud. 'Don't talk like that, Mike,' she said. Then Mike began to sing: 'I'll Take You Home Again, Kathleen,' and she joined in.

Then he offered me a Senior Service cigarette: 'Come on, mate, won't do you any harm. Help you to relax in this madhouse.' The baby was screaming again in the room opposite.

So I took it and smoked it through, enjoying the kick it gave me, but feeling slightly ill. The Cotton priests had been effective role models as smoking enthusiasts.

Terry, who did not smoke, nor ever would, grinned at me oddly: 'You're nuts!' he said.

96

WE WENT TO midnight Mass at the church of Saints Peter and Paul next to my old Secondary Modern school as we were no longer in Saint Augustine's parish. I went into the sacristy to ask the parish priest, a smooth-faced Englishman with a posh voice, if I could serve on the altar; but he told me politely enough that all the servers' places were filled and, in any case, he did not know me. When I told him that I was a seminarian and a new parishioner, he shrugged his shoulders. So for the first time in years I attended a Mass of Christmas like anybody else within the congregation rather than on the high altar. How I missed Father Cooney's 'Wisswiss . . .' and the Mass by gaslight at the Camp. Father Cooney would have squeezed me on to the sanctuary however many servers had turned up.

We walked home through Ilford afterwards and had our traditional ham sandwiches and tea with a dash of whisky sitting around the gas fire of the halfway house. Then we exchanged presents. Mum had bought me an LP record of Toscanini conducting the New York Philarmonic Orchestra playing Beethoven's Fifth and Eighth Symphonies. In one of my letters home I had mentioned how Father Armishaw played Beethoven on his gramophone and how the sound of it filled me with happiness and peace. It was her attempt to make up for the predicament in which I would find myself that Christmas holiday. I was overjoyed, and immediately put the record

on to our ugly grey-and-pink record player, Mum ordering me
to play it softly so as not to wake the baby opposite. But even
as the opening bars of the Fifth struck, I felt a pang of remorse.
A long-playing record was in those days equivalent to the price
of a pair of shoes, and I had noticed that my brother Jimmy
had holes in the only ones he possessed.

97

IMMEDIATELY AFTER CHRISTMAS, Mum and my brother
and sister went back to work. Mum had an office job at one of
the Plessey factories creating a filing system for draughtsmen's
drawings of electronic components. I spent a lot of time lying
on the sofa bed in the living room, smoking cigarettes, listening
to Beethoven and reading Somerset Maugham's *Of Human
Bondage*, borrowed from Father McCallum. My younger
brothers played in the yard outside or roamed Valentine's Park
opposite.

A letter arrived from Paul Moreland the day after New Year.
It was written in red ink; the handwriting and the sentiments
were typically extravagant. I could hear his voice as I read it.
He wrote that he had been walking on the common on a
'sherbert day, sharp, yellow and refreshing'. He was reading
Immanuel Kant slowly, 'like a tortoise'. He had had a tantrum
on the previous evening after reading a book on Aquinas by a
'tawdry British philosopher'. Then a 'meaty mouse' appeared
from below his bed and he had another tantrum. Then, in a
phrase I had heard him repeat before, he wrote: 'So, as Plato
says, life itself is the true tragedy.' In the last paragraph he
complained that he had not spoken to anyone all day: it's so
odd, he went on, when 'no one comes to give one language'.
He finished by suggesting that we meet at Sloane Square

outside the tube station on the day before the Epiphany at twelve o'clock. If I came, that would be 'too dreamy', and if I didn't, no matter, as he would go shopping in the King's Road.

I set off on the tube from Gants Hill, arriving in Chelsea at 11.30. When he had failed to arrive by 12.15, I was beginning to feel annoyed. At 12.20 I saw him coming up from the District Line train with his slight limp, full of apologies.

We walked the length of the King's Road down as far as World's End where we entered an Indian restaurant. I had never eaten Indian food before and Moreland ordered everything for both of us, explaining the different dishes. He ordered lager beer and drank his greedily, ordering another. All this time he had been talking knowledgeably about food. He offered me a cigarette and we both began to smoke. He was looking at me strangely.

He said that he wanted to tell me something in strict confidence. He told me that he suffered from strange 'phenomena'. They were not so much 'visions as *distortions*'. I wondered for a moment whether he wasn't drunk with the lager. He went on to say that he was at times prey to roaring sounds, like a 'thousand lions', and the grotesque distortions of vision were so devastating that he could do nothing but lie for hours in the dark until they had faded. 'I tell people,' he said, 'that I am having migraines.' Afterwards, he said, his mind became clear and penetrating. 'I can see,' he said, 'into the life of things. And I can make such strange connections between things that it frightens me.'

I sat in silence, paralysed, unsure how I should react or respond.

Then he said: 'Do you abuse yourself, Fru?'

I did not want to answer him.

Eventually, he said: 'You've been raped, haven't you?'

I was silent, terrified. I was thinking in a confused fashion of the Rape of Lucrece, wondering what he could mean.

'I know, because it's happened to me too. I can tell.'

I did not need to reply, since he did not wait for an answer. He went on to tell me that he had been forcibly masturbated, repeatedly, for more than two years by the priest who had been his spiritual friend. 'What a friend! What a priest!' he said bitterly. After his father left home, he went on, his mother had become deeply attached to this priest. He was supposed to help her. He converted her to Catholicism. He used to come every day.

'She knew that it was happening, but she pretended to herself that he was my mentor, my special spiritual guide.'

I was dumbfounded. I just sat looking at him.

He said: 'I came to enjoy it in a way, Fru . . . I came to need it, and to need *him*,' Paul said. 'I found my vocation to the priesthood with the priest who destroyed my soul. There's only one answer to the murder of your soul, Fru, which is to receive God's grace through no action of our own.'

'But surely,' I said at last, 'you have been to confession, and any sinfulness is now forgiven.'

Paul laughed, a cold little laugh. 'But evil, Fru, is not just a question of intentions.'

He then told me the story in detail: places, times, circumstances. Moreland had served the priest's Mass, and went to him regularly in confession. The priest, whom he gave a name, was on the surface devout and dedicated. 'He was holy,' Moreland said, 'except when he made me suck his penis.'

Afterwards the priest would hear his confession.

It was almost dark by the time we got up from the table. I felt sick in my soul; and I was conscious that we were just walking distance from where I had been sexually attacked five or six years earlier. Yes, I was thinking, it is true: I have been raped. Before we left the restaurant, he said: 'I am not afraid of sex, Fru . . . Our bodies are just playgrounds.'

I said: 'But our bodies, Moreland, are the temples of the Holy Ghost.'

'Mine,' he repeated, 'is just a playground.'

At that moment, young as he was, his face, strangely beauti-ful to me, appeared ancient and ruined. Was that, I wondered, something he had seen in my face too? His last words to me were: 'You will never tell a soul, will you, Fru?'

98

LENT TERM BEGAN the following week. Cotton was in the grip of winter and I detected an unusual transformation among the senior boys. They were obsessed with the latest pop single, 'Singing the Blues'. For the first few days of term boys were humming the tune and arguing rowdily over the competing merits of Tommy Steele and Guy Mitchell. I heard James, of all people, hotly insisting at supper that one would dance the foxtrot to it, to the amazed derision of those around him. The pop music from home had found its way back to Cotton and created a strangely disruptive mood. Hearing two boys quarrelling about 'Singing the Blues' as he came into his history class, Father Grady slammed a book on his desk and said tartly: 'Oh, how I hate all that Blue-Skies-Round-the-Corner rubbish. Why can't people be happy with real music!'

To my surprise and relief, Mère Saint Luc had insisted that I must remain in the infirmary and had provided me with extra blankets and two hot-water bottles. By a stroke of irony I had not been back a week before I contracted flu, and I was soon joined in the infirmary by several other boys who had caught the same virulent strain.

Father Gavin began to appear in the infirmary after he had said his Mass. He seemed different out of the context of the classroom. Despite his premature baldness there was some-thing angelically youthful, I thought, about his lineless, jovial face; the way he made his mouth small to prevent it breaking out into a broad grin. I was impressed that he was the only priest who visited the sick in the infirmary while the flu was about and I came to see that outside his Latin drills he was a kind and affable human being.

Visiting me after I was on the mend, he asked me if I would like to act in the role of a Jesuit priest, Father Henry Garnet, in a play he was producing about Guy Fawkes and the 5 November plot to blow up the Houses of Parliament. I had enjoyed being on the stage in the previous year and it seemed a stroke of divine providence. Encouraged by the archivist, Mr Roberts, I had been avidly reading about Father Garnet's clandestine missionary activities during the time of the Protestant persecution of Catholics.

The play, 'Gunpowder, Treason and Plot' by the Catholic writer Hugh Ross Williamson, argued that the scheme to blow up king and parliament was actually instigated by the government in order to justify a more vicious persecution of Catholics. The Protestant arch-villain of the piece, Lord Salisbury, sought to blame the Jesuits as the principal traitors, and the alleged ringleader, who might have been called a 'master spy', was Father Henry Garnet.

The play was performed two evenings running, a month into the term, and attended by various Cotton benefactors. Father Doran rose at the end to commend the 'clarity of speech of all the cast'.

Public speaking, and clarity of speech, had become an obsession in the previous year on the initiative of the archbishop, who was a stickler for elocution. Under pressure from the archbishop, the profs had been delivering frequent pep talks about bad pronunciation and working-class accents. At his first Sunday homily that term Father Doran had complained for a full fifteen minutes about the pronunciation of a single word. During a rugby match against a visiting school, in the previous term, he said, he had listened to boys shouting: 'Get it

*Me as Father Henry Garnet SJ in
'Gunpowder, Treason and Plot', 1956.*

back!' The word 'back', he insisted, had been pronounced
by Cottonians, on the touchline, as well as in the team, as in
'Bach', the composer. 'But it isn't Bach,' he insisted, 'it's back!';
he was pronouncing the word, it seemed to me, as in 'beck'.
On and on he went: 'Beck, not Bach.' Then he laboured the
pronunciation of the word 'ghost', as in Holy Ghost. 'It is *not*
Horly Gorst,' he insisted, 'it's Holy Ghost!' But his 'Holy Ghost',
it seemed to me, came out as 'Herley Ghoost'.

Father Gavin initiated a weekly debating club, recording the
proceedings on a new Grundig tape recorder presented by the
archbishop. The idea was to encourage boys to hear themselves
speaking and so improve their delivery. Given that newspapers
were not allowed in the school, the debates tended to be of a
peculiarly abstract nature. Typical motions were: 'This house
believes that tomorrow never comes,' 'This house is of the
opinion that it is the last straw that breaks the camel's back,'

263

and 'This house believes that the longest way round is the shortest way home.'

By the advent of Holy Week my accent was back to a respectable, well-enunciated and emphatic version of Black Country, mainly in emulation of Father Armishaw.

99

I SAW LITTLE of Moreland as the term progressed, since bad weather had precluded afternoon walks. Our paths occasionally crossed and he would give me a look of affectionate complicity; but we had no opportunity to speak.

I had noticed him during the forty hours' devotion when the Blessed Sacrament was exposed in the Lady chapel through nearly two days and two nights surrounded by forests of lighted candles and flowers. Boys took it in turn to maintain watch. I spent more time than most on my knees before the Blessed Sacrament; but Moreland seemed to be there all the time.

During the forty hours I had a strange experience. I had been on my knees before the Blessed Sacrament three hours on the first evening, gazing at that circle of white, the Eucharistic wafer, when I began to feel feverish. Eventually I felt as if my head was about to burst. Just at the moment when I thought I could bear it no longer I saw very clearly hovering around the monstrance, with its radiating gilt sunbeams, an intensely bright spark of light: it had the brightness of the sun itself, and it gave off an impression of supernatural energy. I said to myself: 'I am seeing God: and God is pure energy!' Then the moment and the 'vision' passed.

I continued kneeling, wondering whether the spark would return; then the thought came to me that I should ask God for a miracle. All these years, since my childhood, I had accepted the defective vision in my right eye, akin to peripheral vision. I could not read with my left eye closed, I could only perceive the world in a shadowy fashion. Perhaps I should ask God to cure my right eye; it occurred to me that if I had sufficient Faith then God would grant me a miracle. I covered both eyes with my hands and prayed and prayed with all the Faith that I could muster.

I wanted something dramatic, startling, to occur, revealing God's action in the world in a direct and tangible manner. Slowly I removed my hand from my right eye and opened it. The miracle had not been granted.

Then Moreland was sent to the infirmary.

100

HIS AILMENT, or ailments, lacked specifics, though I had heard rumours from James Rolle. Moreland had been suffering 'severe migraines' and there had been odd incidents: he had been found sleepwalking far from the dormitories in the middle of the night. On one occasion he had been followed by a member of the big sixth down into the refectory where he took his place in the dark at the head of one of the tables. When the sixth former switched on the lights, Moreland screamed. His screams could be heard all over that wing of the college and even as far as Saint Thomas's.

When Moreland arrived in the infirmary he greeted me affably, but he seemed to want his privacy. Dr Hall came to see him and questioned him in a quiet voice. I could not hear the conversation. He was given some sort of sedative and he slept a great deal.

One night Moreland woke up and screamed once, only to fall asleep again immediately. Not long after this, in the early hours I heard him weeping for a while. In the morning I went out to the toilet after breakfast. When I came back he was sitting up in bed with a cup in his hand. 'This is your cup,' he said, laughing in a strange manner. 'When you were outside I licked it where you drank from it. You see, Fru, I long to be intimate with you.' I laughed, too, when he said this, but I was feeling embarrassed.

As he got better, he started to talk. His monologues, once he got going, overwhelmed me. His speech was like a fast-running river, with currents and cross-currents, sudden digressions and tributaries. It was the repetitions more than anything that made me wonder about his sanity; they made him sound irrational. And yet he could control his tongue when the need arose, which was usually when Father Gavin came into the infirmary for his regular visit after Mass in the morning; or when Mère Saint Luc appeared with food or medicine.

The content of this prodigious flow was a kind of mixed-idea salad from his wide reading, most of it religious in nature and philosophical. Yet it seemed to me that there was little depth, and increasingly fewer logical connections; it was mostly flashy, on the surface. After Matron had given him more pills, he became very quiet and slept again for a long time. Some sort of crisis had passed.

Before I fell asleep, he woke up and told me in a lazy voice that he had been having a 'visionary dream' about stigmata. 'It was so *real*, Fru,' he said. 'So real and so beautiful. Do you realise that the stigmata is your body as Christ's cross: you don't replicate Christ in his wounds; that would be a blasphemy. You replicate the cross on which he hung: you are the cross through which the nails penetrate, and the spear too. In stigmata Jesus is nailed to *you* . . .'

We talked for a while that evening in low voices. When I got back into bed he came and sat next to me. He became excited and tearful. He said to me at one point that the Jesuit who had abused him had 'penetrated' his body. 'I can only make reparation for that,' Moreland said, 'by becoming the cross on which Jesus was nailed.' I tried to calm him; but it was a hopeless conversation, which degenerated into Moreland's repetitions. Eventually I fell asleep while he continued to speak.

In the middle of the night I woke up with a fright. Moreland was standing over me. The only light was from the fire in the grate, and the entire world seemed hushed as if after snowfall.

'Fru, I want you to do something,' he said. 'Just lie on your back and stretch out your arms. Please do that for me. Stretch out your arms as if you are on the cross.' He was so earnest and insistent, and I was so sleepy and confused, that I did as he asked me since I wanted him to get it over with.

He pulled back the bedclothes and before I could resist he had climbed on top of me, face down, stretching out his arms as if our bodies were in mirror image. His lips were touching mine and his eyes were looking into mine. I was paralysed with fear. Then he started to gabble something about me being the tree of good-and-evil. I looked into his eyes and I was shocked to see that he was utterly absent. His eyes were wide open looking into mine, but he was not there.

He was sweating through his pyjamas and dribbling into my mouth. Disgusted, I pushed him off and he landed in a heap on the floor. I was shaking, speechless. He picked himself up and went back to his bed. For a moment it occurred to me that there was nothing wrong with him, that he had had himself put into the infirmary precisely to act out this weird ritual.

His last words to me, in a quite normal voice, were: 'Don't tell anybody, Fru. Please.'

I said nothing.

The next morning neither Father Gavin, who slept immediately above, nor Matron, mentioned a disturbance in the night. Moreland was released from the infirmary that day and he and I did not speak of the incident again. The term was drawing to a close, I was preparing for end-of-term exams, and the annual retreat was coming up. Through Holy Week I could barely concentrate on the homilies of the retreat leader. I was worried about returning home again to the halfway-house hostel.

101

ON EASTER MONDAY I travelled down to London. The weather in Ilford was cold and windy. Our temporary home was sunk in an atmosphere of foreboding. The couple next door were arguing and fighting much of the day, and their baby was screaming day and night. Terry, my quiet, long-suffering elder brother, said: 'Looks as if we've exchanged one boxing ring for another!'

The day after Easter Mum, Terry and Maureen returned to work. My younger brothers were in the sitting room all day listening to the radio, watching television or playing in a desultory kind of way. To get some peace I lay on my mother's bed rereading *The Cardinal* and listening to Beethoven. I was getting listless. I wondered if I should get in touch with Moreland, but I now felt afraid of him and therefore afraid for myself. Another danger, however, lurked for me in the bedroom here. All around were items of my mother's and sister's clothes and lingerie. In my boredom and lethargy I began to feel stirrings of those 'irregular motions of the flesh'. After a morning of mounting sexual fantasies I got up off the bed and went out into the cold wind.

I took a bus to Woodford Green to visit the Franciscan church of Saint Thomas. Inside the empty church I prayed before the statue of the Virgin. Then I sat in the pews feeling empty, half-praying, half-daydreaming. Eventually a man in the Franciscan habit came out on the high altar from the sacristy. He straightened the altar cloth and stood back to appraise his work, then came to where I was sitting. He was a youngish man with a bright, open face and closely cropped hair. The sleeves of his habit were rolled up and I could see bare wrists and arms. He smiled and we spoke for a while. When I told him that I was a junior seminarian, he became affable. He was intrigued to know why I had come all the way from Ilford to visit the Franciscan church. On an impulse, thinking that it would catch his interest, I said I had come to pray for a 'special intention'.

He told me about the community of Poor Clares who lived on the other side of the church behind a high wall. 'The prayers of our Franciscan nuns,' he said, 'have the power to perform miracles. The Good Lord cannot refuse them.' He told me about the relationship between Francis and Clare, an aristocratic lady of Assisi who had founded the Franciscan sisterhood.

He now insisted that I accompany him to visit the Poor Clare convent. Leading the way, he took me out of the church and through a door in a wall to a garden in front of an old house with shuttered windows. He rang on a bell, and within a few moments a sister appeared dressed in a brown habit and black veil.

'This young man,' said the friar, 'would like to see Reverend Mother.' Before I could hesitate, or explain myself, the nun ushered me into the dark interior of the house. I heard the friar calling out behind me: 'You'll be all right. Tell Reverend Mother of your intention.'

The nun brought me to a room with bare boards where there was a simple chair facing a grille covered with a gauze curtain. Asking me to sit, the nun disappeared. I heard a door opening and a different nun appeared on the other side of the grille. I could barely see her face because of the gauze, but it appeared to me that her skin was sallow, almost yellow.

She asked me how old I was and where I lived. As we talked,

it occurred to me that the Poor Clares were living a kind of entombed life-in-death. Despite this she seemed cheerful. She said that they had retreated from the world to pray day and night for others. They did not accumulate wealth for future emergencies but relied on what was given to them more or less from day to day. 'Sometimes,' she said, 'we wonder if we're going to eat at all for a whole week. But something usually turns up.'

She brought the conversation to a close by saying that she would ask the sisters to pray for me and my special intention. The intention, she said, could be a secret one. I was relieved as I did not want to talk to this strange nun about my sexual temptations. In my mind, though, I added an intention that I had not thought of for some time – that Dad would come back to us.

She asked me to kneel down with her and pray a little before we parted. She said the Hail Mary followed by the *Memorare*. As she prayed her voice seemed to wrap me around with gentleness. I felt a great surge of warmth for this woman and her strange life of prayer and self-denial. Then she was gone. The moment she disappeared the sister who had met me at the door came in and led me out of the room. Before I knew it the front door had closed behind me and I was standing blinking in the driveway, buffeted by the cold winds.

I went back into the church, hoping to see the friar again, but he had disappeared. After a while I heard voices singing a simple version of the Divine Office in the choir on the other side of the high altar, hidden from the sight of the main church.

102

ON SATURDAY NIGHT I went to confession at Saints Peter and Paul church. Walking down the Ilford High Road afterwards I collided with a boy called Bob Prince who I had known at my old school. I was surprised to see how much he had changed: he was dressed in a tight-fitting suit and his hair was in the new slicked-back style known as a DA ('duck's arse'). He had once covered the back of my blazer in chalk marks and I had bloodied his nose. He kept me in conversation for a long time, leaning up against a shop window. He couldn't get over the way I talked and how 'square' I looked.

He persuaded me eventually to go with him to the Catholic Youth Club next to the school. There were boys mostly of my age; some were playing table tennis, others were listening to the record player which was belting out Bill Haley and the Comets' 'Rock Around the Clock'. A girl called Pat, with jet-black hair and high heels, came up to us and said she was having a party at her house as her parents had gone away for a wedding. She was wearing heavy make-up, as if to hide some prominent spots, but she was vivacious and attractive. She kept flicking Bob's arm and saying: 'Bring your friend.'

We left the youth club, a dozen or so of us including about five girls, and walked out into the road called Green Lane. Everybody was lighting up cigarettes, including me. One of the boys had a sheaf of records. After twenty minutes' walk, via an off-licence where we had a whip-round for quarts of cider, we arrived at a terrace house. There was a lot of joshing about the records, and pushing back of furniture. Then the girls kicked off their shoes and started dancing in their stockinged feet.

I sat on the arm of a chair, carried away by the sound and the hectic beat. They played over and over again a version of 'Pick a Bail o' Cotton' by a skiffle group called The Vipers. The girls danced and whirled with their tight skirts hitched up. Soon everybody was dancing except me. Prince came over to me and pointed at Pat. 'Look at her,' he said. 'Snake-hips we call her.' Then Pat made me get up and dance. She took me through the moves. I felt self-conscious and awkward at first, but when I picked up the rhythm I started to get into it. She cried out: 'Hey, John, you're in the groove!'

We drank and smoked, and danced some more. Then each boy, except me, ended up with a girl on his knee. Some swapping went on; Pat went on several laps, and finally landed on mine. She stayed there.

For the first time in my life I felt and tasted the tongue of another human being inside my mouth. I found it repulsive at first, but I soon got used to it; it was a surprise, like buttered toast, I thought. Pat had a long soft nose. I wanted to stroke her hair, but she wouldn't let me. She was keen on close eye-staring which she called soul-kissing. When I was leaving, just before midnight, Pat said she would like to see me at the youth club again.

I walked back to the hostel to find my younger brothers and Mum in bed. Maureen and Terry were out. So I lay on the sofa in the living room and pondered the evening. I could still smell Pat all over me. I smoked a cigarette. I could see Pat's eyes with huge black pupils staring one inch away into mine, and I could hear Geoff, the patient in Staffordshire Royal Infirmary, saying: 'Tell me what's better! Eh! Tell me what's better!' Then I thought of Paul Moreland's absent eyes staring into mine in his weird visionary state.

I longed for physical closeness: I yearned for it. But did I have to choose between the tongue-in-my-mouth concupiscence of Pat, or Paul's ranting, dribbling stigmatic rapture? The idea of existing just to myself – pounding up and down reading a breviary – seemed to me that night as attractive as ending up in Saint Clement's in the Bow Road with a lobotomy.

When Maureen came in, she sat on the bed and we talked

for a while about a party she had been to. She had left school now and was working in the bank. Her demure convent-school ways had quickly lapsed. She laughed a lot about how some of the girls were dressed and the saucy things the boys got up to. I loved talking to Maureen that night; she had become so smart about people and funny. After she went to bed, I lay awake into the small hours.

103

THE NEXT DAY I got up at seven and went to the early Mass at Saints Peter and Paul. I spent a long time over my thanksgiving, examining my conscience about the night before; anxious that I might have entered an 'occasion of sin.' My mind was spinning with the old scruples again, so thinking of Father Buxton's advice during the retreat the year before I made an act of contrition and left the church.

Back at the hostel I was in the communal kitchen making a cup of tea, when the woman from across the corridor came in. She was half-dressed and weeping. Embarrassed, I said: 'Good morning!' and turned to face the stove where I had the kettle on.

At that moment a voice shouted: 'Fuckin' Christ. You cunt! I turn my fuckin' back and you're chattin' up a fuckin' bloke!'

A man was at the kitchen door, unshaven, in his under-clothes. He was short but tough-looking, with the face of a wino. He was looking directly at me. 'What the fuck are you doin' in my kitchen!' he yelled. Then he grabbed the woman by the hair and smacked her round the face. Turning on me again, he screamed: 'I'll knock your fuckin' block off.'

With this he came around the table, fists clenched. He was a hard labouring man in his forties and I was terrified. I made for the door, but he came around the table to cut me off. Then he had me up against the gas stove, one hard hand at my throat: 'I'll smash your fuckin' face in . . .' he was yelling.

An icy voice cut in: 'Oi! You! . . . Leave that boy alone!'

Mum was at the kitchen door.

She stood there, eyes bulging with violent intent, her left hand opening out and suddenly closing to a fist, the other hand out of sight as if she would take him with one arm tied behind her back.

He loosened his grip. He was staring at Mum. At that moment I knew that I was safe and I adored her with all my heart and soul.

'I'm goin' to smash this bastard's 'ead in,' he said, his fist raised.

'That boy is MY . . . SON!'

'I don't care 'oo 'e is.'

'Don't you!'

From behind her back Mum now produced her kitchen carving knife, a familiar bone-handled instrument she kept whetted to razor sharpness.

He let me go.

'John,' she ordered, 'out through the window over the sink.'

I clambered over the sink and through the open sash window.

Looking back, I cried out with terror as I saw Mum make a rush at the man, thrusting for his belly with the carving knife.

The man skipped around the table, narrowly avoiding the merciless jabs, and disappeared into the corridor. He had locked himself into his room, but Mum went on after him and was rattling at the handle and throwing her shoulder at the door.

'You so much as look at my son again and I'll bloody swing for what I'll do to you! . . .' she growled.

For a few seconds there was silence. 'No one threatens my

sons! Or they have me to deal with!' she yelled, with a final bang on the door with her free fist.

Shortly afterwards I followed Mum into our living room.

She collapsed on a chair, the knife in her lap. Then she had a good cry. 'Scum of the earth!' she kept saying. 'Scum of the earth! That my seminarian son should have to endure this! This is what that dirty rat your father has brought us to.'

There and then she decided that she would telephone the college and ask them to have me back early. I pleaded with her not to, but she was adamant. 'You can't say here, darling. No way. Next time you'll come back to our own home. I promise.'

Locking me in our living room for safety, Mum took herself off to the public phone box on the corner of Cranbrook Road and The Drive. When she returned she told me that she had talked to Father McCallum, the bursar, Father Doran being away. It was agreed that I should return to Cotton straight away.

104

FATHER McCALLUM was waiting at Oakamoor station in a new Morris car. He was initially full of concern about the attack. 'What a business! How simply frightful for you.' Then he began to talk airily about his plans for further decoration at Cotton.

Once again I was established in the infirmary with Mère Saint Luc making a fuss of me. After I told her of the attack at the hostel, she sat with me for a while talking about dangerous moments she had experienced during the Great War.

Later, in the clock cloister, I ran into Father Armishaw who had returned to the college early and also knew about the incident. He asked me up to his room to 'chew the fat'. He seemed more relaxed than at our last meeting in his room. He said that priests were often attacked on sight because of their Roman collars. 'Best policy is to run!' he said with a laugh; but I could see that he was concerned. Sitting in the armchair facing his desk in that meticulously tidy room, I felt secure. I wanted nothing more in life than to be Father Armishaw.

He chose from his record collection Beethoven's Violin Concerto. As we sat listening, he smoked his pipe and read a book. The music and his presence calmed my heart. Occasionally he looked up but said nothing. Before I went to bed he asked me to serve his Mass the next day.

I served Father Armishaw's Mass at the side altar beneath the stained-glass window of Saint Teresa and Saint John of the Cross. The familiar ritual close to Father Armishaw in the cool, silent morning made me light-headed with happiness. Was it possible, I wondered, to reside and rest within the tranquil ambit of music, nature and the liturgy, for the whole of one's life? The heroism of Father Fermoyle in *The Cardinal*, and Father Cooney, did not seem so attractive in the aftermath of the 'halfway house'.

In the sacristy Father Armishaw asked me if I would like to meet him after breakfast by the garages where he was working on his motorbike.

The garages where Father Armishaw kept and maintained his gleaming green motor cycle were the other side of a wall at the end of Top Bounds. When I arrived he was on his knees cleaning engine parts which were laid out on a sheet. He was wearing old trousers and his leather flying jacket. His motorbike was a water-cooled Velocette 192cc, popular with police forces in England, he told me. As he worked he explained what he was doing. I learnt about the chemistry of petrol, and the principles of the combustion engine – carburettor, cylinders, gearbox. As he bent to his task and spoke about the mechanisms, he would hand me a piece to examine and feel its weight.

Father Armishaw photographing himself.

That afternoon he took me for a ride as far as the Rocks. As he opened up along a straight stretch, he called out for me to hold on to him tightly around his waist. I pressed my head against his back, watching the drystone walls zipping by.

The hours and the days leading up to the beginning of term passed like a paradisal interlude. Father Armishaw showed me the intricacies of his camera, and how to take pictures at the right speed and with the appropriate film without artificial lighting. He talked books, and we listened to music.

One night he took the blanket from his bed and led me down to the lawn in front of the old hall, out of bounds to boys. As we lay side by side under a clear sky he pointed out stars and planets, and the constellations. He told me a mnemonic by which I could remember the order of the planets from Mercury to Pluto, starting with the one closest to the Sun: 'Married virgins eat mango jam sitting under nanny's piano.'

He did not speak to me in an intimate way, nor did he once talk about religion or the spiritual life. I asked him practical questions, or just remained silent waiting for him to say something.

I longed to give him something back, and it was this desire that prompted me to talk about Paul Moreland. The night after our star-gazing Father Armishaw lent me a book by Sir James Jeans titled *The Stars in their Courses*. He had won it as a school prize and it was precious to him. He had just marked a passage for me about the method of calculating the weight of the moon and the earth, when I said: 'I'm worried about Paul Moreland, sir . . .'

'What do you mean?'

I told him about the episode in the infirmary, when Paul had talked of stigmata. Then I described how he had lain on top of me. Father Armishaw was listening intently and gravely. His face was taking on such a serious expression that I began to feel afraid. But wasn't that the effect I had sought? Then I went on to tell him about the abuse Moreland had experienced at the hands of the family priest.

I thought that one confidence might lead to another. We would become closer, more intimate. But when I finished, he was suddenly offhand, although his face remained pale and intense.

'These things happen,' he said shortly. Then he told me to go to bed.

As I made my way down to the infirmary I knew that I had made a mistake.

105

As the profs and boys returned and the new term began I learnt that I had a new berth in Top Dorm. My infirmary privileges had come to an end. For several days I hardly saw Father Armishaw except in class where he treated me like everybody else and betrayed no indication that there was anything special between us. I saw Paul Moreland only fleetingly, hurrying to the sixth form library with piles of books.

I explained to James what had happened at the hostel for the homeless and he was sympathetic. We were walking up and down Top Bounds, James gossiping, just being companionable. Then Derek came up to join me at break, wondering why I had not been on the train from Saint Pancras. He tried to get our private game going; but my heart wasn't in it.

Two days into the term I collided with Father Armishaw in the cloister and he asked me to come and see him after night prayers. The house was in silence as I knocked. He told me to come in and shut the door.

'Would you like to hear some music?' he asked. He put a Beethoven violin sonata on the turntable. While we listened he read a book and I sat in the armchair looking into the fire. I was expecting him to say something about Paul Moreland; but he said nothing. Later we talked for a while about photography; then he said: 'Time for your bed.' Before I left, he said: 'You can come here if you feel like it any Thursday after night prayers . . . but keep it to yourself, if you get my drift.'

I got his drift.

The next day Father Doran sent for me. It was a late spring morning, the distant hills blue with the promise of a glorious day. He was at his desk, his back to the open bay windows.

He asked me to repeat what I had told Father Armishaw about Paul Moreland. His seriousness and cold voice scared me. After I had told him everything, he wanted to know whether I had 'participated' when Paul lay on top of me; whether I had attempted to resist. His tight-lipped questions put me on my guard. Under his stern cross-examination I stressed again and again Paul's forcefulness and my unwillingness. Eventually he dismissed me without comment.

I felt perplexed; betrayed. Father Armishaw had gone to Father Doran with what I had told him. We had not been speaking under the seal of confession, but I now realised, painfully, that his first loyalty was to his religious superior. My biggest disillusionment was that he had put me in danger no less than Paul. In alerting Father Doran to Moreland's behaviour, I had been expendable. Yet I, too, had been guilty of a betrayal. Paul had begged me to treat what he had told me, and done to me, with confidence. Had I betrayed that confidence in his interests? Or the interests of the seminary? It had not for one moment escaped me, ever since that evening's confidence, that I had betrayed Paul in my eagerness to get closer to Father Armishaw.

The college was now entering the rhythm of its usual routines, and the rest of the morning proceeded as usual. At the end of classes we went into church in ranks for prayers before lunch. Moreland was not at his place in church. When we arrived in the refectory for lunch he was not at his place at table. Then I learnt that he had left.

Sitting there, unable to eat, I remembered Paul sitting by the railway tunnel in the Churnet valley. It struck me that Paul was capable of doing something reckless, and I would be to blame. After lunch, ignoring the lists that had gone up on the noticeboard for cricket practice and athletics, I slipped down the valley path and hurried towards Oakamoor. I wanted to know that Paul had not harmed himself, and I was desperate to say goodbye to him and to be forgiven. My eyes were blinded with tears; I stumbled and fell again and again as I ran down the steep pathways. And all the way I was imagining Paul's body lying on the railway track, his limbs severed, his beautiful head smashed in.

I found him on the platform at Oakamoor, sitting amidst his bags. He was reading a book. He looked at me with that absent gaze he sometimes affected, and said nothing.

I was crying. I told him I was sorry, over and over again.

Eventually he said very softly: 'I did ask you, didn't I, Fru, not to tell anybody . . . Poor Fru!'

After a while he said in a small voice: 'I think I'm probably a better fit with the Jesuits.' It did not occur to me then that he was being ironic.

When the train came in, bound for Uttoxeter, I stood on the platform gazing up to where he sat in the carriage by the window. But he opened his book and did not look at me again.

Later that day Father Doran sent for me. He told me that Paul Moreland was suffering from a form of mental illness; that he had left of his own volition and I was not to think badly of him. He hoped I would settle down to the good work of which I was capable. He had heard of my attack at home and he believed that such incidents strengthened a person's character.

I came away from Father Doran's office feeling calmer, and I decided to steel myself against feeling guilty for my part in Paul's departure.

106

Now that I was in the sixth form I came under the direct spiritual influence of Father Doran. After night prayers we would come forward to the front of the church, filling the first three benches on both sides of the aisle. Carrying his copy of the New Testament, Father Doran would rise from his prie-dieu and come to sit behind us in the fourth row to give us 'meditation points', themes for our silent prayer the following morning.

He would read a passage from the Gospels and draw reflections for our consideration. He stressed our human weaknesses, repeatedly contrasting our disobedience with the acquiescence of the Virgin Mary. His personality came across strongly during these nightly talks: an ascetical, disciplined man, with a jaundiced view of human nature and of boys in particular. After he had finished he would walk back to his prie-dieu, his heavily shod shoes echoing through the church. We remained kneeling in contemplation until we heard him rising and passing through the double doors of the church and out into the cloister.

The next morning we would be on our knees in our normal places, towards the back of the church, to begin half an hour's meditation on Father Doran's points before the rest of the school joined us for their morning prayers before community Mass.

I seemed to be living through much of the week on autopilot, sustained by the rhythm of the religious round. Father Doran's meditations dominated my mind, but there was an area of my life which remained independent of the routine – my weekly visits to Father Armishaw's room on Thursday nights. He saw other boys on Saturday evenings, but I was the only sixth former to be invited alone to his room. This special privilege was, I knew, an act of kindness in response to my home circumstances, but I was convinced that he saw me as someone special. I was tempted to broach the affair of Paul Moreland, but I never did. Instinctively I knew that never again should I attempt to take our relationship further than the limits he had set.

Our evenings followed a pattern. There would be music, invariably Beethoven to begin with, then Bach or Brahms, then Mozart. He would smoke a cigarette or two, but he never offered me one. He liked to talk music and the merits of different performances. He would compare, for example, the precision of Toscanini with the flexibility of Furtwängler, then he would expound the balance and contrast between freedom and control in writing: inspiration and intuition versus hard, conscious graft. He would lend me books, not all of them to my liking, and he would ask me what I thought when I returned them. The books were always outside our class work: Joyce, Shaw, George Eliot, D. H. Lawrence, Flaubert, Dostoevsky, Tolstoy.

There were times, especially after haymaking, when I almost fainted with the fragrance of the grass and the wild flowers, a mood of longing in the distant hills, the beauty of our sunsets. I was reading the early books of Wordsworth's *Prelude* which seemed to articulate these feelings, creating an even deeper sense of mystery and presence than I had felt in earlier years. We talked of this one evening in his room, and he warned me of the danger of pantheism, the heresy that would reduce God to the level of his own creation.

We did not talk spirituality, or about spiritual reading, although I knew that he had a special interest in mystical poetry. One day I asked him what he thought of the autobiography of Saint Thérèse of Lisieux. He looked over his spectacles, the way he did when he was about to say something quizzical, and asked if I had read the poetry of Richard Crashaw. I had not. He took a book down from his shelf and marked a page: it was Crashaw's 'The Flaming Heart', dedicated to the earlier, Spanish Teresa.

Before handing it over, he read out a passage from another Crashaw poem which spoke of God taking up residence in the 'mild and milky soul of a soft child'. He said that description was more apt for the French Saint Thérèse than the Spanish Santa Teresa. The problem of great mystics, he said, was their tendency to hurt as well as to *be* hurt.

> For in love's field was never found
> A nobler weapon than a Wound.

107

COTTON HAD A newly appointed spiritual director from outside the college – Father Joseph Connelly, a former professor at the senior seminary, who worked on a parish five miles distant, and who came to Cotton every Thursday afternoon. I had another idea. A combination of curiosity and rashness attracted me to Father 'Rainbow' McCallum. I had found his attentions flattering when I was in the infirmary and he offered the prospect of real engagement.

I knocked on his sitting room door one lazy Thursday afternoon beyond mid-term. His windows were wide open and he was standing looking out towards the meadow at the head of the valley. He was wearing one of his coloured silk shirts. He said that he would be delighted to act as my spiritual director. He shut the door and turned the key in the lock, inviting me to sit in an armchair.

He offered me a drink of 'something strong' and a cigarette, which I declined. Sitting close to me on a higher chair, he said that anything I told him would be under the seal of confession. I could talk freely and with confidence.

He started by asking me about how his predecessor Father Browne had conducted spiritual direction. He affected to be shocked when I told him about Father Browne's recommendation of the life of Saint John Vianney. 'How utterly preposterous!' he said. 'John Vianney was a sado-masochist. He would whip himself until his bedroom was spattered with blood.'

When I told him about Father Browne's counsel on custody of the eyes, he burst out laughing. He was still laughing when his phone rang. He answered it and spoke for a few minutes, before putting down the receiver and bringing the meeting to an end.

'I have to go out,' he said. 'One of our local parishioners is sick.'

I had found his spiritual direction disappointing, and I had not been to confession, but I decided I should give it another try.

I returned to Father McCallum a week later, this time determined to make my confession. He again offered me a drink and a cigarette. Again I declined, adding that I wanted to make my confession properly on my knees. Despite the fact that I was already kneeling by his chair, he got up and poured a glass of sherry. 'Sit down,' he said, 'and now drink this.' I did as I was told. As I sat sipping the sherry he came and sat next to me, very close. I proceeded with my list of sins, feeling silly as I did so, with the glass in my hand.

Looking at me intensely, he interrupted: 'Have you had problems with sexual sins, John?'

Something about the abrupt and intrusive way he asked this made me uneasy. I began to tell him about my difficulties two years earlier. I did not have the opportunity to explain the influence of the retreat father, Father Buxton, in my second year, because he interrupted me again.

'Oh,' he broke in. 'You must not feel any guilt about masturbation. It's now regarded by experts in sexual development as perfectly normal. In fact, it's abnormal not to do so. You may have heard of the Kinsey report in America. Masturbation is a natural form of growing up ... mutual masturbation is not such a bad thing either ... all part of growing to maturity. Did you know that 99.9 per cent of all males masturbate at puberty? Don't worry, they're all sure to have done it: Father Doran, Father Armishaw, Father Owen, Father Browne ... all of them.' He was leaning towards me, looking at me intently and touching me lightly on the arm and on the knee.

Then he said: 'On the other hand, there are individuals who suffer from abnormal forms of over-stimulation. Because of a deformation of the penis some boys are prone to excessive erections. If you were to show me your penis now, John, I could easily tell by manipulating it whether you have a problem of this kind . . . Will you let me examine your penis now?'

Suddenly I could not breathe. The question, his silk shirt, his hand on my knee, a heady smell (hair oil, aftershave, stale cigarette smoke, a faint hint of alcohol) filled me with terror. I remembered the face of the man in South Kensington subway: that same predatory look.

I stood up: 'No, Father McCallum, I don't think so.'

I walked to the door, turned the key in the lock, and went out into the cloister.

I looked back. He was standing in the middle of the room in an obvious state of agitation, his hands held out towards me, shaking his head. He appeared to be pleading with me not to say anything. I had a feeling as I stood in the cloister, free of him, that I had got off lightly.

108

I WAS TO say nothing to anyone about Father McCallum. I knew that it would be my word against his; and it was too close to the Paul Moreland affair. I thought of telling Father Armishaw, but I was sure that he would take it straight to Father Doran. And Father Doran, I suspected, would be obliged to believe Father McCallum before me.

For several days I could think of nothing else. Passing Father McCallum in the cloister occasionally, he would smile and greet me as if nothing had happened. But the incident had altered for ever my view of the priesthood. Throughout my time at Cotton nothing like this had ever occurred. Father McCallum had shown me what individual priests were capable of. McCallum was a 'shitten' priest, as Chaucer had put it in the *Prologue* to the *Canterbury Tales*. The fact of receiving the oils of ordination did not eradicate corruption in the heart of an individual priest. Never again, it occurred to me then, could I trust a priest unconditionally and implicitly.

A week or so after the incident, I went to Father Connelly for spiritual direction. He was a man of military bearing, well groomed and friendly. He took confessions and direction in the archbishop's suite. On my first visit, he brought me straight back to basics. His spiritual direction coincided with Father Doran's nightly talks in church. We are by nature imperfect, he said, but by unrelenting self-discipline we can work towards perfection. Holiness had to be worked for every day of our lives. We can never lower our guard, or be complacent.

Meanwhile, night after night Father Doran talked about temptation. We cannot control, he stressed, the suggestions that come our way through chance and imagination. The crucial issue was consent. 'Faced with temptation, as soon as its self-seeking pleasure is perceived, if we momentarily hesitate, if we resist in a half-hearted manner, we are on the way to failing.'

If I had entertained any doubts up to this point about the relentlessly ascetical, monastic nature of our sixth form formation, the experience with Father McCallum had allayed that anxiety. Any remaining concerns I had on this score evaporated after reading a book which now fired me with ascetical enthusiasm. I had been attracted initially by Evelyn Waugh's name on the cover. The title was *Elected Silence* by the Cistercian monk Thomas Merton, and Waugh had written the preface. There was an epigram on the title page by Gerard Manley Hopkins:

> Elected Silence, sing to me
> And beat upon my whorlèd ear,
> Pipe me to pastures still and be
> The music that I care to hear.

I read this book in one sitting on the Ascension Day choir outing. I took it with me to Dovedale and sat reading it all afternoon by the river. I read it on the bus back, and then right through the evening, missing the feast-day film. What struck me, to begin with, was its similarity in mood and prose style to *The Cardinal*. It was written in the style of a popular American novel. Like *The Cardinal*, it moved to and fro between Europe and the United States during the same historical period, ending in the early 1950s. *Elected Silence* (entitled *The Seven Storey Mountain* in the American edition), describes a coming-of-age spiritual quest which ends in Louisville, Kentucky, at a Trappist monastery where monks live in austere and permanent retreat from the world. The journey takes Merton from Prades in the French Pyrenees, where he was born in 1915, to Long Island, to Paris, to Bermuda, to Clare College, Cambridge, to Columbia University in New York City, and thence to the Abbey of Gethsemani where he enters the novitiate.

Since the writer is a young monk approaching ordination, his perspective both on his own life and on the history of the period, is God's shaping providence. God's 'purpose' for Thomas Merton, as he perceives it himself, is evident from the very first page. With resonances of Augustine's *Confessions*, the author frankly admits his sins, and the sinfulness of the entire world.

On his spiritual journey there are false trails, adventures and misadventures of the mind and the heart, as well as acts of lechery, leading to self-disgust. If I had any doubts about the stern strictures of Fathers Doran and Connelly they were resolved by Merton's astounding statement: 'There has never yet been a bomb invented that is half so powerful as one mortal sin – and yet there is no positive power in sin, only negation, only annihilation.'

Merton insisted that the life of the soul had far-reaching consequences beyond himself and his own spiritual destiny.

Through Merton's book, and as a result of the incident in Father McCallum's room, I felt that I had reached a better understanding of our strict, monastic disciplines within the seminary, which often seemed tedious and mechanical, and remote from the world, but which were aimed at instilling long-term perseverance and resistance to temptation. But nagging questions nevertheless arose about our seminary formation, which challenged, if not undermined, my new convictions.

109

I WAS STUDYING long hours, preparing for public A-level examinations. When I wasn't digging ditches I was taking long walks. I enjoyed long fast walks with Peter Gladden. Peter was interested in politics and science, and he had become preoccupied with the possibility of a Third World War which, he assured me, would be nuclear. He would inform me from time to time about news of the Soviet threat following the Suez crisis, when Britain and France invaded Egypt after Nasser had nationalised the canal. Peter, who would return to Cotton having read the *Manchester Guardian* every day during his holidays, would say: 'It's coming! Make no mistake.' He had made himself an expert, so it seemed, on the technology of the hydrogen bomb: 'Compared with an H-bomb the bombs that we dropped in Japan were just fire crackers.' Now, he was telling me, experts were convinced that an H-bomb test could cause a chain reaction through the entire matter of the earth. 'It could happen at any time,' he assured me, 'and when it does we shall all go up in a trice. Armageddon.'

As he walked, hunched and long-legged, his eyes narrowed with speculation, his mouth slightly open and moist, his prominent Roman nose bright red with exertion, Peter invariably turned to the question of the Third Secret of Fatima, the prophecies imparted to three peasant children in Portugal in 1917. The Third Secret, he assured me, had been read by a bishop in Portugal, who had leaked the information that unless Russia converted to Catholicism the world would come to an end in a more terrible war than the previous world wars.

Peter's preoccupations, it occurred to me, challenged at least one aspect of our strictly cloistered existence at Cotton. The point of protecting us from knowledge of current affairs was in part, as I understood it, to reduce distractions, mundane anxieties and temptations. But these Cold War crises were invading and filling our secluded uninformed lives with apocalyptic fantasies precisely *because* of our isolation. For a time Peter Gladden's circle became obsessed with the idea that at any moment the Russians would drop atom bombs on us, or invade Britain and come racing in tanks up the valley from Oakamoor to imprison and torture us for our Faith.

I had another problem with Peter, which was not unconnected with our emotional isolation: his continuing interest in the boys in Saint Thomas's. From time to time he would attempt to draw me into discussion about the looks and demeanour of the prettiest boys, asking me what I thought of this one and that one.

'They're just boring little urchins,' I would say, before attempting to change the subject.

'But some of them are gorgeous, Fru. Have you really studied little Brunning, for example? Why would God make such beautiful creatures if he didn't want us to adore them?'

'But aren't men meant to enjoy looking at women?' I said. 'And aren't we meant to resist the temptation to do that?' Even as I said it, I was aware of being unbearably priggish.

'Oh, I'm not in the least interested in women,' said Peter. 'They're too voluptuous and they smell.'

These conversations about smaller boys left me feeling anxious for Peter. He would go on at length about the 'frigid beauty' of his latest soprano crush in the choir, extolling 'his austerely pure voice, those icy notes that only boys can attain', and the 'pure, pure loveliness of little Brunning'.

One day, taking a rest on the top of a hill called Below, a burial mound high above the surrounding countryside on the road to Farley, Peter said: 'Sometimes, Fru, I daydream about Brunning. He is lying naked on an altar, and I'm stroking him and giving him pure kisses all over . . .'

'Peter,' I said, echoing what I had once told Paul Moreland, 'our bodies are the temples of the Holy Ghost.'

'But our souls are separate from our bodies,' said Peter. 'What I do to someone's body doesn't necessarily affect his spiritual, immortal soul.'

I looked at Peter, his full lips invariably parted as if he was incapable of breathing through his nose. I saw a young man who might well be mistaken for being innocently gormless: intelligent, kind in so many ways, and practical; but a minor seminarian approaching graduation to senior seminary, trapped in a delirium of warped, childish desire.

Meanwhile, despite my dogged commitment to Father Doran's and Father Connelly's spiritual formation, I was also aware that I was often thinking about people and the world that owed less to our seminary spirituality and much to the quiet influence of Father Armishaw's English classes and my weekly trips to his room after night prayers.

We were reading Dryden and Pope; learning about the art of satire's 'fine raillery'. He liked to quote from Samuel Johnson, trenchantly proclaiming the Doctor's didactic utterances. He would look over his spectacles, a smile playing about his lips, and come out with such lapidary phrases as: 'The metaphysical poets were men of learning, and to show their learning was their whole endeavour.' Or: 'Anything so little in the power of man as language, cannot but be capriciously conducted.' We were reading John Donne, Shakespeare's sonnets, Marlowe,

Me and my siblings, on being 'rehoused'.

George Herbert. Whatever the set books, he would send us off to the library to explore a wider circuit of texts.

One afternoon he took the sixth form in a hired bus to the theatre at Stratford-on-Avon where we saw an ageing Michael Redgrave playing Hamlet to Googie Withers's Gertrude. I sat next to him on the long drive back and he talked all the way, passionately, excitedly, about details of design and direction. I had never seen him so happy. In turn, I had never been so happy for him.

Father Armishaw approached the study of English literature in a tense frame of mind. Qualities of genius, taste, originality, creativity, were constantly set at odds with grossness, convention, feeble imitation and 'invincible obtuseness'. Then there were the key qualities to be noted: energy, concreteness, melody, sensibility, precision, wit, *irony*. There was a hint of alternative enlightenment in his lessons that complemented, and rivalled, the spiritual imperatives of Father Doran and Father Connelly. It was dawning on me that one could learn how people should behave towards each other, how one should think and feel, not only through prayer and the sacraments, nor alone through ascetical disciplines, but in realms of literature, poetry, novels, plays. As we explored and discussed the undercurrents of motive, emotion and desire in Father Armishaw's classes, I sensed a quiet countervailing influence to our seminary formation that felt more like creative tension than dislocation. By then, having read *Elected Silence* for a second time, I realised that Merton was perhaps more deeply a writer than a monk.

At the end of that summer term I went home to a new three-bedroomed council flat near Barkingside cemetery. Mum had at last been rehoused and she was much happier.

PART FOUR

PUBLIC MAN

110

RETURNING TO COTTON at the beginning of my final year, Father Ryall greeted me as I came in from the bus. He was smiling – a self-conscious boyish grin. He asked me up to his room where he shook my hand and told me that I had been appointed school captain, or 'Public Man', a title that had been used in the first century of the school's existence, and which had now been reinstated. I had also been appointed captain of my house. To be both school captain and house captain simultaneously was an honour that had rarely been bestowed in the history of the college. He said that I should go straight away to see Father Doran as he had something to say to me.

Father Doran was standing as usual by his fireplace fiddling with a pipe. He greeted me affably. He said: 'I have a feeling that you will blossom with responsibility, John Cornwell. I sometimes think that you lack self-confidence.' He went on to talk about how well I had done in my studies, and how it seemed to him that I was shaping into an ideal candidate for the priesthood. Dropping a heavy hint, he said that the last Cottonian from my diocese to be school captain had been sent to the English College in Rome. 'That's something we may allow ourselves to hope for in your case,' he said. 'I am convinced that you would benefit enormously and take the greatest advantage of the Rome experience . . .'

My happiness knew no bounds. Titles, responsibilities and a promise of proceeding to Rome, England's premier seminary, for the completion of my studies for ordination. As I took my

John Cornwell, Public Man.

place at the head of my table in the refectory, and at the head of the entire college, I felt ecstatic. I was assailed by just one scruple: that these honours were in part a reward for having betrayed Paul Moreland.

The duties of the Public Man were mainly devotional and disciplinary. He led morning and night prayers from the back of the church, and grace in the refectory in the absence of the Prefect of Discipline. He led the school in ranks to and from the cloisters on the way to church.

He had a room-sized cubicle in Top Dorm where he wrote up the school chronicle each day. He roused the sixth form every morning, making sure that every boy was down in church in time for the start of morning meditation. The Public Man was a link between Father Doran and the college, and he assisted the Prefect of Discipline in all matters relating to the rules and sanctions. He would ensure that his peer group did not smoke; that they obeyed the Greater Silence. He made sure that the big sixth, the monitors, were doing their jobs. In recognition of all these duties, the Public Man, Father Doran told me, would receive five pounds at the end of the year.

But for me the greatest honour in prospect was the possibility of being sent to Rome at the end of the year to complete my studies. There was only one Roman prof and that was Dr 'Laz' Warner. Laz was still taking me for one lesson a week in New Testament Greek. I went to see him after tea early in the term and asked him about the Roman seminary life. He eulogised for an hour about the Venerabile: the 'best college in the world', he called it. He talked of the ceremonies in the great basilicas, the works of art, the catacombs, the tombs of the popes. He told me that one only came home from Rome once in seven whole years, at the end of the third year: that, I thought, would suit me very well. Each summer, he said, was spent at an idyllic summer house, a former Trappist monastery, known as Palazzola, twelve miles from Rome and high above the shores of Lake Albano, where the students swam every day and lazed in the Italian sun. My whole being yearned for Rome.

111

IT SEEMED TO me that most of the profs were happy with my elevation to Public Man; especially Father Armishaw who said it was an 'inspired choice'. Father Grady, my housemaster, was delighted and hinted, with his polite little cough, that it would put me in good stead in future years. There was only one prof who appeared discountenanced and failed to congratulate me. This was Father 'Bunny' Manion, the priest who had written 'poor' on my botany report. There had been another more recent incident involving Bunny during the Michaelmas term of my first year in the sixth form. During the days when I was lodged in the infirmary I had settled one afternoon with a book on the stoop of the cricket pavilion which looked out over the deserted cricket field just above Top Bounds. Father Manion and one of the Saint Thomas's first-year boys came walking by: the boy was good-looking, pretty in fact, possibly of mixed English and Asian origin, with a shock of black hair; he was dressed in shorts and rugby shirt and he was holding his arm up a little as if he had been injured. Father Manion, who was also in shorts, had his arm around the boy's shoulder and appeared to be speaking to him endearingly. This seemed strange for the boy did not look to be in pain and he was walking perfectly well without assistance. I must have stared with blatant curiosity; I had never seen a priest put his arm affectionately around a boy at Cotton. When Father Manion at last noticed my presence he looked shocked; then his eyes blazed, as if to say: 'Who the hell are you looking at?' They walked on and disappeared in the direction of Saint Thomas's, the priest's arm around the boy all the way.

I knew as I entered my final year that Father Manion disliked me, but I was not unduly anxious, as it seemed to me that he had no power over my career in the college. I put his jaundiced view of me down to nothing more than personal chemistry, and the fact that a former boy of Saint Thomas's had not been made Public Man.

112

As I GOT into the rhythm of my new role with all its duties, I was asked by Father Ryall to show consideration to a new member of the teaching staff called Philip Pargeter, a fleshy, clerical-looking young man with limp hair and gold-rimmed spectacles. Philip Pargeter was a deacon at the senior seminary, Oscott, who decided that he needed an extra year before taking the plunge of priestly ordination. The archbishop suggested that he spend a year teaching at Cotton while he pondered his vocation further. He opted to wear lay clothes in the college, but nevertheless looked like a young prelate. Since he was in limbo between the teaching staff and the boys, I was recruited to accompany Deacon Pargeter on country walks to give him exercise. The walks were enjoyable as he had a pleasant turn of wit and was widely read.

I was also asked to take walks with a very civilised, somewhat pedantic elderly man called Eric Partridge, a prolific author of books on English usage and a friend of 'Whisky' Roberts, the archivist. Mr Partridge would come to the college to stay for several weeks at a time and loved walking in the valley. On one of our walks we talked about the derivation and usage of the word 'smog' for the length of three miles. Father Armishaw considered Partridge's preoccupations trivial and would show me his latest book, reading out items of pedantry for my amusement.

This role I now had of being a walker for the junior prof Pargeter and the ageing etymologist, in addition to my dual captaincy, gave me an elevated sense of my own self-importance. Smugness, and the undeniable fact that I looked and felt mature for my seventeen years, rising eighteen, were about to contribute to the single most important event of my final year and involved the disgruntled Father Bunny Manion.

One of my duties as captain of Challoner House was to choose and direct a play. This proved an added burden to my already loaded routine, especially as I insisted on designing the set and casting myself in the lead role: Cornwell the actor-manager! The piece I chose was a drawing-room farce, *See How They Run*, in which I played the part of a silly vicar, the Reverend Lionel Toop. On the day before the performance, which was to take place in the evening after supper, Father

Grady, Challoner's housemaster, came to watch the dress rehearsal. He and I were now, as I saw it, on equal terms. He was then in his early thirties. At a pause in the rehearsal we were standing next to each other, chatting pleasantly, when he said: 'I think the set lacks something. It looks a bit sparse. Why don't you go over to the profs' common room, John, and fetch one of the coffee tables.'

I set off across Top Bounds from the assembly hall. I leapt up the Bounds Steps two at a time, past the noticeboards where I chided a knot of boys for idling, and walked purposefully and not a little bumptiously along the clock cloister, turning into the area where the profs had their refectory and common room. I had never entered the profs' common room during my entire time at Cotton, and I was conscious that I was approaching hallowed territory; through the glazed front doors of the hallway I could see the gardens at the front of the house from an unfamiliar viewpoint. The inner sanctum of the common room lay ahead, door wide open, apparently deserted, and there in the middle of the room was the item described by Father Grady. I strode up to the coffee table and bent down to lift it. At that moment from somewhere behind and to the right of me I heard a sound like the querulous bleat of a trapped sheep.

Looking back I saw the figure of Bunny Manion, hands deep in his cassock pockets, his face vermilion, his pale blue eyes starting from his head. His presence had been hidden by the open door and he was standing well back by the side of the fireplace. Before I could apologise and explain my presence and my errand, he cried out in a shrill voice: 'Never, *never*, in all my years in this place has a *boy* come into this room without a by-your-leave. How dare a *boy* walk boldly into this room without knocking, asking permission and explaining the nature of his business . . .'

I felt a confused mix of angry emotions. Here I was, on the verge of manhood, accorded respect both by superiors and peers, being referred to as a disembodied third person: 'How dare a boy!' Then there was the injustice of the thing: I was in the room legitimately. Certainly I should have asked his permission had I known that he was present. But what hit me bang in the solar plexus of my pride was being referred to as '*boy*', twice in a single sentence, and with relish; for I had the distinct impression that he was exultant.

I should have adopted a demeanour of humility and self-recrimination. I should have said: 'I'm so sorry, sir, I really did think that the room was empty . . .' Had I said something along these lines, events, and perhaps my whole life, might have turned out differently.

What I did was this: I slammed the coffee table down on the floor with a bang and rounded on him. I was head and shoulders above him, and judging by the frightened look on his face (not for nothing was he nicknamed 'Bunny'), my demeanour was obviously menacing. There he stood: the embodiment of all those in my life who had failed to see my worth.

'How dare *I*?' I roared. 'Don't be so ridiculous! You know full well that I couldn't see you lurking back there. I came in because Father Grady asked me to pick up a coffee table for our play rehearsal. And how dare *you* speak to *me* in such a manner!'

I was conscious as I let rip that my eyes were bulging and my fists were clenched. I concluded, pompously, disastrously: 'And I am not a *boy*. I am the Public *Man*.' With which I picked up the coffee table and made my exit.

Only in retrospect do I see that my action was learnt behaviour. The years of discipline at Cotton had been a poor antidote to my hot-headed maternal role model, but there was something else beyond the knee-jerk anger of my adolescent injured merit. I barely knew it at that moment, but I would have ample opportunity to ponder the incident's significance and consequences in the coming months. I was saying an emphatic 'No!' to acquiescence in the face of humiliation. I was saying 'No!' to the 'Little Way' of Saint Thérèse, who repeatedly rejoiced in such opportunities to eat dirt.

Father Manion, I learnt later, hastened as fast as his legs could carry him to Father Doran's office to recount the outrage. According to Deacon Pargeter, who reported back to me the agitated discussion in the profs' refectory that evening, Bunny Manion asserted to the assembled staff over their soup: 'He marches into the common room without so much as a by-your-leave and when I remonstrate with him reasonably, he bawls at me, fists clenched as if to hit me: "I am not a boy, I am the Public Man!"' The story, according to Deacon Pargeter, prompted gasps of horror and nervous laughter: although not on the part of Father Doran.

That evening Father Grady asked me to come to his room. 'Oh dear,' he said ruefully, 'you've caused a terrible brouhaha.' I tried to explain the circumstances, and he seemed to appreciate what had happened. But he made it clear that I had been guilty of an act of insolence that would admit of no excuse or explanation. Father Doran had told Father Grady that I should apologise at once to Father Manion without reservation, or pack my bags.

So I apologised to the priest on the Bounds Steps the next day as he made his way across to the main building from Saint Thomas's. He took my apology with poor grace; with such a sense of chronic outraged dignity, in fact, that I felt like punching him. My feelings probably showed. I suspected that he was disappointed that I had apologised, devoutly wishing me to be on a train home.

113

THAT I HAD offended not just one schoolmaster in a trivial incident but the entire Roman clerical caste, became clear to me in the course of the following days. Only one prof, apart from Father Grady, offered me a straw of understanding and sympathy, and that was Father Armishaw. But our friendship, too, was about to become a casualty of the precarious situation in which I had landed myself.

I went up to his room after night prayers two days after the house play. It was cold; he was having difficulty with the fire, and he was sitting huddled in his cloak. I asked him if he had heard about the rumpus. He took the stem of the pipe from his mouth and gave me a broad grin. 'Heard about it? I imagine by now that it's being hotly discussed in the offices of the Holy Inquisition in Rome.'

'I didn't see him in the room.'

'It's all right. You don't have to explain. Father Manion has a short fuse. Anybody would think you'd made love to Mère Saint Luc in the clock cloister. But that's not the point. The point is, Cornwell, how you behave when you find yourself at odds with clerical authority. What you do *not* do is lose your rag . . . Anyway, not to worry, life is full of little irritations and disappointments.'

With this he went over to his gramophone and selected a record. 'What with one thing and another . . .' he said, sighing to himself. 'I don't know. I fancy some Mozart. How about you?'

Father Armishaw never got as far as putting the record on the turntable. We were disturbed by a harsh rap on the door.

Before he could call out: 'Come in,' or even walk to the door to open it, Father Doran burst in.

The priest was white in the face and trembling. He did not look at Father Armishaw. He just glared at me, shaking a finger in my direction. 'Go to your dormitory this instant,' he ordered. 'I cannot have a situation where a boy is alone in a master's room after night prayers.' There it was again, that de-personalised, third-person '*boy*!'

This time I was not in the least angry. I felt entirely cool and in charge. I turned to Father Armishaw, who was standing with a faintly amused look of surprise, and said: 'Thank you, sir. Goodnight.' As I passed Father Doran, and looked him directly in the face, I had a mischievous urge to come out with a catchphrase from the popular *Carry On* films at that time: 'Ding Dong! Anything Wrong!' Instead I said politely: 'I'm sorry, sir. Goodnight.' My survival instincts were in working order.

As I made my way to my cubicle in Top Dorm I felt as if a thread had loosened in the fabric of my vocation; it might take a long time unravelling, but it seemed to me that the process was irreversible. What was the value, I asked myself as I lay in bed that night, of all the prayers, and Masses, and commitment to liturgy and the divine office, and celibacy, and meditation, if you ended up treating people like things rather than as persons? Had Father Manion and Father Doran once learnt all those lessons about forbearance, understanding, charity and respect, and forgotten them? Or had they never taken them in? That, prompted by injured pride, was my first thought. My next inclined towards self-castigation. Surely it had been childish, as well as unrealistic, not to accept the rules of clerical hierarchy. In losing my temper with Father Manion I had shown not how grown-up I was, but how immature: still a boy! And yet, no, on reflection I was not prepared to be acquiescent. Perhaps I *could* be: but I *would* not.

114

FATHER DORAN never spoke to me again. And for all the trouble it had occasioned, my ridiculous play, *See How they Run*, had not impressed the anonymous reviewer in the college magazine. He had judged the performance 'amusing enough . . . which better done could have been a truly hilarious affair'. My own performance was described as 'a little too deliberate' and the rest of the cast were 'inaudible from bad elocution'. Despite all the campaigns for speech purged of local accents, Cottonians seemed intent on speaking in a way that came natural to them.

My sessions of spiritual direction and Father Doran's evening talks seemed increasingly dry and tedious to me after the Manion incident. Yet my spiritual life took a surprising turn for the better during my remaining months at Cotton. This was not so much due to the influence of a priest as, yet again, to a book.

I was still a member of the League of Christ the King. Sitting in Father Grady's room during one of our sessions, I noticed a new volume on his shelves entitled *Jesus in His Time*, by Daniel-Rops. It was a long book, five hundred pages, and the preface claimed that its object was to study the life of Christ as if it were the life of any other historical person. Daniel-Rops was a distinguished French historian who had attempted to place Jesus biographically within a social and political as well as a religious milieu. He had studied the Gospels as historical documents rather than points for pious meditation. He brought to bear a wealth of parallel sources, while making many personal journeys to Palestine and Jerusalem.

I asked Father Grady whether I could borrow his copy, and his face lit up. 'It's a wonderful book,' he said. 'You will never think about Jesus in the same way again.'

I carried it around with me for a month until he begged for it back.

Father Grady was right. After reading *Jesus in His Time* I was never to see Christ again in the same light. I felt that for the first time I was encountering the 'real' Jesus, a man of striking sincerity and simplicity, yet a master of every event: firm, unswayed by applause or opposition. He had authority, and also tenderness: 'Suffer the little children to come unto me,' and he could be brilliantly ironic: 'Render unto Caesar the things that are Caesar's.' He could be angry, too, and radical. 'This is a man,' Daniel-Rops wrote, 'with blood in his veins, not a pallid conventional *seminarian*.' Pallid conventional seminarian! It was the first time I had read the word 'seminarian' employed as a term of abuse.

I began to meditate on the character of Jesus neither as the sweet Galilean of the *Key Heaven*, nor as the moral finger-wagging creation of Father Doran, but as a man of flesh and blood; a man who put love above the laws of the prophets, and who revealed his preferences for the poor and the dispossessed; a man who gathered women about him, and to whom women were attracted. Daniel-Rops asserted that the psychological portrait of Jesus of the Gospels is so powerful that it can be said to provide one of the most striking proofs of the veracity of scripture. He cited Gide: 'The best intentions make the worst literature.' The Gospel writers had drawn a portrait of perfect virtue without insipidity, and perfect charity without sentimentality. Yet how should one think of him also as God? Who did he think that he was? Who did he say that he was? The divinity, the godliness, of Christ now seemed to me so problematic that I put it to the back of my mind. Like my vocation I put it on hold. The book was a timely antidote to a recurring suspicion that the spiritual life was unreal, a state of make-believe. Danel-Rops wrote:

Nowhere is the perfect balance of his character more apparent than in Jesus's sense of reality. It is one of the traits which does most to humanise him for us and it is continually in evidence. There are visionaries for whom the real world hardly seems to exist, they live on that borderland where the dream and the experience merge, where madness lies in wait to open the door to their soaring ambitions ... But there is no trace of it in the words and the thought of Jesus; his feet are firmly on the ground and the visible world is real.

My spiritual life in those final months at Cotton was dominated by a down-to-earth image of Jesus, who haunted my prayers and meditations, and my reading of the Gospel stories.

115

MY LAST WEEKS at Cotton passed swiftly and busily as I sat the examinations that would qualify us for university entrance should we fail to make it through to the senior seminary and to the priesthood. I seldom considered my graduation to senior seminary, nor how I was feeling about leaving Cotton. I already suspected that I was not to be sent to Rome, but I had been told nothing; it was possible that I could end up in any of England's four senior seminaries.

My last important duty as Public Man was to greet the visitor of honour on prize-giving day and show him around the college. He was a stout, pink-faced auxiliary bishop of the diocese of Westminster, sparkling with interest and humour. It seemed odd to me to be talking with a bishop who was not being distantly grave and ceremonious.

Mum came up from London for the special day; it was her first and only visit. Uncle Mike drove her in his temperamental Vauxhall, taking seven hours including time for break-downs.

Mum looked smart in a fashionable flared cream-white coat. Uncle Mike looked odd. His tie and collar were loose, and I counted six ballpoint pens in his top pocket. During the speeches in the assembly hall he kept his trilby hat firmly on the back of his head.

Father Doran managed to get through the entire day without exchanging a single word or glance with me. Nor did he speak to Mum. The bishop had taken a liking to me. He evidently asked Father Doran where I was bound after Cotton, for it was from the bishop that I got confirmation that I was to be sent to Oscott, Cotton's sister college in Birmingham. The bishop said, as he wished me goodbye: 'What a pity you're not going to Rome, you would have enjoyed it so much.' It was obvious to me that Father Doran had intimated my disgrace, and that it was going to dog me for the rest of my clerical life.

On the evening before the last day of the college year Father Doran entertained the big sixth to dinner in the drawing room of the old hall. This was an annual event intended to reveal to working-class ordinands the mysteries of civilised dining. It was a beautifully proportioned room with a semicircular bay, regency-striped wallpaper, and a copy of the *Monarch of the Glen* on the wall. Over the marble fireplace there were the official framed documents granting the college its coat of arms. The table was laid up with a variety of cutlery and glasses. It was a four-course affair, ending with cheese, the nuns bobbing and bowing in silence as they waited upon us.

Father Doran told us how to use our cutlery, starting from the outside and working inwards. He served two kinds of wine and gave a little lecture on how we should savour the aroma, and drink sparingly, not 'just slurp it *beck*'. He said he was once invited to the officers' mess of a USAF base during the war and an unscrupulous colonel spiked his beer with gin. He crashed his car in a ditch as a result and narrowly missed being jailed for drunk driving. Nobody else seemed to think the story funny, but the image of a plastered Father Doran behind the wheel amused me and I laughed out loud. My companions looked embarrassed; Father Doran looked down at his plate with pursed lips.

'Never touch spirits or fortified wines such as port,' he said, 'except after the age of forty and then only as a medicine.' He went on to say how impressed he was with the archbishop, 'who makes a glass of wine last an entire meal'. Priests, he told us, because of their lonely lives were often prone to alcoholism; but this could be avoided by the formation of good habits early on.

At this point I decided to tell a story about how my Uncle Mike had given me a glass of very strong 'scrumpy' cider from Somerset, and how I had passed out under the table. As I attempted to relate this to the entire table, Father Doran, who had just lit a cigarette, went into a coughing fit so that I was effectively drowned out. When he finished, I remarked quietly: 'Actually, excessive smoking is not such a good idea either.'

The following day I waited for a call to receive my five pounds from Father Doran's hands for my services as Public Man. He did not send for me. In the end I asked Father Ryall if he would let Father Doran know that I wanted to see him. Father Ryall invited me to sit in his room while he went down to the profs' common room. When he came back he said that the headmaster was not available.

I was not to receive the five pounds that had been awarded to school captains ever since the end of the war. I wanted Father Doran to tell me to my face, and give his reasons. He intended me, though, to draw my own conclusions. Father Ryall looked sympathetic. He said I could have the run of his room for the evening. I played his record of *Eine Kleine Nacht Musik*, but I soon got bored and went down to the sixth form common room and joined James and Derek. They were talking about their holiday plans, but I hardly heard them. I was angry. Five pounds would have been a welcome sum for my mother, and I had already promised it to her. I wondered what Father Armishaw would have to say about it.

I left the common room and climbed the stairs to his room. I thought he might ask me in on this my last evening at Cotton, despite Father Doran's proscription. The door was wide open; he was sitting at his desk reading a book. When he saw me he rose at once and put an unlit pipe into his mouth. As he came to the threshold there was something forcedly jovial about the angle of the pipe-stem between his teeth; his eyes were apologetic. He sounded as if he was speaking through a brace: 'Oh, yes, Cornwell, you're off to Oscott. I'm sure I'll hear news of you.' He shook my hand vigorously and immediately retreated, shutting the door firmly. I stood staring at the door, fit to cry. He had been a true father-figure when I most needed one. I needed him now. But he had submitted unconditionally to Father Doran's prohibition of lone visits to masters' rooms in the evening.

Many years later, when the terrible extent of Catholic priestly abuse was exposed, I found myself wondering about that moment outside Father Armishaw's closed door. Was Father Doran's repression necessary in order to thwart McCallum's brand of emancipation? Did a priest have to choose between being a Father Doran and a Father McCallum? Was there no alternative to prudent repression and self-seeking 'emancipation'? Abuse crises were nothing new in the Catholic Church, they had recurred down the centuries, imprinting themselves indelibly on the folk memory of the priestly caste; shaping its ideals of detachment. Religious superiors cannot be spared responsibility for enforcing prudence. Yet prudence, even in the form of a closed door, carries the risk of wounding and self-wounding consequences. On the night Father Doran ordered me out of Father Armishaw's room I had felt the bond of my vocation loosening. On my last night at Cotton, as I walked away from Father Armishaw's closed door, that premonition was confirmed. I imagined Father Armishaw sitting down again on the other side of the door, staring into an empty hearth, and I sorrowed for him and for the priesthood.

The next day, my last at Cotton, I rose while it was still dark and went outside. I sat in the cold air on the steps above Lower Bounds. As the birds began to sing and the sunlight touched the distant crests of the landscape, I took my leave of the valley. I was ready to go. Yet I sensed a painful nostalgia in prospect: *ad multos annos . . . ad multos annos . . .* Five years earlier I had travelled to this valley, a recently reformed hooligan, rescued from ruin by an austere parish priest who avoided personal engagement with all but the very old. Without Father Cooney, without Cotton, and without Father Doran and his staff, my prospects had been dismal. Cotton had saved me, and made me. As the sun rose over the valley, I had an intuition that Cotton would possess me for the rest of my life.

Shrine of Saint Wilfred in Cotton Valley.

RECONCILIATIONS

116

FIVE WEEKS AFTER leaving Cotton I travelled to a suburb of the city of Birmingham to enter Oscott College, a neo-Gothic edifice with a proliferation of towers, spires and gables. The famous nineteenth-century Catholic architect, Augustus Welby Pugin, had designed much of the college which with leaking roofs and crumbling plaster, was in need of restoration. Pugin was also responsible for designing many of the chapel's decaying vestments.

Oscott had been a focus of the rebirth of Catholicism in England. In 1852 John Henry Newman preached his famous 'Second Spring Sermon' from the chapel pulpit, anticipating a great revival of the Catholic faith in England. By the late 1950s, however, the college, albeit filled to capacity, had an autumnal atmosphere. In my class, known as First Year Philosophy, were seven other Cottonians as well as six or seven mature men who were some years out of school. There were about a hundred and twenty students in the college and we were obliged to dress in cassocks and Roman collars at all times within the buildings and the grounds. I had bought a celluloid collar like Father Cooney's that could be wiped clean with a damp cloth before I went to bed at night. However loose I tried to wear it, I felt that it was slowly choking me.

To my dismay, James Rolle and Peter Gladden had decided during their summer holiday not to proceed to the senior seminary. They did not reply to my letters, and I was never to see them again. Such defections between junior and senior

John Cornwell, fourth from left, back row on arriving at
Oscott College, 1958.

seminary, even on the part of the most promising priestly candidates, were not uncommon. For the sake of his prospective sacristy boys I was glad that Peter had decided not to persevere. James, I heard some years later, got married and raised a family. Derek had been kept back at Cotton for a further year to improve his Latin.

At Oscott we each had our own sparsely furnished room. Unless given express permission we were not allowed outside the grounds. When we did gain permission, usually to make a visit to the local shops or walk on the nearby common, we were required to go in groups of three, wearing black suits, black raincoats and Roman collars. We were instructed to walk one in front and two behind, or vice versa, so that we should not 'crowd' the pavements and inconvenience other pedestrians. The mature students, many of whom had spent time in the armed services, seemed to endure these disciplines with good humour. I heard one of them say: 'Seminary's a doddle after sar'nt-major!' We had manual labour, mostly weeding and raking leaves, once a week. There was no obligation to take exercise or play games, and there was no gymnasium.

The elderly rector was suffering from spasmodic senile dementia. He would address students by the names of men who had long ago departed the college, and even this life. His Masses were occasionally invalid; some days he missed out the consecration altogether. College discipline was in the charge of the vice-rector, a bustling martinet of a man, who had spent the summer previous to my arrival studying the regimes in the strictest Spanish seminaries in order to tighten up discipline at Oscott. He would patrol the outside of the building after 10.15 at night to ensure that lights were out in every room. After supper each evening he would stand outside the refectory accepting apologies from any who had broken the rules of the house: there were usually about a dozen self-confessing miscreants. The teaching staff comprised ten 'professors', who seemed languid and mournful. There were heavy bars on the windows of their ground-floor studies off the main cloister: to keep unwanted visitors out.

Many of my companions appeared to be thriving. Yet I was not entirely alone in finding the regime difficult. Every few weeks a student would slip quietly away without farewells. By my first winter I became afflicted with a form of depressive introversion, so overwhelming that I found it difficult to concentrate or sleep. The condition was exacerbated by the influence of our ascetical theology tutor, a gentle, dough-faced individual called Father Peter Lawler. Father Lawler counselled moment-to-moment 'recollection'. He gave us instructions on how to dispose our minds as we studied, took a walk, enjoyed a view or read a book. 'It's important to time yourselves,' he said. 'Stop every five minutes for one minute's reflection on what you have read ... Always read with your eye on the clock...' Most students cheerfully ignored all this. I took it seriously.

I was lonely, but my agitated interiority made me a poor companion. I found it difficult to make new friends with students of my own age, including former Cottonians. In our new setting my old companions seemed stand-offish. Avoidance of special friendships was taken even more seriously at Oscott than at Cotton. I was interested in making friends with some of the mature students in the college, but they regarded the boys from Cotton as 'mere boys'. I fell in with a set of garrulous would-be intellectuals in first-year theology who would sit around in one of our rooms, smoking and drinking instant coffee after lunch. We talked abstruse topics. One of our group was obsessed with ethical dilemmas presented in our moral textbook, H. Noldin SJ's *Summa Theologiae Moralis*. For example, would one break the Eucharistic fast by chewing a piece of mahogany? Or swallowing dust? Or by accidentally swallowing a gnat? Would it be possible to eat without sin as much as one liked on a fast day by travelling from Louvain in Belgium to Oscott, via Paris, thus passing through different canonical abstinence zones?

I made friends with a mature student who had been an army officer and had read natural sciences at Cambridge. He broke the rules of the house to entertain me in his room after lights out (he covered his windows with wartime blackout material). He always had an open bottle of claret hidden in his wardrobe and he was never short of cigarettes. As he poured the wine, he would murmur ceremoniously: 'Drink up, it's sacramental!' I confided my problem of self-consciousness to him, and he told me of the French theologian Teilhard de Chardin's 'practice of self-forgetfulness'. 'It is possible,' he said, 'to forget the self in a sympathetic union with all men.' It was this kind of language, 'the *practice* of self-forgetfulness', that drove me straight back into my self. But there was something unctuous about the way he said 'sympathetic union'. I was not aware of a homosexual clique in the college, but I suspected without evidence that he was a homosexual when he dropped me suddenly for an effeminate-looking youth, also in first-year philosophy.

The six-year seminary course of studies began with two

years' metaphysics. I found the numbered-paragraph spoon-feeding of this abstract mode of thought tedious. We were also dictated a potted version of the multi-volume history of philosophy by Frederick Coppleston SJ. Most of the major philosophers in the history of Western thought were set up to be knocked down by our superior 'scholastic' critiques. We were not encouraged to read original texts. The mature students were mostly content with the spoon-feeding since they had been away from books for some years. I managed to cadge a lot of cigarettes and alcohol by helping older students with their shaky Latin. I was getting through more than twenty cigarettes a day. I started to suffer from a stomach ache which the college doctor thought was 'an incipient ulcer'.

We had a well-stocked library that included not only theological works, but aslo large collections of 'secular' books, mostly donated by wealthy Catholics in the hope that future priests would read widely. Some of us did. I began to read and to be influenced by recent British philosophy as an antidote to metaphysics. I started to read anthropology, history of science, sociology and biography. Due to Father Armishaw's encouragement at Cotton, I was interested in astronomy and cosmology. I became a library cormorant, but my reading lacked direction and opportunity for discussion.

I missed Father Armishaw's subtle intelligence: his encouragement of independent thinking and debate, and of exploring different sides of a question. I missed reading and talking literature; I desperately missed listening to music and choral music. Oscott's music was exclusively Gregorian chant, and although it was done expertly and possessed an austere beauty, it lacked the rich variety of the four-part descant motets we sang at Cotton. We were not allowed radios or gramophones in our rooms. The landscape of our private grounds, bordered by a busy highway and a Catholic cemetery, was flat and enclosed by trees. I felt in exile from Cotton's valley with its wild weather and steep woods.

The prospect of six years at Oscott stretched ahead like a life sentence. We stayed in the college for the whole of Easter and Christmas, and rarely went home. On my occasional visits to London, Mum and the family seemed to treat me distantly and uncertainly. Back in Barkingside I spent a lot of time pacing the streets and public parks, saying my beads which I held inside my clerical raincoat pocket. One day in Valentine's Park, Ilford, a girl passed me who took my breath away. I turned and followed her at a distance. The beads of the rosary continued to pass through my fingers, but I was looking at her swaying hips and her head of beautiful dark hair.

By the beginning of my second year at Oscott I felt that I had been buried alive. Like Thomas à Kempis I was attempting to claw my way out of the tomb. In second-year philosophy I began to experience sexual torment, quite different from those earlier years at Cotton. I was thinking about women, and my fantasies were mostly fed by films I was seeing in Birmingham. I would sneak out of the college and down to the city centre, covering my clerical collar with a scarf. I never once joined the queue after supper to confess these misdemeanours.

At Easter during my second year I received a reprimand from the vice-rector. I must mend my ways or a poor report would be sent to the Bishop of Brentwood, my sponsor. I forestalled further acrimony by leaving of my own accord after a brief interview with the rector, who seemed to think I was somebody called Andrew. The vice-rector, who knew exactly who I was, was relieved. And so I left, without saying goodbye to my companions. I slipped out of the college while the community Mass was in progress. I travelled all the way to Ilford wearing my black suit and Roman collar. I took it off at home in the presence of Mum.

'I always thought you were acting a part when you got to that Oscott,' she said. 'It never was you.'

Standing in front of the mirror, she tried the collar and black stock round her own neck. It was a terrifying sight:

Canon Sheehy-Egan. In a Dublin brogue she cried: 'Y'are all sinners! And y'are all goin' ter Hell!' We burst out laughing.

The next day I called on Father Cooney in his presbytery. He seemed unaffected by the news. He said: 'Ah, wisswiss . . . Do you say so! Well now. Keep the Faith.' Then he shut the door. I was never to see him again.

117

DUE TO COTTON's education I earned a place at Oxford University to study English literature, supported on a full state grant. At Oxford I was intellectually and imaginatively stretched. I continued to practise as a Catholic although I no longer attended Mass every day, nor did I pray regularly. Increasingly I was finding a different kind of spiritual sustenance in literature, especially in the Romantic poets: Wordsworth and Coleridge in particular, reviving memories of the landscapes around Cotton and a sense of a spirit 'that rolls through all things'. I went to Mass on Sundays, but my devotions were as perfunctory as a prayer wheel. The scourge of malign interiority I had experienced at Oscott receded. I was living life on the surface, going to parties and meeting girls. The Cottonian misogynist attitudes evaporated on getting to know them. I loved dancing. I went to dances in the colleges and a weekly nurses' 'hop' at the Radcliffe Hospital. We jived to the strains of the Marvelletes' 'Please Mr Postman', and to Jimmy Dean's 'Big Bad John'. We twisted to Chubby Checker. Through my years at Oxford, Cotton seemed a world away, but with the power to affect me – like a strong, emotionally charged dream. There were nights when I dreamt that I was back there, trying to find my place in the refectory or the church, and being turned away. Somebody would say: 'You don't belong here any more.' And I would wake feeling miserable and abandoned. I thought of Father Armishaw sometimes when we revisited in university tutorials some of the texts I had studied in his class.

At last I wrote to him. It was a long descriptive letter, a result of many drafts. I told him that I was disappointed that F. R. Leavis had no influence in the English faculty at Oxford, but it was just an excuse to tempt him into a correspondence. He wrote a few lines in response, telling me that he himself was no longer enamoured of Leavis. He recommended that I read C. S. Lewis's *Experiment in Criticism* as an antidote to Leavis's 'stocktaking'. The important thing, he told me, was to learn how to read and write. I was crestfallen that he had not congratulated me on having got into Oxford. There was nothing about himself or Cotton. Only when I read Lewis's book did I realise that Father Armishaw's advice had not been an insult. I never wrote again.

By the time I went on to Cambridge as a post-graduate student everybody was dancing to the Beatles' 'From Me to You', but I had become a fan of Bob Dylan and Joan Baez. The times were indeed a-changing. I had stopped going to Communion, because I no longer went to confession. As a young man in love in the early 1960s, I could not make a firm purpose of amendment, while failing to abide by the mores of the Catholic Church on sex outside marriage; but I was convinced that my lapse would be temporary. I missed the Eucharist. Sometimes I dreamt that I was receiving Communion and would wake in tears. Then, as a result of a crisis, came a decisive, conscientious decision that had been creeping up on me for some time.

I was a member of Christ's College, Cambridge, where John Milton and Charles Darwin had been students. During my third term at Christ's I had spent many hours in the college library acquainting myself with two distinct world pictures. I had been reading, more or less side by side, *Paradise Lost* and *The Origin of Species*. The underlying tension between these two versions of reality, I realised, had been forcing me into a kind of intellectual schizophrenia.

One afternoon I was walking across a stretch of grassy open ground called Parker's Piece in central Cambridge; it was a sunny day and there were students sitting around on the grass reading and chatting. In the distance I could see the neo-Gothic tower of the Catholic church on Hills Road where I still attended Mass occasionally, without going to Communion. The sight of the tower, rising huge and solid, filled me with unbearable tension. The tower represented for me at that moment two irreconcilable choices. My old Cotton dilemma, make-believe versus reality, had returned.

One world picture involved the supernatural realm beyond the veil of appearances where resided the Holy Trinity, the angels and the saints, and the dead from the beginning of time – in hell with the Devil and all his demons, or suffering in purgatory, or enjoying celestial happiness in the presence of God. Here the powers of light were pitched against the powers of darkness. Here was the Creator, who sustained from moment to moment all of his creation in being. Here the shape of human history was determined, depending on the extent to which we appealed to the mediating power of the Virgin Mary. This sacred cosmology, moreover, was entirely subject to belief and imagination rather than direct empirical knowledge and reason.

The other world picture, admittedly skewed by my youthful Cambridge optimism and sense of certitude, acknowledged the wonder and mystery of the vast material universe, and the emergence, through blind evolution, of the stupendous fertility of life on the planet. It paid homage to the dignity, genius and resourcefulness of humankind. It was a world picture that could be constructed and perceived by direct knowledge, underpinned by the natural sciences and unaided reason. The shape of human history, within this world picture, depended not on contending unearthly powers, but on the responsibility of individuals and groups of individuals working out their destinies in communities and societies.

It struck me that I could no longer hold these mutually exclusive world pictures in parallel, let alone reconcile them. What was more, while science allowed for scepticism and healthy falsification of theory, Catholic truth made outrageous and dogmatic demands on my acquiescence, and with everlasting penalties. No intelligent, educated Catholic, it seemed to me, was spared the choice that had to be made between these contrasting world pictures. On that day I made my choice. I abandoned the Faith. It was a decision that seemed to bring instant relief. There were no pangs of conscience and no heart-searching. Importantly, it suited all the plans I had for myself; how I wanted to lead my life.

I did not renounce my belief in the historical reality of Jesus Christ, as described by Daniel-Rops, nor did I entirely renounce that great Gospel account of the Sermon on the Mount. But was he God? *Was* there a God? If there was a God, I reasoned, He must be a God who lay beyond all rational understanding, all proof and all human description. He was a God who was indifferent to the universe, detached from the emergence and evolution of life. He was remote from the problems of evil and suffering in the world. I was none of God's business, nor He mine: I no longer believed in a life after death when I would come to know Him face to face. I had become an agnostic. Yet what had happened to all that accumulated religious experience at Cotton? The years of daily ritual, spiritual reading, meditation, the disciplines of spirituality? The shaping of my younger soul? On that last morning, sitting above the valley, I knew that Cotton had claimed part of my soul. That day in Cambridge I decided to bury that claim deeply.

This is not the place for the narrative of a life journey that, twenty years on, would find me a returning Catholic, except to say that my marriage to a Catholic woman, and the birth of our children, whom she brought up as Catholics, kept the spark of Faith alive in me by proxy. But there was always a thread, tenuous, subconscious, that led back to Cotton.

In the meantime there had been rumblings in Rome, which to some presaged damaging storms, and to others, rain for famished lands. The Second Vatican Council of the early 1960s shook the Catholic Church to its foundations, and the reverberations were certainly felt at Oscott and at Cotton. Half of the twenty students who started in our year at Oscott did not make it to the priesthood. Of those who did, half had abandoned their calling by 1980; they were part of the army, a hundred-thousand strong, that left the priesthood during the 1970s. Those who remained, both profs and students, have to the best of my knowledge remained good and faithful priests: some in parishes, some in seminaries, and some on remote missions in Africa and South America.

The Cotton staff priests of my time were all of them faithful survivors except Father McCallum, whose predatory ways were soon exposed. He was removed from Cotton shortly after I left and died of a heart attack during the 1960s. Father Doran was appointed to a parish in Oxford, where he died in the early 1990s. When I was doing research in Oxford in the early 1970s, I telephoned him to suggest that we meet. He said: 'Give me at least a month's warning for an appointment, and not at all during Lent.' Lent was three weeks away. I never attempted to contact him again. He was said to be a dutiful parish priest, if a little dry.

And what of Cotton itself? In the 1950s there were five minor seminaries in England, several hundred in Western Europe, and more than seventy in the United States. Most were filled to capacity and the system appeared to be expanding. By the late 1960s liberated social attitudes and a growing youth culture had set the minor seminary formation at odds with the times. Many boys were failing to proceed to senior seminary and the priesthood after minor seminary. As a result of the reforms of the Second Vatican Council, moreover, bishops had doubts about recruiting boy ordinands. By the late 1970s the minor seminaries were as abandoned as the monasteries of England in the late Middle Ages. Cotton attempted for several years to make it as a regular boarding school for Catholic boys who had no intention of becoming priests, but it never got over its long reputation as a minor seminary. It closed its doors in 1987.

118

FATHER ARMISHAW retired from Cotton in 1976 and was appointed to a parish in Oxfordshire. I went without appointment to call on him in the summer of 1983. He was living in a bungalow by the side of his church. It was a noisy spot: at the end of the overgrown garden was a high wire fence marking the perimeter of an American air base, and every few minutes a jet aircraft took off.

He was much altered physically, deeply stooped and grey. He recognised me instantly at the doorstep. At first he was tense. He said that he was 'tied up' and could not entertain me. But eventually he invited me into his kitchen. I had arrived at noon and I was still there at six in the evening. He talked mostly about Cotton in the old days. There were a lot of harmless anecdotes about Cottonian characters, and especially about Father Piercy's genius with a screwdriver and spanner; but nothing personal. I asked him at one point whether there had been repercussions for him after Father Doran had ordered me from his room. He shrugged and said: 'Time heals most things.' Then he changed the subject.

He had lost his aptitude for neatness. He lived in a muddle, surrounded by his hundreds of books, now dust-laden. He had

At home with Father Armishaw, 2002.

a huge hi-fi set, and was neglecting Beethoven, Bach and
Mozart for Elgar and Holst. His sharp and attentive mind
seemed to have sunk into a state of discursive reminiscence.
He asked me no questions about myself, whether I was married
or had children. No talk about books, or about music. The
light seemed to have gone out of his eyes; but he was a surviv-
ing disciplined priest. He showed me with pride around his
church, and we knelt together in silent prayer for a few minutes
before I departed.

I saw him rarely through the 1980s; then he called me in
1989. I guessed that it had taken an effort. He wanted to see
me. I began to visit him more regularly. Eventually we would
talk on the phone two or three times a week. He was lonely,

and he had overcome the embarrassment that prevented him from reaching out. He always announced himself in a low voice: 'It is *I* . . .' He wanted to dispense with the formality of 'Father Armishaw', and yet to announce himself as 'Vincent' was a step too far. Much of his conversation was an evasion of intimacy. He liked to have a minor quarrel about historical dates or the meanings of words. He liked to 'settle questions' that had arisen in his mind. He had never ceased to be amused by Eric Partridge, the etymologist who used to visit Cotton. So a phone call usually went like this: 'It is *I* . . . Can you settle a question in my mind?' he would say, imitating Partridge's plaintive voice: 'Would it be true to say that "as yet" is redundant in a sentence such as "his mind was not as yet completely ossified"?' Then he would chuckle.

After turning down repeated invitations, he eventually came to stay in our home; then he became a regular visitor. We found him shy before strangers, self-centred and a little crotchety; there was never enough salt on his food (although he suffered from hypertension); he could never get my wife's name right: she was always Danielle instead of Gabrielle. He was fond of Gabrielle, I could tell, but he found it difficult to look at her directly. He was uncomfortable around women.

By this time I had returned to the Church and I had questions for him. But he disliked talking about spiritual and doctrinal matters. He refused to discuss the divide between so-called traditionalists and liberals. He seemed to harbour the worst kind of traditionalist attitudes. He confessed to me on one occasion that he had angered a forty-year-old woman parishioner by telling her that she should not go to Communion because she had not been to confession all year. As a result, he told me indignantly, she had stopped going to church. He said to me once: 'I sit in that confessional box every Saturday, and hardly anyone comes.'

He once told my wife that being late for Mass constituted 'a mortal sin'. It was not said tongue-in-cheek. Talking of the scarce vocations to the priesthood, he said: 'The absence of priests is due to all those boys who failed to be born through contraception and abortion.' We stared at him across the dinner table, stunned into silence.

In more recent years, as the scandal of priestly abuse of minors spread like a bushfire across America, I told him about Father McCallum. He appeared uncomfortable. It was obvious that he knew about the priest's tendencies and deplored them; but the need to close ranks against the laity, whatever the issue, reasserted itself. He refused to discuss Father McCallum directly. He said: 'If a priest must have sex, why the bloody hell doesn't he get himself a woman, or a man for that matter? And leave the kids alone.'

I asked him on that occasion whether he thought that Cotton with its isolation had trapped boys in immaturity, '*infantalised* them'. He looked at me intensely for a moment, almost as he did when I was boy. 'But from all you've told me,' he growled, 'you were better off at Cotton than at home. Where would you be without Cotton?' I guessed he was thinking, too: 'Where would *I* be without Cotton?' Yes, where *might* he have been?

We never mentioned these matters again, but occasionally he betrayed his sorrow and fear that all he had lived for, all that he had spent his life serving, was in peril, if not in vain. He said once that the corps of the clergy, as he had known it, was about to 'disappear over the precipice.'

In the summer of 2002, aged seventy-seven, Father Armishaw was about to move to Aston Hall, a retirement home for priests in the Birmingham archdiocese. He wanted to give me his books; the room he had been assigned at the home was too small to house a personal library. Two or three days before the move I went to Carterton with a van to collect them: they exuded the tobacco scent of his old room at Cotton. We sat together drinking tea out of mugs in the empty room that had been his study for more than twenty-five years. I could see that he was grieving the loss of his books. I said: 'Your books will always be in our home, and our home is your home. So they will always be with you.'

He replied: 'I've worked out the precise number of miles from Aston Hall to your front door.' It was the closest he had ever come to an admission of emotional attachment to us.

Three days later I had a call from the Aston nuns who cared for the retired priests to say that he was seriously ill in hospital. He had not spent a single night at the home, having collapsed on arrival. He had been suffering for some time from cancer of the lymph glands.

I went to see him in Stafford general hospital. He was on a noisy public ward with an unwatched television blaring. He was propped up on the pillows and did not seem to be in pain, but I could see that he was very ill. I sat by his bed holding his hand for a long time. Then he tried to say something to me. At first I could not hear, so I put my ear close to his mouth. He said faintly: 'My master calls, and I must go.'

Before I left him, I kissed him on the forehead. It was the first time I had ever kissed a priest. He looked up at me, shut his eyes, and nodded his head – as if to say: 'Thank you.' When I left, I turned at the end of the ward to look back at him. At that moment I was transported back to the day in the Staffordshire Royal Infirmary when, as a handsome young priest in a flying jacket, he had given me, the seminary boy, a thumbs-up sign as I lay sick in bed with pericarditis. From his deathbed Father Armishaw stirred an arm impeded by festoons of tubes. He raised his thumb in a firm farewell. He died on 7 July 2002, well 'fortified', as they used to say, 'by the rites of Holy Mother Church'.

I went to his funeral Mass a week later at Saint Chad's cathedral in Birmingham. As I crossed the road at the traffic lights to approach the cathedral doors, I could see a group of middle-aged and elderly priests. Several of them shouted out: 'Here comes Fru!' I had not heard my nickname in decades.

There were a lot of old faces gathered for the requiem: including Canon Piercy, Canon Grady, Bishop Pargeter, Monsignor Gavin, Monsignor Ryall, Father Derek and many others: survivors all. As they bore the coffin out from the cathedral at the end, we sang the old Cotton Easter hymn: 'Battle is o'er, hell's armies flee'. He was buried late that afternoon in a graveyard in Carterton.

119

I FELT THAT summer of 2002 that I had lost a father. By a strange turn of events I had rediscovered my real father several weeks before Father Armishaw's death. Not long after I watched Dad disappearing into the Majestic cinema in Woodford in the September of 1957, he left London for Portsmouth taking Grandma Lillian with him. He had achieved his ambition to settle in the town of his dreams and start a new life far away from Mum and sports fields. Over the years I had heard that he had worked at temporary jobs like tending the central reservations of the highways of Hampshire and Dorset. Then he was employed in the naval dockyards dipping corroded machinery in acid. In the mid-1960s came the divorce from my mother, and the death of Grandma Lillian. In the 1970s he married a woman called Ivy and departed from his last-known abode without leaving a forwarding address. From time to time down the decades I made small efforts through cousins on his side of the family to find him; to no avail.

By 1990, when he would have been approaching eighty, I was anxious to know whether he was alive or dead. I contacted the Salvation Army's missing persons' department. They drew a blank. An officer told me: 'He might be alive but bedridden.' In 2001 my brother Terry picked up his trail through the

Internet. On a people-search website we found an individual with my father's initials in Kent. The record showed that he was sharing a house with a single widow called Freda. Through directory enquiries I found a telephone number for her.

She had a kind, reassuring voice. I said that I was trying to contact a long-lost friend and mentioned his first name. 'Yes,' she said. 'There's a man of that name living with me. I've been looking after him for twelve years since his wife, my cousin, died of cancer.' What sort of age would he be, I asked. He was ninety, she told me, 'last February'.

I had found Dad. I said: 'Well, I am his son.'

There was a shocked silence. Eventually she said: 'He always told us that he never had any children.'

There was, of course, no going back now. I had broken in, perhaps clumsily, on his secret life; and in the subsequent spasmodic conversation I learnt that he had not only kept back important facts about himself, but that he had invented some as well. He had told his deceased wife, and all connected with him going back thirty years, that he had injured his leg when his submarine was blown up during the war.

I spoke just a few words with Dad that day. The conversation was difficult and hedged around with equivocation. But I judged there and then that Freda was a remarkable woman. I decided to write to her and tell the truth of our family's story: which was also *his* story and therefore hers.

For almost a year I corresponded with Freda and spoke with them both on the telephone from time to time. I did not want to rush a reunion, as there were emotions and versions of lives to be sorted out before we could meet in person. Then one day Freda called me to say that she was grateful that I had persisted in finding Dad, and even more so for insisting on enabling him to talk about his family. 'He cried for three days after he admitted to having five children,' she said. 'He had hidden the fact for all those years, and it had been a terrible burden.'

On 25 April 2002, I went with my son, Jonathan Samuel, to see Dad. From London's Waterloo East we took a train which trundled across the wastelands of the Thames estuary to Rochester. We drove in a taxi to where they lived, a quiet winding suburban road in the Medway valley. It was a small detached house standing on a crest. The bottom half was painted bright red; the top half white. The front garden was filled with daffodils.

Freda, who was eighty, met us at the door dressed in a housecoat; she was frail and moved with difficulty. She showed us into the single downstairs sitting room. Dad was sitting in the corner facing a huge television set on the opposite side of the fireplace. His bad leg was placed on a footstool. I recognised him instantly, although he was much heavier than he had been in his forties. He had a wide open face, a fresh complexion with very few lines and youthful observant eyes.

He was laughing; and as he laughed his shoulders heaved a little. He had huge muscular forearms and large strong hands. When he spoke, his accent was ripe old cockney with a faint nasal twang.

Freda served tea and cakes while Dad, who was hard of hearing, embarked on a series of monologues. There was no scope for questions, nor for interjections that would have made for a true conversation. He took charge.

'You probably had a good laugh about the submarine days, son. But you've got to understand that no one gave you a chance if you were just a cripple. If you had a war wound, you were OK. My Ivy knew the truth of it. In fact, she was the one who suggested it.'

Was this the truth, or yet another fabrication? It hardly seemed to matter now. In any case, he had launched into what was to prove a lengthy account of his childhood, and the origin of his handicap. As he spoke, he pulled out a red handkerchief and dabbed his eyes from time to time.

He told me that when he fell down the stairs as a child 'the wound went in instead of out'. He got TB in the bone and was in and out of hospitals and sanatoria from the age of four until the age of twelve. 'My father never visited me once in hospital, he was ashamed of me,' he said, tears welling in his eyes.

'My leg when I was twelve was twenty-five degrees out from true at the knee, excruciatingly painful and permanently bent; so I could only walk awkwardly on my toe. They took me back in the hospital, they broke the leg at the knee and took the kneecap out to straighten it. Just so that I could stand up straight.'

There were many more stories of Custom House and his childhood, mostly in explanation of his mid-life depressions and failures. How his brother Earnie became the favourite son; how he became an unpaid drudge at home. I had heard none of these stories when I was a boy. I could see that it was doing him good to unburden himself. Just before it was time for us to depart for London, he asked me: 'How's your mother?'

It was a difficult question to answer in the space of a few minutes to an old man who was hard of hearing. I should have liked to tell him how she had kept the family together, maintaining a home for us all until we started families of our own. How she had taken up painting and pottery, and had written her autobiography; how she had become an expert in designer knitwear, then a librarian; then joined a choir and sang the part of a nun in *The Sound of Music*. Among her many jobs she had been a credit controller at the gas board with a team of men under her and, briefly, the housekeeper of a priest. She had travelled widely, to the United States, Italy and Spain. She was arrested in Moscow for setting her hotel bedroom on fire. Against explicit instructions to the contrary she had plugged her curlers into the bedside lamp socket. She had married, unsuccessfully, for a second time. She had kept the Faith and was still alive and well, aged eighty-eight.

Dad did not wait for an answer.

I had not expected any great epiphany on achieving reunion

My father and I, 2002.

with Dad. But I felt a sense of ripeness at being able to locate him in my mind and heart. As for Mum, when I reported an account of his situation after meeting him, she said: 'You make him sound like an old reprobate, instead of what he really is . . .'

What was he, really? It had never occurred to me when I was a child that Dad was a clever man with a range of subtle emotions. Nor had I appreciated what it took for him to survive despite a childhood of pain, isolation and humiliation. Who knows what webs of fantasy he was obliged to construct in order to survive those lonely years of hospital and sanatoria beds? As a young married man during the war his tendency to lie undoubtedly cost others dearly. But he had found, despite that weakness, two women in his life who over a period of more than thirty years saw his qualities, experienced his ability to love, and enabled him to flourish and be loved in turn.

120

AFTER MANY YEARS' absence, my journey back to the Faith of my Fathers has not been easy. At the Mass I attended on the first Christmas of my return to practice, the choir in our local church sang 'Happy Birthday to You' at the consecration. I staggered out into the open air, thinking: 'I'm not going to make it.' Where were the ancient rhythms, the sacred repetition, the Catholic musical splendours of my youth? I had to learn the benefits of the new 'participation', while sorrowing over the lost liturgy of my boyhood.

I soon discovered that I could not 'return' to Faith by attempting to recapture what I had left behind at Cotton all those years ago. Yet I found myself thinking about Cotton as if it contained a secret to be discovered, a riddle to be solved. I continued to return there in dreams which seemed to contrast my boyhood innocence with a sense of adult shame. It was not until the early 1990s that I understood what drew me restlessly back.

I returned by car one summer's afternoon to look at the valley and the old buildings. Driving down the last stretch of the lane, I thought the outline of the college on its promontory looked much the same from a distance. But as I parked on Top Bounds I saw the extent of the devastation that had befallen the place. The refectory, classrooms, libraries and cloisters had been looted, vandalised. The floors, doors, windows and most of the roofs had gone. Saint Thomas's had been burnt to the ground (by vandals, I was told later). The gardens, once beautifully tended, were overrun with weeds. Faber's Retreat had been smashed by a fallen tree, and the church was locked up.

As I wandered the ruins of Cotton, I remembered how I had walked its pathways and cloisters during the Easter retreat, seeking God in fasting and silence and seclusion from the world. Now, decades on, it struck me that the desert places of spirituality are not to be found alone in religious houses where men and women shut themselves away to find God in self-denial and abstinence. The desert can lie at the very heart of a person's life, amid the turmoil of worldly distractions.

Many who have turned away from religion to embrace agnosticism and atheism, as I had done, are perhaps as much in a state of desert spirituality, the 'dark night of the soul', as any contemplative. What we are escaping is not God at all, but the false representations, the 'trash and tinsel', as W. B. Yeats once put it, that pass for him. So, 'hatred of God may bring the soul to God'. At Cotton that summer's day I recognised the truth of that 'darker knowledge', and it eased the feelings of a former apostate's remorse. Yet I sensed that for years my younger self, the seminary boy, had still to forgive me for having turned my back on the auspices that had saved his soul all those years ago from ruin. As I walked through the over-grown pathways of Cotton that seminary boy came to meet me: without reproach or condemnation on his part, and with a sense of healing reconciliation on mine.